The Ultimate Guide To NHRA Drag Racing Statistics

THE NITRO EDITION: 1997-2012:

Patrick J. Keenan

PublishAmerica
Baltimore

© 2013 by Patrick J. Keenan.
All rights reserved. No part of this book may be reproduced, stored in a retrieval system or transmitted in any form or by any means without the prior written permission of the publishers, except by a reviewer who may quote brief passages in a review to be printed in a newspaper, magazine or journal.

First printing

PublishAmerica has allowed this work to remain exactly as the author intended, verbatim, without editorial input.

Softcover 9781462656783
PUBLISHED BY PUBLISHAMERICA, LLLP
www.publishamerica.com
Baltimore

Printed in the United States of America

INTRODUCTION

Passion is the operative word when it comes to discussing any specialized activity, and that certainly includes drag racing. It takes passion to participate in any aspect of the sport, be it as driver, car builder, team owner and yes, even as journalist. Those of us who have been lucky enough to have spent our working lives in drag racing understand the importance of our passion because the harsh reality is, with very few exceptions, none of us has amassed significant financial rewards from our efforts. I'm certainly not complaining about that, and I've rarely heard others bemoan their financial fates as a result of drag racing. We all went into this with our eyes wide open.

Many have suggested that drag racing is an addictive activity, and from where I'm sitting, it's difficult to dispute that. Almost everyone I know who's involved with it acknowledges that it's an impossible habit to kick once it gets into your blood, and no form of motorsports does that quicker than drag racing.

In many respects Patrick Keenan's eyes are open wider than other observers of the sport—but unlike those who are enthralled by the visceral aspects of the endeavor, Keenan has taken the sometimes mundane esoterica of statistical information and turned it into a highly readable and informative tome. Let's face it, statistical information isn't for everyone, but drag racing truly is an endeavor ruled by numbers. While the general public can't get much beyond the speeds recorded—and those are indeed critically important—it's the elapsed times and Reaction Times that make drag racing an ever fascinating sport. Where else but in drag racing could you record a quicker elapsed time and still lose the race? And how the hell does that happen? Patrick Keenan has the answer to this and hundreds of other interesting questions.

Not yet 30, this is Keenan's first book about drag racing—and it certainly won't be his last. He's moving into fiction now, but drag racing remains his first love and main passion—and we're all benefitting from that.

The information Keenan has compiled here is invaluable as a research source for serious writers, but it's not just for them. It's for the rest of us, too, because it contains a tremendous amount of never-before-written-about personal information on the sport's most famous and infamous individuals. As Keenan has so aptly recognized, drag racing is about a lot more than drivers, so inside you'll find out what makes the best tuners tick as well. And if you read between the lines you'll see that some of those guys have (possibly) unintentionally revealed some of the their best-kept speed secrets!

A final word of advice. You'd better keep this book handy, because the next time you're arguing over an adult beverage about who actually won how many Whatever Nationals wins in Whatever season, this will be your source material!—Jon Asher

The Ultimate Guide To NHRA Drag Racing Statistics is the ultimate book when it comes to NHRA Drag Racing statistics because unlike any drag racing book ever published, this book will be the first book NHRA racers, team members, and fans alike will pick up and never have to look further to find out more. Although this book covers 1997-2011, this book will carry major statistics that were made prior to 1997. So enjoy, answer your question, answer some else's question; overall expand your knowledge of the NHRA in an easy, very simple, fun filled way. What is the national record? How successful was the driver's season? Who won the most out of everybody? Who cuts the best lights? Find out all this and more in a matter of minutes! Best of all, you even get an inside look at what it takes to own, drive, and be a crew chief from the most well-known stars of the sport, in an unedited form, about the most addicting sport in the world.

Jon Asher is veteran drag racing editor, photojournalist, and entrepreneur with over 50 years of experience. He has worked with the NHRA, AHRA, IHRA, many, many publications and magazine, and is an innovator in many ways. Here is a look at the history of all the past publications and projects you could see his talent in:

- BBDO Advertising Photographer for Dodge. (1966)
- Editor of All American Drags. (1967)
- Contract writer for AHRA's Drag World (sanctioning bodies leading publication) covering in-depth information of the Grand American Series of National Events. (1968-1971)
- Wrote a combined more than 100 articles a year for Hot Rod, Car Craft, Popular Hot Rodding, Hi-Performance CARS, Rodder & Super Stock, Super Stock & F/X, Speed & Supercar, Super Stock & Drag Illustrated, Drag Racing and Drag Strip Magazines. (1968-1972)
- Wrote monthly editorials for HI-Performance CARS Magazine and additional editorial for other Magnum Royal Publications titles under the name "Dave Johnson." (1968-1972)
- Produced national advertising photography for Budweiser, Dodge, Winston and many industry-related companies. (1968-1972)
- NHRA contract writer for Autoweek and competition press publication. (1970-1972)
- IHRA contract writer/photographer for Drag Review. (sanctioning bodies leading publication) (1971-1972)
- Competition Editor for Car Craft Magazine (1973-1979)
- Program Producer for Car Craft Magazine's All American Drag Racing Team (1974-2002)
- Editor of Car Craft Magazine (1979-1983)
- Freelance contributor to numerous print publications, such as Hot Rod and Car Craft. Also, he provides photography for numerous motorsports-related calendars. (1984-Present)
- Contract Editor for Petersen's Drag Racing Magazine. He was also a coach and mentor to the new Editor as well as doing the same for the succeeding Editor in hopes that they could run a successful publication. (1989-1991).
- Publisher and Editor of American Drag Racing Magazine. (1996)

- Senior Editor and Senior Photographer for RACER Magazine and provided all of their drag racing coverage on a freelance basis. (1996-2005)
- Contributed articles and Editorial writing for Japan's Daytona Magazine and was the American correspondent for Australia's Motorsport News (1997-'02).

He can be credited with bringing the Miller Brewing Company into drag racing in 1982, as well as signing the first major sponsorship with Summit Racing Equipment in the late 1980's. He served as a Corporate Marketing and Promotions Advisor for Summit Racing Equipment for 15 years. He received the Founding Editor's Award from the International Drag Racing Hall of Fame in 2006, and he is one of only two individuals to have received two Special Recognition Awards as part of the All-Star Drag Racing Team program, the first in 1984 and the second in 2000. In 2010, he received the Straight Shooter Award from AARWBA (American Auto Racing Writers And Broadcasting Association in 2010. Recently, you can find as him as the Senior Editor on CompetitionPlus.com, the largest drag racing web magazine, a Founding and Senior Editor for Drag Racing Action Magazine, and a Photo Journalist at select NHRA National Events.

Every statistic is current as of April 29, 2012, except for interview content which is current as June 4th. This book does not address many stats as a stat could be created for any situation, it could be almost endless. Feel free to e-mail me any time a new question arises about a stat or if you would like to possibly explore a stat not provided in this book at PatrickJKeenan@KeenanBooks.com—Patrick Keenan

The sources are from my knowledge as a big stats buff that I have always been with the sport, the Internet, and a select group of individuals. The Acknowledgements section will provide more on this. Every fact in this book is 100% correct as of publication.

The interview topics and the list of people interviewed is just a guide for you to see who was interviewed about what, as the interview content goes beyond exactly what they are listed for. Wherever the person's name was listed first is the section where you will find their entire interview, if they are listed for any additional sections. This was done with the intention to make it best for the reader and to publish the entire interview as one instead of cutting it up and making you flip back and forth.

Other Books By Patrick Keenan:

Forever Endeavor: 'Till Death Do Us…Alive

TABLE OF CONTENTS

INTRODUCTION..3
NHRA ALL-TIME LISTS..13
TOP 25 DRIVERS ON THE WINS LIST IN TOP FUEL...............22
TOP 25 DRIVERS ON THE WINS LIST IN FUNNY CAR..........27
NHRA PROFESSIONAL CLASS DRIVERS...............................32
A POINTS HISTORY ANALYSIS:1997-2011...........................267
CREW CHIEFS WHO HAVE TUNED IN BOTH NITRO CLASSES 281
COUNTDOWN ATTITUDES: FEELINGS FROM THE MOST POSITIVELY AND NEGATIVELY AFFECTED DRIVERS ABOUT THE COUNTDOWN..287
1320 VS. 1000 FEET: A FULL DEBATE..317
WHAT DOES IT TAKES BE A SUCCESSFUL DRIVER?..........325
WHAT DOES IT TAKES BE A SUCCESSFUL CREW CHIEF? 344
WHAT DOES IT TAKE TO BE A SUCCESSFUL TEAM OWNER 357
AN EASY AND FAIRLY ACCURATE WAY TO CONVERT A 1000FT. E.T. TO A 1320FT. E.T..360
INTERNET AND ENTERTAINMENT DRAG RACING FIX.....362
ACKNOWLEDGEMENTS...367

NHRA ALL-TIME LISTS:

Top 25 Drivers With The Most Wins

#	Driver	Wins
1.	John Force	134
2.	Warren Johnson	97
3.	Frank Manzo	96
4.	Bob Glidden	85
5.	David Rampy	80
6.	Dan Fletcher	76
7.	Pat Austin	75
8.	Greg Anderson	72
9.	Kenny Bernstein	69
10.	Jeg Coughlin	67
11.	Tony Schumacher	67
12.	Larry Dixon	62
13.	Joe Amato	57
14.	Bob Newberry	50
15.	Don Prudhomme	49
16.	Edmond Richardson	45
17.	Dave Schultz	45
18.	Gary Scelzi	43
19.	Tony Pedregon	43
20.	Peter Biondo	43
21.	Angelle Sampey	41
22.	Jeff Taylor	41
23.	Jay Payne	40
24.	Kurt Johnson	40
25.	Cory McClenathan	38

Note: This Page And The Next Are The Only Pages You Will See John Force Having The NHRA Correct Wins/Final Rounds Total.

Top 25 Drivers On The Final Rounds List:

1. John Force	215
2. Warren Johnson	151
3. David Rampy	131
4. Bob Glidden	122
5. Kenny Bernstein	120
6. Frank Manzo	120
7. Pat Austin	118
8. Dan Fletcher	114
9. Tony Schumacher	113
10. Larry Dixon	108
11. Joe Amato	107
12. Greg Anderson	107
13. Jeg Coughlin	106
14. Bob Newberry	90
15. Kurt Johnson	78
16. Tony Pedregon	76
17. Jay Payne	73
18. Cory McClenathan	71
19. Dave Schultz	71
20. Cruz Pedregon	71
21. Gary Scelzi	70
22. Ron Capps	69
23. Don Prudhomme	69
24. Angelle Sampey	68
25. Antron Brown	67

TOP 25 DRIVERS WHO HAVE WON THE U.S. NATIONALS THE MOST:

1.	Bob Glidden	9	1973-1974, 1978-1979, 1983, 1985-1988: Holds All-Time And PS Record: 4 Consecutive Wins
2.	Tony Schumacher	8	2000, 2002-2004, 2006-2009: Tied All-Time And Holds TF Record: 4 Consecutive Wins
3.	Don Garlits	8	1964, 1967-1968, 1975, 1978, 1984-1986
4.	Don Prudhomme	7	3 – TF: 1965, 1969-1970 4 – FC: 1973-1974, 1977, 1989, First Driver Ever To Win In Both Nitro Classes
5.	Ed McCulloch:	6	1 – TF: 1992 5 – FC: 1971-1972, 1980, 1988, 1990
6.	Warren Johnson	6	1984, 1992-1995, 1999: Tied PS Record: 4 Consecutive Wins
7.	Greg Anderson	6	2001, 2003-2006, 2011: Tied PS Record: 4 Consecutive Wins
8.	Dave Schultz	6	1987-1988, 1990, 1992-1994: Hold PSM Record: 3 Consecutive Wins
9.	Larry Dixon	4	1995, 2001, 2005, 2010, Won As A Rookie
10.	John Force	4	1993, 1996, 1998, 2002
11.	Terry Vance	4	1979, 1981, 1985-1986
12.	Jeg Coughlin	3	2000, 2002, 2009
13.	John Myers	3	1989, 1996-1997
14.	Cruz Pedregon	3	1992, 1994-1995: Holds FC Record: 2 Consecutive Wins, Won As A Rookie
15.	Kenny Bernstein	3	2 – FC: 1983, 1987 1 – TF: 1991
16.	Gary Beck	3	1972, 1973, 1983
17.	Antron Brown	3	2 – PSM: 2000-2004 1 – TF: 2011: Only Driver To Win In TF And PSM
18.	Joe Amato	3	1987-1988, 1990
19.	Cory McCleanathan	2	1996, 1999
20.	Jim Head	2	1 – TF: 1997 1 – FC: 1984
21.	Raymond Beadle	2	1975, 1981
22.	Kurt Johnson	2	1996-1997
23.	Lee Shepherd	2	1980-1981
24.	Ronnie Sox	2	1969, 1971
25.	Matt Hines	2	1998-1999

Top 25 Percentages For The Drivers Who Have Won The Most When Having Gone To A Final Round: 31 Shown In Fairness Of Having 25 Different Drivers:

1. Bob Bode (FC Leader)	1/1 =	100%
2. Melanie Troxel (FC Career)	1/1 =	100%
3. Cristen Powell (TF Career) (TF Leader)	1/1 =	100%
4. Johnny Gray (TAFC Career)	2/2 =	100%
5. Johnny Gray (TAD Career)	1/1 =	100%
6. Shelly Anderson (TAD Career)	1/1 =	100%
7. Cruz Pedregon (TAD Career)	3/3 =	100%
8. Shelly Anderson (PM Career)	1/1 =	100%
9. Shelly Anderson (Career)	6/7 =	85.7%
10. Don Garlits	35/43 =	81.3%
11. Shelly Anderson (TF Career)	4/5 =	80%
12. Don Prudhomme (FC Career)	35/44 =	79.5%
13. Morgan Lucas (TAD Career)	11/14 =	78.5%
14. Shawn Langdon (Sportsman Career)	7/9 =	77.7%
15. Mike Dunn (FC Career)	10/13 =	76.9%
16. Gordie Bonin (FC Leader)	9/12 =	75%
17. J.R. Todd	6/8 =	75%
18. Paul Lee (TAFC Career)	3/4 =	75%
19. Leroy Goldstein	3/4 =	75%
20. Del Worsham (TF Career)	8/11 =	72.7%
21. Rod Fuller (Sportsman Career)	13/18 =	72.2%
22. Darrell Gwynn (TF Career)	18/25 =	72%
23. Todd Simpson (TAFC Career)	5/7 =	71.4%
24. Don Schumacher	5/7 =	71.4%
25. Don Prudhomme (Career)	49/69 =	71%
26. Bill Walsh (TAD Career)	12/17 =	70.5%
27. Shirley Muldowney (TF Career)	18/27 =	66.6%
28. Darrell Gwynn (TAD Career)	10/15 =	66.6%
29. Eric Medlen	6/9 =	66.6%
30. Lori Johns	4/6 =	66.6%
31. Steve Torrence (TAD Career)	4/6 =	66.6%

Note: List features only drivers who have driven in a Top-Fuel And Funny Car. If any of the drivers listed has had a successful career in any other pro or sportsman class, it was listed. There could be segments of driver's careers that have overall career numbers that could make this list, but exact career information could not be found. This is the only page in the book where the list is not 100% accurate due what may be missing, but what is listed is 100% accurate.

Top 25 Percentages For The Drivers Who Have The Best Record For Left First/Left On: 29 Shown In Fairness Of Having 25 Different Drivers:

1. Leah Pruett (FC Leader)	1/0 =	100%
2. Justin Schriefer	1/0 =	100%
3. Andy Kelley	1/0 =	100%
4. Scotty Cannon (TF Career) (TF Leader)	1/0 =	100%
5. Spencer Massey	105/20 =	84%
6. Clay Millican	134/45 =	74.8%
7. Kenny Bernstein (FC Career) (1997-2011)	20/7 =	74%
8. Paul Romine (1997-2011)	51/21 =	70.8%
9. Shawn Langdon	91/40 =	69.4%
10. Antron Brown (TF Career)	173/81 =	68.1%
11. Brady Kalivoda	17/8 =	68%
12. Tony Pedregon (FC Career)	481/232 =	67.4%
13. Brian Thiel	4/2 =	66.6%
14. Todd Simpson (TF Career)	2/1 =	66.6%
15. Tim Boychuk	2/1 =	66.6%
16. John Smith (TF Career)	76/39 =	66%
17. John Smith (Career)	81/42 =	65.8%
18. Scott Palmer	25/14 =	64.1%
19. Bob Gilbertson	114/65 =	63.6%
20. Jim Head (TF Career)	90/52 =	63.3%
21. Jeff Arend	116/69 =	62.7%
22. Antron Brown (Career)	315/189 =	62.5%
23. John Smith (FC Career)	5/8 =	62.5%
24. Dale Pulde (1997-2011)	5/8 =	62.5%
25. Tommy Johnson Jr. (Career) (1997-2011)	198/125 =	61.3%
26. Tommy Johnson Jr. (1997-2011)	194/122 =	61.3%
27. Steve Torrence	50/32 =	60.9%
28. J.R. Todd	68/44 =	60.7%
29. Del Cox	3/2 =	60%

TOP 25 PERCENTAGES FOR THE DRIVERS WHO HAVE THE BEST ELIMINATION ROUND WIN/LOSS RECORD: 35 SHOWN IN FAIRNESS OF HAVING 25 DIFFERENT DRIVERS:

1. Gary Scelzi (TF Career) (TF Leader)	223/89 =	71.4%
2. John Force (FC Leader)	1105/444 =	71.3%
3. Del Worsham (TF Career)	57/23 =	71.2%
4. Antron Brown (TF Career)	189/82 =	69.7%
5. Tony Schumacher	599/268 =	69%
6. Spencer Massey	92/43 =	68.1%
7. Larry Dixon	637/314 =	66.9%
8. Kenny Bernstein (TF Career) (1997-2011)	255/126 =	66.9%
9. Antron Brown (Career)	413/213 =	65.9%
10. Kenny Bernstein (Career) (1997-2011)	269/412 =	65.2%
11. Joe Amato (1997-2011)	137/79 =	64.9%
12. Gary Scelzi (Career)	380/214 =	63.9%
13. Robert Hight	237/134 =	63.8%
14. Antron Brown (PSM Career)	224/121 =	63%
15. Mike Dunn (1997-2011)	114/184 =	61.9%
16. Jack Beckman (FC Career)	171/109 =	61%
17. Tony Pedregon (FC Career)	501/331 =	60.2%
18. Brandon Bernstein	268/178 =	60%
19. Tony Pedregon (Career)	503/337 =	59.8%
20. Doug Kalitta	424/289 =	59.4%
21. Whit Bazemore (FC Career) (1997-2011)	289/197 =	59.4%
22. Jack Beckman (Career)	175/121 =	59.1%
23. Eric Medlen	95/66 =	59%
24. Whit Bazemore (Career) (1997-2011)	306/215 =	58.7%
25. Darrell Russell	106/76 =	58.2%
26. Cory McClenathan (1997-2011)	512/369 =	58.1%
27. Ron Capps (FC Career)	425/306 =	58.1%
28. Mike Neff	95/69 =	57.9%
29. Ron Capps (Career) (1997-2011)	436/322 =	57.5%
30. Cruz Pedregon (FC Career) (1997-2012)	449/333 =	57.4%
31. Cruz Pedregon (Career) (1997-2012)	452/343 =	56.8%
32. Rod Fuller	127/101 =	55.7%
33. Gary Scelzi (FC Career)	157/125 =	55.6%
34. Ashley Force Hood	105/84 =	55.5%
35. Matt Hagan	87/70 =	55.4%

NOTABLE ALL-TIME NHRA STATS:

Debut: 1951 First National Event Winner: 1955—Calvin Rice

Most Wins: 135—John Force Most Finals: 216—John Force

Most Elimination Rounds Won: 1105—John Force

Most Elimination Round Appearances: 1549—John Force

Most Consecutive Elimination Round Wins: 35—Bob Glidden

Most Elimination Rounds Won In A Single Season: 76

TF: Tony Schumacher In 24 Events PS: Greg Anderson In 23 Events

Most Consecutive Rounds Won In A Single Season: 31—Tony Schumacher

Most Wins In A Single Season: 15

TF: Tony Schumacher In 24 Events PS: Greg Anderson In 23 Events

Most Final Round Appearances In A Single Season: 19—Greg Anderson

Most Consecutive Wins: 9—Bob Glidden

Most Consecutive Finals: 17—Bob Glidden

Most Wins At A Single Event: 11 In Brainerd—John Force

Most Consecutive Wins At A Single Event: 7 In Atlanta—Dave Schultz

Most Finals At A Single Event: 15 In Indianapolis—Bob Glidden

Most Consecutive Final Rounds At A Single Event: 13 In Indianapolis—Bob Glidden

Most Qualified Starts: 577—John Force

Most Consecutive Qualified Starts: Current: 215—Greg Anderson

Record: 397—John Force, Streak Ended In 2007 And Started in 1988

Most # 1 Qualifiers: 139—John Force

Most # 1 Qualifiers In A Single Season: 16

Greg Anderson In 23 Events/Mike Edwards In 24 Events

Most Consecutive # 1 Qualifiers: 23—Bob Glidden

Most Championships Won By A Driver: 15—John Force

Most Consecutive Championships Won By A Driver: 10—John Force

Most Championships By A Won By A Team Owner: 17—John Force

Most Championships Won By A Crew Chief: 17—Austin Coil

Most Consecutive Championships Won By A Crew Chief: 10—Austin Coil

Most Consecutive Top Ten Finishes: 27—John Force

Most Consecutive Seasons With A Win: Current: 12—Greg Anderson Record: 22—John Force

Most Consecutive Seasons With A Final Round:

Current: 17—Tony Schumacher/Larry Dixon Record: 24—John Force

Largest Championship Winning Points Margin: 742—Greg Anderson

Smallest Championship Winning Points Margin: 2—TF: Tony Schumacher PSM: Hector Arana

Youngest NHRA Championship Winner: 20—LE Tonglet Oldest: 61—John Force

Youngest National Event Winner: 18—Jeb Allen Oldest Winner: 66—Warren Johnson

Youngest Driver Ever: 17—Jeb Allen Oldest: 83—Chris Karamesines

TOP 25 DRIVERS ON THE WINS LIST IN TOP FUEL:

1. Tony Schumacher	67
2. Larry Dixon	62
3. Joe Amato	52
4. Kenny Bernstein	40
5. Don Garlits	35
6. Cory McClenathan	34
7. Doug Kalitta	32
8. Gary Scelzi	25
9. Gary Beck	19
10. Shirley Muldowney	18
11. Brandon Bernstein	18
12. Darrell Gwynn	18
13. Scott Kalitta	17
14. Antron Brown	16
15. Dick LaHaie	15
16. Don Prudhomme	14
17. Gary Ormsby	14
18. Eddie Hill	13
19. Mike Dunn	12
20. Doug Herbert	10
21. Connie Kalitta	10
22. Spencer Massey	9
23. Del Worsham	8
24. Kelly Brown	8
25. Rod Fuller	7

TOP 25 DRIVERS ON THE FINAL ROUNDS LIST IN TOP-FUEL:

1. Tony Schumacher	113
2. Larry Dixon	108
3. Joe Amato	99
4. Kenny Bernstein	71
5. Cory McClenathan	65
6. Doug Kalitta	64
7. Don Garlits	43
8. Gary Scelzi	39
9. Brandon Bernstein	36
10. Scott Kalitta	34
11. Gary Beck	34
12. Antron Brown	34
13. Eddie Hill	33
14. Dick Lahaie	31
15. Doug Herbert	27
16. Mike Dunn	27
17. Shirley Muldowney	27
18. Darrell Gwynn	25
19. Gary Ormsby	25
20. Don Prudhomme	25
21. Connie Kalitta	22
22. Rod Fuller	18
23. Darrell Russell	17
24. Spencer Massey	16
25. David Grubnic	15

Top 25 Percentages For The Drivers Who Have Won The Most When Having Gone To A Final Round In Top-Fuel:

32. Cristen Powell	1/1 =	100%
33. Don Garlits	35/43 =	81.3%
34. Shelly Anderson	4/5 =	80%
35. J.R. Todd	6/8 =	75%
36. Del Worsham	8/11 =	72.7%
37. Darrell Gwynn	18/25 =	72%
38. Shirley Muldowney	18/27 =	66.6%
39. Lori Johns	4/6 =	66.6%
40. Mark Oswald	2/3 =	66.6%
41. Gary Scelzi	25/39 =	64.1%
42. Pat Austin	5/8 =	62.5%
43. Kelly Brown	8/13 =	61.5%
44. Tony Schumacher	67/113 =	59.2%
45. Larry Dixon	62/108 =	57.4%
46. Ed McCulloch	4/7 =	57.1%
47. Kenny Bernstein	41/72 =	56.9%
48. Spencer Massey	9/16 =	56.2%
49. Gary Ormsby	14/25 =	56%
50. Don Prudhomme	14/25 =	56%
51. Gary Beck	19/34 =	55.8%
52. Richard Tharp	5/9 =	55.5%
53. Morgan Lucas	6/11 =	54.5%
54. Joe Amato	99/52 =	52.5%
55. Cory McClenathan	34/65 =	52.3%
56. Doug Kalitta	32/64 =	50%

Notable All-Time Stats In Top-Fuel Dragster:

Class Debut: 1955—Known As Top Eliminator Until 1963
First National Event Winner: Calvin Rice
Most Elimination Rounds Won: 637—Larry Dixon
Most Elimination Round Appearances: 951—Larry Dixon
Most Rounds Won In A Single Season: 76—Tony Schumacher
Most Consecutive Rounds Won In A Single Season: 31—Tony Schumacher
Most Wins: 67—Tony Schumacher Most Finals: 113—Tony Schumacher
Most Wins In A Single Season: 15—Tony Schumacher
Most Final Round Appearances In A Single Season: 18—Tony Schumacher
Most Consecutive Wins: 7—Tony Schumacher
Most Consecutive Finals: 11—Tony Schumacher
Most Wins At A Single Event: 8—Indianapolis Don Garlits/Tony Schumacher
Most Consecutive Wins At A Single Event:
4—Joe Amato In Denver/Tony Schumacher In Indianapolis/Pomona-2
Most Finals At A Single Event:
10—Larry Dixon In Englishtown/Indianapolis/Tony Schumacher Chicago/Indianapolis
Most Consecutive Finals At A Single Event: 8—Tony Schumacher In Chicago/Indianapolis
Most Qualified Starts: 403—Cory McClenathan
Most Consecutive Qualified Starts: 206—Tony Schumacher
Most # 1 Qualifiers: 67—Tony Schumacher
Most # 1 Qualifiers In A Single Season: 13—Tony Schumacher
Most Consecutive # 1 Qualifiers: 9—Gary Beck

Most Championships Won By A Driver: 7—Tony Schumacher

Most Consecutive Championships Won By A Driver: 6—Tony Schumacher

Most Championships By A Won By A Team Owner: 7—Don Schumacher

Most Championships Won By A Crew Chief: 11—Alan Johnson

Most Consecutive Championships Won By A Crew Chief: 6—Alan Johnson

Most Consecutive Top Ten Finishes:

Current: 15—Doug Kalitta Record: 19—Joe Amato

Most Consecutive Seasons With A Win: Current: 5—Larry Dixon

Record: 9—Tony Schumacher

Most Consecutive Seasons With A Final Round: Current: 17—Tony Schumacher/Larry Dixon

Largest Championship Winning Points Margin: 415—Tony Schumacher

Smallest Championship Winning Points Margin 2—Tony Schumacher

Quickest Bump 1000/1320: 3.884—Morgan Lucas/4.577—David Grubnic

National E.T. Record 1000/1320: 3.735—Del Worsham/4.428—Tony Schumacher

National Speed Record 1000/1320: 332.18—Spencer Massey/336.15—Tony Schumacher

Quickest E.T. And Speed Ever Run: 1320: 4.420—Doug Kalitta/337.58—Tony Schumacher

Youngest Championship Winner: 18—Jeb Allen Oldest: 57—Eddie Hill

Youngest National Event Winner: 18—Jeb Allen Oldest Winner: 60—Eddie Hill

Youngest Driver Ever: 17—Jeb Allen Oldest: 83—Chris Karamesines

TOP 25 DRIVERS ON THE WINS LIST IN FUNNY CAR:

1.	John Force	135
2.	Tony Pedregon	43
3.	Don Prudhomme	35
4.	Ron Capps	32
5.	Kenny Bernstein	30
6.	Cruz Pedregon	30
7.	Robert Hight	27
8.	Del Worsham	25
9.	Whit Bazemore	20
10.	Ed McCulloch	18
11.	Mark Oswald	18
12.	Tim Wilkerson	17
13.	Al Hofmann	15
14.	Chuck Etchells	13
15.	Raymond Beadle	13
16.	Gary Scelzi	12
17.	Jack Beckman	12
18.	Billy Meyer	11
19.	Mike Dunn	10
20.	Gordie Bonin	9
21.	Gary Densham	8
22.	Tommy Johnson Jr.	7
23.	Bruce Larson	7
24.	Frank Hawley	7
25.	Mike Neff	7

TOP 25 DRIVERS ON THE FINAL ROUNDS LIST IN FUNNY CAR:

1. John Force	216
2. Tony Pedregon	76
3. Ron Capps	68
4. Cruz Pedregon	67
5. Kenny Bernstein	50
6. Whit Bazemore	46
7. Don Prudhomme	44
8. Ed McCulloch	43
9. Robert Hight	41
10. Del Worsham	39
11. Mark Oswald	38
12. Al Hofmann	32
13. Tim Wilkerson	29
14. Raymond Beadle	28
15. Jack Beckman	27
16. Chuck Etchells	26
17. Gary Densham	20
18. Gary Scelzi	20
19. Billy Meyer	20
20. Bruce Larson	19
21. Tommy Johnson Jr.	17
22. Mike Neff	18
23. Ashley Force Hood	16
24. Dean Skuza	14
25. Mike Dunn	13

Top 25 Percentages For The Drivers Who Have Won The Most When Having Gone To A Final Round In Funny Car:

57. Bob Bobe	1/1 =	100%
58. Melanie Troxel	1/1 =	100%
59. Don Prudhomme	35/44 =	79.5%
60. Mike Dunn	10/13 =	76.9%
61. Gordie Bonin	9/12 =	75%
62. Leroy Goldstein	3/4 =	75%
63. Don Schumacher	5/7 =	71.4%
64. Eric Medlen	6/9 =	66.6%
65. Leonard Hughes	2/3 =	66.6%
66. Robert Hight	27/41 =	65.8%
67. Raymond Beadle	13/20 =	65%
68. Del Worsham	25/39 =	64.1%
69. John Force	135/216 =	62.5%
70. Kenny Bernstein	30/50 =	60%
71. Gary Scelzi	12/20 =	60%
72. Mike Ashley	3/5 =	60%
73. Tim Wilkerson	17/29 =	58.6%
74. Frank Pedregon	4/7 =	57.1%
75. Tony Pedregon	43/76 =	56.5%
76. Frank Hawley	7/13 =	53.8%
77. Billy Meyer	11/20 =	55%
78. Chuck Etchells	13/26 =	50%
79. Jerry Toliver	5/10 =	50%
80. Frank Pedregon	4/8 =	50%
81. Scott Kalitta	1/2 =	50%

Notable All-Time Stats In Funny Car:

Class Debut: 1969 First National Event Winner: Clare Sanders

Most Elimination Rounds Won: 1105—John Force

Most Elimination Round Appearances: 1549—John Force

Most Rounds Won In A Single Season: 65—John Force (Out Of 76 Rounds Or 19 Events)

Most Consecutive Rounds Won In A Single Season: 30—Don Prudhomme

Most Wins: 135—John Force Most Finals: 216—John Force

Most Wins In A Single Season: 13—John Force

Most Final Round Appearances In A Single Season: 16—John Force

Most Consecutive Wins: 7—Don Prudhomme

Most Consecutive Finals: 13—Don Prudhomme

Most Wins At A Single Event: 11—John Force In Brainerd

Most Consecutive Wins At A Single Event: 5—John Force In Gainesville

Most Finals At A Single Event: 12—John Force In Brainerd

Most Consecutive Finals At A Single Event: 9—John Force In Atlanta

Most Qualified Starts: 578—John Force

Most Consecutive Qualified Starts: Current: 80—John Force Record: 397—John Force

Most # 1 Qualifiers: 139—John Force

Most # 1 Qualifiers In A Single Season: 13—John Force

Most Consecutive # 1 Qualifiers: 7—Don Prudhomme/John Force

Most Championships Won By A Driver: 15—John Force

Most Consecutive Championships Won By A Driver: 10—John Force

Most Championships By A Won By A Team Owner: 17—John Force

Most Championships Won By A Crew Chief: 18—Austin Coil

Largest Championship Winning Points Margin: 636—John Force

Smallest Championship Winning Points Margin: 8—Gary Scelzi

Most Consecutive Championships Won By A Crew Chief: 10—Austin Coil

Most Consecutive Top Ten Finishes: 27—John Force

Most Consecutive Seasons With A Win:

Current: Active: 8—Robert Hight Inactive: 10—Whit Bazemore Record: 22—John Force

Most Consecutive Seasons With A Final Round:

Current: 8—Robert Hight Inactive: 10—Whit Bazemore Record: 24—John Force

Quickest Bump 1000/1320: 4.134—Tony Pedregon/4.795—Jim Head

National E.T. Record 1000/1320: 3.991—Matt Hagan/4.661—Jack Beckman

National Speed Record 1000/1320: 318.99—Jack Beckman/334.83—Mike Ashley

Quickest E.T. And Speed Ever Run: 1320: 4.636—Robert Hight/334.83—Mike Ashley

Fastest Speed Ever 1000: 322.27—Matt Hagan

Youngest Championship Winner: 26—Frank Hawley Oldest: 61—John Force

Youngest National Event Winner: 21—Del Worsham Oldest: 62—John Force

Youngest Driver Ever: 19—Billy Meyer Oldest: 62—John Force

NHRA PROFESSIONAL CLASS DRIVERS:

- ALL STATS ARE UP TO DATE AS OF 4/29/12, CONCLUSION OF RACE 6.
- All Left First Stats For Drivers/Riders: A Drag Race Had A Pair Of Reaction Times To Qualify For The Stat. Driver Red-Lights, Bye Runs, Opponent Red-Light, Opponent Break Before Taking The Tree, Or An R/T Tie, Did Not Count. 4 Wide Races Determined By Driver's R/T Against Their Lane Opponent. (1-2, 3-4)
- In-depth Shootout Class Results Not Included, Non Point Races In Pro-Stock And Pro-Stock Motorcycle Count Toward Driver Stats, Top-Fuel And Funny Car Bonus Race Stats From Bristol Not Included, But Stats From '97 And '98 Winston Invitational Did Count. My Parameters For This Stat Are Somewhat Different When Compared To How This Stat Is Usually Counted. I Consider My Way To Be The Most Direct Way To See Flat Out Who Won/Who Lost At The Tree, But My Only Flaw Is That It Will Not Tell The Story On How Many Times A Driver May Have Been In A Situation That Disqualified The Stat.
- A Note Of How Close A Driver DNQ'ed By Was Only Given If The E.T. Was Within A Hundredth (10 Thousandths) Of A Second And The MPH Was Faster Than # 16, Or The E.T. Was The Same And The MPH Was Slower. When A Driver Has Wins/Finals/# 1 Qualifiers From Any NHRA Sportsman Series Class, Only The Wins/Finals/# 1 Qualifiers Received At National Events Counted Toward Driver's Total. All At The Tree, Win Percentage In Final Round, (Must Have Won To Have Stat Recorded) Average Career Qualifing Spot, Most Successful Event Stats Are Taken From Stats In The Drivers

Pro Class Careers Only. Any Information Found On A Driver In Another Series Other Than The NHRA Was Shown, But Not Counted Toward Overall Stats Since This Is Strictly NHRA. Consecutive Qualified Starts Means The Number Of Consecutive Starts The Driver/Rider Has Made In Their Career Without A DNQ.

- What Determined How A Driver Received A Profile In This Book? The Driver Had Three Ways To Accomplish This. The Driver Either Won A Championship Or Appeared In A Final Round Between 1997-2012 In A Pro Class, Have Made At Least One Pass In Their Respective Class Since 2009, Or Have Made At Least One Pass In Their Respective Class From 1997-2012 And Are One Of The Top 50 NHRA Drivers From The 2001 List.

- Sportsman Statistics Of A Drivers Career Are From What Was Easily Be Found. I Feel Confident That I Covered Every Driver, But There is A Small Chance I Missed Season Or Class Information. Divisional Championships Don't Count Toward A Drivers Championship Total. Points Data Was Not Available For All Drivers In-depth Prior To 2000, Especially If They Finished Outside The Top Ten. 1999 For Divisional Information. *

- Differences In Engine Cubic Inch Displacement Varies Between Teams Due To The Teams Combination Of Bore And Stroke Of The Engine Block And Type Of Pistons Used. It Is Roughly Closer To The 500 CID Rule Limit After The Engine Is Together.

- Data On The 1997 Indianapolis Provisional # 1 Qualifiers Could Not Be Found.

Top-Fuel Dragster Drivers:

Khalid alBalooshi Date Of Birth: July 27, 1979 From: Brownsburg, IN Formally: Dubai, UAE

Sponsor: Al-Anabi Crew Chief: Jason McCulloch/Ronnie Thompson Owner: Alan Johnson

Chassis: '11 Hadman Engine: TFX 500

Pro Debut: 2012 Starts: 6 Consecutive Qualified Starts: 6

Win Percentage In Final Round: 66.6% PM: 66.6% Average Career Qualifying Spot: 6.66

AT THE TREE:

Career Holeshot Win/Loss Record: 0/3 Career Left Firsts/Left On: 1/4 = 20%

STATS:

Championships: 1 PM: 1

ADRL: US: PM: 1 ADRL: PM: 2 EMC: 5 PM: 1 SS: 1 SS8: 1 SS7.5: 1 SS6: 1

Career Best E.T./Speed: 1000ft.: 3.808/323.58

Career Wins: 2 PM: 2 ADRL: US: PM: 1 ADRL: PM: 9 EMC: PM: 14 SS: 1

Career Finals: 3 PM: 3

Most Successful Event: All Starts: 0/1

Elimination Round Win/Loss Record: 0/6 = 0%

Career # 1 Qualifiers: 2 PM: 2

Career Provisional # 1 Qualifiers: 4 PM: 4

Top Five Point Finishes: 1 PM: 1
Top Ten Point Finishes: 1 PM: 1

YEARLY CAREER SUMMARY:

* Distinction Between Which ADRL Is Which Is Only Made In This Driver's Profile. ADRL In All Other Future Pages Is Known As The American Drag Racing League *

2012: 13th-208 (-329), 0/6, Average Qualifying Start: 6.66, Left First: 20%
2011: Won NHRA And Arabian Drag Racing League Pro Mod Championship
2010: Won Arabian Drag Racing League Pro Mod Championship
2009: Won American Drag Racing League Pro Mod Championship
2006: Won Emirates Motor Club Super Street 8, Super Street 7.5, Super Street 6 and Pro Mod Championships
2005: Won Emirates Motor Club Super Street Championship

Joe Amato Date Of Birth: June 13, 1944 From: Exeter, PA RETIRED

Pro Debut: 1982 Starts: 1997-2011: 90 Consecutive Qualified Starts: 23

Win Percentage In Final Round: 53.2% TF: 52.5% TAD: 60% PC: 66.6% IHRA: TF: 57.1%

Average Career Qualifying Spot: 1997-2011: 4.33

AT THE TREE: 1997-2011:

Career Holeshot Win/Loss Record: 7/2 Career Left Firsts/Left On: 106/95 = 52.7%

Career Final Rounds Won/Lost On A Holeshot: 2/0

STATS:

Championships: 5 U.S. Nationals Wins/Finals: 3/4

Career Best E.T./Speed: 1320ft.: 4.516/326.67

Career Wins: 57 TF: 52 TAD: 3 PC: 2 IHRA: TF: 4

Career Finals: 107 TF: 99 TAD: 5 PC: 3 IHRA: TF: 7

Last Win: 2000 Reading

Last Final: 2000 Reading

Most Successful Event: Englishtown: 6 Wins, 9 Finals

Elimination Round Win/Loss Record: 1997-2011: 137/74 = 64.9%

Career # 1 Qualifiers: 56

Career Provisional # 1 Qualifiers: 1997-2011: 17

Top Five Point Finishes: 15, 4 Consecutive IHRA: TF: 2

Top Ten Point Finishes: 19 Consecutive IHRA: TF: 3

Career Best Points Finish: 1st-16058

YEARLY CAREER SUMMARY:

2001: # 9 On The Top 50 NHRA Drivers List

2000: 4th-1422 (-468), 31/21, 2 Wins, 4 Finals, Average Qualifying Spot: 4.34, Qualified # 1 Three Times, Left First: 30.6%

1999: 3rd-1345 (-143), 30/16, 5 Wins, Including 2 Consecutive, 6 Finals, Average Qualifying Spot: 5.28, Qualified # 1 Four Times Including 2 Consecutive, 1 DNQ, Left First: 48.8%

1998: 3rd-1522 (-259), 36/19, 4 Wins, Including 2 Consecutive, 6 Finals, Including 3 Consecutive, Average Qualifying Spot: 4.34, Qualified # 1 Five Times, Including 2 Consecutive, Left First: 71.1%

1997: 3rd-1597 (-240), 40/18, 5 Wins, Including 2 Consecutive, 8 Finals, Average Qualifying Spot: 3.43, Qualified # 1 Nine Times, Including 4 Consecutive, Left First: 58.1%

1996: 6th-1141 (-274), 2 Wins, 4 Finals

1995: 10th-775 (-800), Qualified # 1 Once

1994: 5th-10244 (-3356), 1 Win, 3 Finals, Qualified # 1 Once

1993: 7th-8844 (-3954), 2 Wins, 2 Finals

1992: 1st-12232, 3 Wins, 5 Finals, Qualified # 1 Once

1991: 1st-14388, 4 Wins, Including 3 Consecutive, 8 Finals, Qualified # 1 Five Times, Including 3 Consecutive

1990: 1st-16058, 6 Wins, Including 2 Consecutive, 10 Finals, Qualified # 1 Seven Times, Including 3 Consecutive

1989: 2nd-14178 (-774), 4 Wins, Including 2 Consecutive, 8 Finals, Qualified # 1 Four Times, Including 3 Consecutive

1988: 1st-14104, 4 Wins, Including 2 Consecutive Twice, 9 Finals, Qualified # 1 Four Times

1987: 2nd-13110 (-42), 3 Wins, 8 Finals, Qualified # 1 Three Times

1986: 4th-9484 (-2452), 2 Finals, Qualified # 1 Once

1985: 2nd-9874 (-2204), 1 Win, 4 Finals, Qualified # 1 Five Times, Including 3 Consecutive

1984: 1st-10646, 3 Wins, Including 2 Consecutive, 7 Finals, Qualified # 1 Three Times, Including 2 Consecutive

1983: 2nd-8806 (-2124), 3 Wins, Including 2 Consecutive, 5 Finals

1982: 6th-5155 (-2747)

Mike Ashley Date Of Birth: July 30, 1965 From: Melville, NY

Pro Debut: TF: 2011 FC: 2005 Starts: 42 TF: 1 FC: 41 Consecutive Qualified Starts: 1

Win Percentage In Final Round: 60% FC: 60% PM: 60% IHRA: FC: 100% PM: 33.3%

Average Career Qualifying Spot: 7.86 TF: 16 FC: 7.66

AT THE TREE:

Career Holeshot Win/Loss Record: 2/4 FC: 2/4

Career Left Firsts/Left On: 25/45 = 35.7% TF: 0/1 = 0% FC: 26/45 = 36.6%

STATS:

Championships: 2 PM: 2 U.S. Nationals Wins/Finals: 1/1 FC: 1/1

Career Best E.T./Speed: 1000ft.: TF: 3.904/314.39 1320ft.: FC: 4.694/334.32

Career Wins: 9 FC: 3 PM: 6 IHRA: FC: 1 PM: 1

Career Finals: 15 FC: 5 PM: 10 IHRA: FC: 1 PM: 3

Last Win: 2007 Indianapolis

Last Final: 2007 Indianapolis

Most Successful Event: TF: Pomona-2: 0/1 FC: Indianapolis: 5/1, 1 Win, 1 Final, 1 DNQ

Elimination Round Win/Loss Record: 36/39 = 48% TF: 0/1 = 0% FC: 36/38 = 48.6%

Career # 1 Qualifiers: 7 FC: 5 PM: 2

Career Provisional # 1 Qualifiers: 10 FC: 6 PM: 4

Top Five Point Finishes: 3 FC: 1 PM: 2 IHRA: PM: 1

Top Ten Point Finishes: 3 FC: 1 PM: 2 IHRA: PM: 1

Career Best Points Finish: Countdown: 6th-2337 (-841)

Pre-Countdown (2006 And Before): 13th—787 (-849)

Best/Worst Points Finish If Countdown Never Was: 6th

YEARLY CAREER SUMMARY:

2011: 33rd-31 (-2596), 0/1, Average Qualifying Spot: 16, Left First: 0%

2008: 23rd-87 (-2474), 1/1, Average Qualifying Spot: 2, Left First: 0%

2007: 6th-2337 (-841), 26/15, 3 Wins, 4 Finals, Average Qualifying Spot: 4.88, Qualified # 1 Five Times, Including 3 Consecutive, 5 DNQ's, 1 By 8 Thousandths, 6 Thousandths, 1 Thousandth, Left First: 39%, Ran The Fastest Speed Ever At Las Vegas-1, 334.61, (Missed Backing By 80.52 MPH) Mark Oswald And Brain Corradi Were The Crew Chiefs

2006: 13th-787 (-849), 8/18, 1 Final, Average Qualifying Spot: 9.5, 4 DNQ's, 1 By 2 Thousandths, Left First: 34.7%

2005: 22nd-157 (-1359), 1/4, Average Qualifying Spot: 11.2, Left First: 40%, Won Pro Mod Championship

2004: Won Pro Mod Championship

Ron August Jr. Date Of Birth: N/A From: Pleasanton, CA

Pro Debut: 2009 Starts: 4 Consecutive Qualified Starts: 2

Win Percentage In Final Round: 50% TAFC: 50% Average Career Qualifying Spot: 13.2

AT THE TREE: 1997-2011:

Career Left Firsts/Left On: 0/3 = 0%

STATS: 1997-2011:

Career Best E.T./Speed: 1000ft.: 3.892/316.90

Career Wins: 1 TAFC: 1

Career Finals: 2 TAFC: 2 IHRA: TF: 1

Most Successful Event: Pomona-1, Sonoma, Las Vegas-2: 0/1

Elimination Round Win/Loss Record: 0/4 = 0%

Career # 1 Qualifiers: 1 TAFC: 1

Career Provisional # 1 Qualifiers: 1 TAFC: 1

Career Best Points Finish: Countdown: 26th-114 (-2513)

YEARLY CAREER SUMMARY:

2011: 26th-114 (-2513), 0/3, Average Qualifying Spot: 14, 1 DNQ, Left First: 0%

2010: 32nd-52 (-2632), 0/1, Average Qualifying Spot: 11, 2 DNQ's, Left First: 0%

2009: 46th-20 (-2551), 3 DNQ's, Finished 10th In The Division 7 Top Alcohol Funny Car Points, 57th Nationally

2008: Finished 5th In The Division 7 Top Alcohol Funny Car Points, 35th Nationally

2007: Finished 3rd In The Division 7 Top Alcohol Funny Car Points, 23rd Nationally

2006: Finished 8th In The Division 7 Top Alcohol Funny Car Points, 29th Nationally

2005: Finished 17th In The Division 7 Top Alcohol Funny Car Points, 44th Nationally

2004: Finished 9th In The Division 7 Top Alcohol Funny Car Points, 32nd Nationally

2003: Finished 6th In The Division 7 Top Alcohol Funny Car Points, 25th Nationally

2002: Finished 12th In The Division 7 Top Alcohol Funny Car Points, 51st Nationally

2001: Finished 17th In The Division 7 Top Alcohol Funny Car Points, 52nd Nationally

2000: Finished 9th In The Division 7 Top Alcohol Funny Car Points, 62nd Nationally

David Baca Date Of Birth: January 30, 1958 From: Brentwood, CA
Pro Debut: 2002 Starts: 81 Consecutive Qualified Starts: 12
Average Career Qualifying Spot: 8.81

AT THE TREE:

Career Holeshot Win/Loss Record: 3/7 Career Left Firsts/Left On: 36/81 = 30.7%

STATS:

Career Best E.T./Speed: 1000ft.: 3.910/313.51 1320ft.: 4.485/331.69

Career Finals: 4 TF: 3 TAD: 1 Last Final: 2006 Pomona-1

Most Successful Event: Atlanta: 5/4, 1 Final

Elimination Round Win/Loss Record: 40/81 = 33%

Career # 1 Qualifiers: 5 TF: 2 TAD: 3

Career Provisional # 1 Qualifiers: 7 TF: 3 TAD: 4

Top Ten Point Finishes: TF: 1

Career Best Points Finish: Countdown: 24th-90 (-3096)

Pre-Countdown (2006 And Before): 7th-1041 (-953)

YEARLY CAREER SUMMARY:

2009: 28th-127 (-2444), 0/4, Average Qualifying Spot: 9, Left First: 25%

2007: 24th-90 (-3096), 1/2, Average Qualifying Spot: 4, Left First: 33.3%

2006: 12th-908 (-773), 10/22, 1 Final, Average Qualifying Spot: 9.77, 1 DNQ, Left First: 33.3%

2005: 13th-617 (-1364), 7/14, 1 Final, Average Qualifying Spot: 9.64, 3 DNQ's, Left First: 38%

2004: 13th-663 (-1331), 8/15, Average Qualifying Spot: 8.66, 1 DNQ, Left First: 31.8%

2003: 7th-1041 (-953), 14/23, Average Qualifying Spot: 7.73, Qualified # 1 Twice, Including 2 Consecutive, Left First: 24.3%

2002: 36th-42 (-1909), 0/1, Average Qualifying Spot: 12, Left First: 0%

2001: Finished 12th In The Division 7 Top Alcohol Dragster Points, 30th Nationally

2000: Finished 6th In The Division 7 Top Alcohol Dragster Points, 26th Nationally

Bobby Baldwin Date Of Birth: 1954 From: Upland, CA Died In 2001— Brain Aneurism

Pro Debut: TF: 1988 FC: 1997? Starts: 18 Consecutive Qualified Starts: TF: 7

Average Career Qualifying Spot: 1997-2011: TF: 13.6

AT THE TREE: 1997-2011:

Career Left Firsts/Left On: TF: 3/17 = 15%

STATS:

Career Best E.T./Speed: 1320ft.: TF: 4.757/305.70 FC: 5.325/260.86

Career Finals: TF: 1 Last Final: 2000 Houston-2

Most Successful Event: 1997-2011: TF: Houston-2: 3/1, 1 Final FC: All DNQ's

Elimination Round Win/Loss Record: 1997-2011: TF: 6/18 = 25%

Career Best Points Finish: 15th-309 (-1581)

YEARLY CAREER SUMMARY:

2001: 16th-353 (-1749), 3/10, Average Qualifying Spot: 13.2, 1 DNQ, Left First: 8.3%

2000: 15th-309 (-1581), 3/8, 1 Final, Average Qualifying Spot: 14.2, 3 DNQ's, Left First: 25%

1999: 3 DNQ's

1998: 7 DNQ's, 1 By 16.98 MPH

1997: 3 DNQ's, TF Only Following Seasons

Whit Bazemore Date Of Birth: March 12, 1963 From: Bend, OR RETIRED

Pro Debut: FC: 1992 TF: 2007 Starts: 1997-2011: 235 TF: 18 FC: 217

Consecutive Qualified Starts: 3 TF: 3 FC: 2

Win Percentage In Final Round: 1997-2011: 42.5% FC: 43.4% IHRA: FC: 50%

Average Career Qualifying Spot: 1997-2011: 5.86 TF: 5.66 FC: 5.88

AT THE TREE: 1997-2011:

Career Holeshot Win/Loss Record: 12/12 TF: 1/1 FC: 11/11

Career Left Firsts/Left On: 215/217 = 49.7% TF: 16/18 = 47% FC: 199/199 = 50%

Career Final Rounds Won/Lost On A Holeshot: 1/1 FC: 1/1

STATS:

U.S. Nationals Wins/Finals: FC: 2/4

Career Best E.T./Speed: 1320ft.: 4.498/332.51 FC: 4.674/333.25

Career Wins: 20 FC: 20

Career Finals: 47 TF: 1 FC: 46 IHRA: FC: 1

Last Win: FC: 2006 Seattle

Last Final: TF: 2007 Denver FC: 2006 Indianapolis

Most Successful Event: 1997-2011: Seattle: 25/8, 3 Wins, 5 Finals TF: Denver: 3/1, 1 Final FC: 1997-2011: Seattle: 24/7, 3 Wins, 5 Finals

Elimination Round Win/Loss Record: 306/215 = 58.7%

TF: 17/18 = 48.5% FC: 289/197 = 59.4%

Career # 1 Qualifiers: 1997-2011: 29 TF: 1 FC: 28

Career Provisional # 1 Qualifiers: 1997-2011: 25 TF: 1 FC: 24

Top Five Point Finishes: 5 FC: 5 IHRA: FC: 1

Top Ten Point Finishes: 15, 14 Consecutive TF: 1 Consecutive FC: 14, 13 Consecutive IHRA: FC: 2

Career Best Points Finish: Countdown: 8th-2182 (-1004)

Pre-Countdown (2006 And Before): 2nd-1748 (-252)

Best/Worst Points Finish If Countdown Never Was: 8th/11th

YEARLY CAREER SUMMARY:

2007: 8th-2182 (-1004), 17/18, 1 Final, Average Qualifying Spot: 5.66, Qualified # 1 Once, 3 DNQ's, 1 By 2 Thousandths Of A Second, 1 By 6 Thousandths, Left First: 47%

2006: 9th-956 (-680), 19/16, 1 Win, 3 Finals, Average Qualifying Spot: 6.76, 1 DNQ, Left First: 53.1%

2005: 9th-1192 (-324), 23/20, 2 Wins, 2 Finals, Average Qualifying Spot: 9.31, Qualified # 1 Once, 1 DNQ, Left First: 53.6%

2004: 6th-1338 (-545), 27/21, 2 Wins, 5 Finals, Including 4 Consecutive, Average Qualifying Spot: 5.17, Qualified # 1 Four Times, Left First: 64.4%

2003: 2nd-1628 (-140), 43/19, 3 Wins, 8 Finals, Including 3 Consecutive, Average Qualifying Spot: 3.86, Qualified # 1 Three Times, 1 DNQ, Left First: 44.4%

2002: 5th-1204 (-572), 24/19, 2 Wins, Including 2 Consecutive, 3 Finals, Average Qualifying Spot: 5.38, Qualified # 1 Three Times, 2 DNQ's, Left First: 48.7%

2001: 2nd-1748 (-252), 44/21, 3 Wins, 8 Finals, Including 2 Consecutive Twice, Average Qualifying Spot: 4.87, Qualified # 1 Nine Times, Including 3 Consecutive Twice, Left First: 29.5%

2000: 7th-1088 (-904), 16/21, 1 Win, 3 Finals, Average Qualifying Spot: 6.27, Qualified #1 Three Times, Including Three Consecutive, 1 DNQ, Left First: 41.4%, Made First Ever 4 Second Pass At Denver, Tim And Kim Richards Were The Crew Chiefs

1999: 3rd-1413 (-658), 30/21, 1 Win, 5 Finals, Including 4 Consecutive, Average Qualifying Spot: 4.4, Qualified # 1 Twice, Left First: 56.2%

1998: 5th-1281 (-382), 27/22, 1 Win, 3 Finals, Average Qualifying Spot: 6.6, Qualified # 1 Once, Left First: 63%

1997: 3rd-1405 (-460), 36/17, 4 Wins, 5 Finals, Including 2 Consecutive, Average Qualifying Spot: 6.47, Qualified # 1 Twice, 2 DNQ's, Left First: 46%

1996: 9th-742 (-2765)

1995: 7th-884 (-806)

1993: 10th-6290 (-11784)

1992: 9th-7162 (-8084), 1 Final

Brandon Bernstein Date Of Birth: August 2, 1972 From: Lake Forest, CA
Sponsor: MavTV Crew Chief: Joe Barlam/John DeFilippis   Owner: Morgan Lucas
Chassis: '11 McKinney Engine: TFX 500
Pro Debut: 2003 Starts: 196 Consecutive Qualified Starts: 111
Win Percentage In Final Round: 51.2% TF: 50% TAD: 60%
Average Career Qualifying Spot: 5.59

AT THE TREE:

Career Holeshot Win/Loss Record: 5/21 Career Left Firsts/Left On: 171/243 = 41.3%

Career Final Rounds Won/Lost On A Holeshot: 1/3

STATS:

U.S. Nationals Wins/Finals: 0/1

Career Best E.T./Speed: 1000ft.: 3.784/325.77 1320ft.: 4.457/333.74

Career Wins: 21 TF: 18 TAD: 3

Career Finals: 41 TF: 36 TAD: 5

Last Win: 2009 Richmond

Last Final: 2011 Las Vegas-1

Most Successful Event: Las Vegas—1: 21/9, 1 Wins, 3 Finals

Elimination Round Win/Loss Record: 268/178 = 60%

Career # 1 Qualifiers: 18 TF: 14 TAD: 4

Career Provisional # 1 Qualifiers: 14 TF: 13 TAD: 1

Top Five Point Finishes: 4 TF: 4 TAD: 1

Top Ten Point Finishes: 8 Consecutive TF: 8 TAD: 1

Career Best Points Finish: Countdown: 3rd-3149 (-37)

Pre-Countdown (2006 And Before): 3rd-1565 (-116)

Best/Worst Points Finish If Countdown Never Was: 4th/7th

YEARLY CAREER SUMMARY:

2012: 11th-236 (-301), 2/6, Average Qualifying Spot: 6.83, Left First: 12.5%

2011: 6th-2381 (-246), 19/22, 1 Final, Qualified # 1 Once, Average Qualifying Spot: 5.59, Left First: 47.5%

2010: 7th-2366 (-318), 31/23, 3 Finals, Average Qualifying Spot: 6.6, Left First: 57.7%

2009: 5th-2438 (-133), 33/23, 1 Win, 5 Finals, Including 2 Consecutive, Average Qualifying Spot: 6.54, Left First: 64.1%

2008: 7th-2327 (-376), 26/24, 4 Finals, Average Qualifying Spot: 6.29, Qualified # 1 Twice, Left First: 29.7%, Lost 5 Rounds, Including 2 Consecutive Finals, On Holeshots

2007: 3rd-3149 (-37), 37/15, 5 Wins, Including 2 Consecutive, 7 Finals, Average Qualifying Spot: 5.4, 2 DNQ's, 1 By A Thousandth, Substitute Driver In Reading Due To Illness, Left First: 32%

2006: 3rd-1565 (-116), 38/19, 4 Wins, 7 Finals, Including 2 Consecutive, Average Qualifying Spot: 4.91, Qualified # 1 Three Times, Left First: 41.5%

2005: 7th-1344 (-637), 28/21, 2 Wins, Including 2 Consecutive, 2 Finals, Average Qualifying Spot: 5.69, Qualified # 1 Twice, Left First: 34.7%

2004: 3rd-1531 (-463), 36/20, 3 Wins, 4 Finals, Including 2 Consecutive, Average Qualifying Spot: 4.21, Qualified # 1 Four Times. Left First: 29.4%, Lost 5 Rounds On A Holeshot, Best Start Of Any Professional Winning In 5 Of Their First 13 Starts

2003: 15th-629 (-1365), 18/5, 3 Wins, Including 2 Consecutive, 3 Finals, Average Qualifying Spot: 3, Qualified # 1 Twice. Left First: 38%, Had A Season Ending Crash At Englishtown, Won Auto Club Road To The Future Award

2001: Won Division 7 Top Alcohol Dragster Championship, 4th Nationally, Shared Wins With His Dad As They Both Dominated In TF And TAD In Las Vegas-1, Chicago-2

Mike Bowers Date Of Birth: N/A From: Plano, TX

Pro Debut: 2009 Starts: 1 Consecutive Qualified Starts: 0 Average Career Qualifying Spot: 16

AT THE TREE:

Career Left Firsts/Left On: 0/1 = 0%

STATS:

Career Best E.T./Speed: 1000ft.: 4.018/296.50 Most Successful Event: Dallas: 0/1, 1 DNQ

Elimination Round Win/Loss Record: 0/1 = 0%

Career Best Points Finish: Countdown: 41st-31 (-2540)

YEARLY CAREER SUMMARY:

2010: 42nd-10 (-2674), 1 DNQ

2009: 41st-31 (-2540), 0/1, Average Qualifying Spot: 16, Left First: 0%

2003: Finished 7th In The Division 4 Top Alcohol Dragster Points, 55th Nationally

2002: Finished 10th In The Division 4 Top Alcohol Dragster Points, 73rd Nationally

2001: Finished 11th In The Division 4 Top Alcohol Dragster Points, 80th Nationally

Tim Boychuk Date Of Birth: N/A From: Alberta, Canada

Pro Debut: 2008 Starts: 3 Consecutive Qualified Starts: 0

Win Percentage In Final Round: 0% IHRA: 57.1% TF: 60% PFC: 55.5%

Average Career Qualifying Spot: 14.6

AT THE TREE:

Career Left Firsts/Left On: 2/1 = 66.6%

STATS:

Career Best E.T./Speed: 1000ft.: 3.890/305.49
Career Wins: 0 IHRA: 8 TF: 3 PFC: 5
Career Finals: 0 IHRA: 14 TF: 5 PFC: 9
Most Successful Event: Pomona-2: 0/1
Elimination Round Win/Loss Record: 0/3 = 0%
Career # 1 Qualifiers: 0 IHRA: TF: 1
Top Five Point Finishes: 0 IHRA: 1 TF: 1
Top Ten Point Finishes: 2 IHRA: 4 TF: 2 PFC: 2
Career Best Points Finish: Countdown: 24th-113 (-2590)

YEARLY CAREER SUMMARY:

2010: 42nd-10 (2674), 1 DNQ

2009: 48th-10 (-2561), 1 DNQ

2008: 24th-113 (-2590), 0/3, Average Qualifying Spot: 14.6, 2 DNQ's, Left First: 66.6%

Antron Brown Date Of Birth: March 1, 1976 From: Pittsboro, IN
Sponsor: Matco Tools Crew Chief: Mark Oswald/Brian Corradi
Assistant Crew Chief: Brad Mason Owner: Don Schumacher
Chassis: '11 DSR Engine: TFX 500
Pro Debut: PSM: 1998 TF: 2008 Starts: 245 TF: 98 PSM: 147
Consecutive Qualified Starts: TF: 75 PSM: 146
Win Percentage In Final Round: 47.7% TF: 47% PSM: 48.4%
Average Career Qualifying Spot: 5.17 TF: 4.81 PSM: 5.41

AT THE TREE:

Career Holeshot Win/Loss Record: 34/17 TF: 13/6 PSM: 21/11

Career Left Firsts/Left On: 315/189 = 62.5% TF: 173/81 = 68.1% PSM: 142/108 = 56.8%

Career Final Rounds Won/Lost On A Holeshot: 2/0 TF: 1/0 PSM: 1/0

STATS:

U.S. Nationals Wins/Finals: 3/3 TF: 1/1 PSM: 2/2

Career Best E.T./Speed: 1000ft.: 3.766/325.92 1320ft.: TF: 4.495/331.94 PSM: 6.930/192.55

Career Wins: 32 TF: 16 PSM: 16

Career Finals: 67 TF: 34 PSM: 33

Last Win: TF: 2012 Phoenix PSM: 2006 Brainerd

Last Final: TF: 2012 Houston PSM: 2006 Memphis

Most Successful Event: Brainerd: 30/9, 5 Wins, 5 Finals

TF: Sonoma: 10/2, 2 Wins, 2 Finals PSM: Brainerd: 23/6, 4 Wins, 4 Finals, Including 2 Consecutive

Elimination Round Win/Loss Record: 413/213 = 65.9%

TF: 189/82 = 69.7% PSM: 224/131 = 63%

Career # 1 Qualifiers: 29 TF: 18 PSM: 11

Career Provisional # 1 Qualifiers: 27 TF: 14 PSM: 13

Top Five Point Finishes: 11 TF: 4 Consecutive PSM: 7

Top Ten Point Finishes: 14 Consecutive * Never Finished Outside The Top 10 *

TF: 4 Consecutive PSM: 10 Consecutive

Career Best Points Finish: Countdown: TF: 3rd-2542 (-85) PSM: 10th-708 (-2503)

Pre-Countdown (2006 And Before): TF: 3rd-1565 (-116) PSM: 2nd-1175 (-157)

Best/Worst Points Finish If Countdown Never Was: TF: 1st/4th PSM: 10th

YEARLY CAREER SUMMARY:

2012: 1st-537, 16/5, 1 Win, 4 Finals, Average Qualifying Spot: 6.16, Left First: 57.1%

2011: 3rd-2542 (-85), 50/16, 6 Wins, Including 3 Consecutive, 8 Finals, Average Qualifying Spot: 5.18, Qualified # 1 Three Times, Left First: 77.4%

2010: 4th-2460 (-224), 36/22, 1 Win, 7 Finals, Including 2 Consecutive, Average Qualifying Spot: 4.82, Qualified # 1 Five Times, Left First: 69.8%

2009: 3rd-2522 (-49), 51/18, 6 Wins, Including 3 Consecutive, 10 Finals, Including 2 Consecutive Twice, Average Qualifying Spot: 3.75, Qualified # 1 Seven Times, Pomona-1 Ran A 3.708 For # 1 When 1/2 Track 3.074 Is About A 3.84; Still Good Enough For # 1, But A Timing Error, Left First: 68.7%, Won 4 Rounds On A Holeshot, Swept Western Swing And Won "Quest For The Full Throttle Moment" For That Feat

2008: 5th-2370 (-333), 36/21, 2 Wins, 5 Finals, Including 3 Consecutive, Average Qualifying Spot: 5.21, Qualified # 1 Three Times, 1 DNQ, Left First: 59.2 %, Won 4 Rounds On A Holeshot, First Season In Top Fuel, Only Driver In History To Win Races In TF And PSM

2007: 10th-708 (-2503), 9/16, Average Qualifying Spot: 7.62, Left First: 66.6%

2006: 2nd-1076 (-23), 28/13, 2 Wins, 5 Finals, Including 3 Consecutive, Average Qualifying Spot: 6.06, Qualified # 1 Once, Left First: 47.8%

2005: 6th-901 (-199), 19/14, 1 Win, 3 Finals, Including 3 Consecutive, Average Qualifying Spot: 4.73, Qualified # 1 Once, Left First: 60.8%

2004: 3rd-1131 (-53), 30/13, 2 Wins, 6 Finals, Including 3 Consecutive, Average Qualifying Spot: 4.33, Qualified # 1 Three Times, Left First: 74.1%, Won 4 Rounds On A Holeshot

2003: 6th-809 (-327), 16/14, 1 Win, 2 Finals, Average Qualifying Spot: 9.2, Left First: 61.9%

2002: 4th-982 (-363), 25/13, 1 Win, 3 Finals, Including 3 Consecutive, Average Qualifying Spot: 5.21, Left First: 60.7%, Won 4 Rounds On A Holeshot

2001: 2nd-1175 (-157), 32/11, 3 Wins, 7 Finals, Including 3 Consecutive, Average Qualifying Spot: 2.21, Qualified # 1 Six Times, Left First: 43.7%

2000: 4th-956 (-300), 26/12, Includes Bristol Non-Points Race, 3 Wins, Including 2 Consecutive, 3 Finals, Average Qualifying Spot: 3.6, Left First: 48.2%, Doubled Up U.S. Nationals Weekend Winning Shootout And Event Netting $25,000

1999: 3rd-1033 (-175), 27/12, 3 Wins, 4 Finals, Average Qualifying Spot: 4.06, Left First: 48.1%, Automobile Club Of Southern California Road To The Future Award Winner

1998: 7th-676 (-811), 12/13, Average Qualifying Spot: 6.92, Fuel DNQ At Debut, Left First: 61.1%

Troy Buff Date Of Birth: January 12, 1963 From: Spring, TX

Sponsor: Bill Miller Engineering Crew Chief: Bill Miller Owner: Bill Miller

Chassis: '10 Bill Miller Engine: BAE 500

Pro Debut: 2006 Starts: 51 Consecutive Qualified Starts: 2

Win Percentage In Final Round: 60% TAD: 60% Average Career Qualifying Spot: 12.6

AT THE TREE:

Career Left Firsts/Left On: 20/45= 30.7%

STATS:

Career Best E.T./Speed: 1000ft.: 3.840/309.27 1320ft.: 4.586/325.69
Career Wins: 3 TAD: 3
Career Finals: 5 TAD: 5
Career # 1 Qualifiers: 1 TAD: 1
Career Provisional # 1 Qualifiers: 1 TAD: 1
Top Ten Finishes: 1 TAD: 1
Most Successful Event: Seattle: 2/3
Elimination Round Win/Loss Record: 10/51 = 16.3%
Career Best Points Finish: Countdown: 12th-460 (-2224)
Pre-Countdown (2006 And Before): 20th-159 (-1522)

YEARLY CAREER SUMMARY:

2012: 14th-103 (-434), 0/3, Average Qualifying Spot: 15, 1 DNQ, Left First: 33.3%

2011: 15th-329 (-2298), 0/10, Average Qualifying Spot: 12.2, 2 DNQ's, Left First: 55.5%

2010: 12th-460 (-2224), 3/12, Average Qualifying Spot: 12.3, 2 DNQ's, Left First: 26.6%

2009: 13th-382 (-2189), 3/9, Average Qualifying Spot: 12.8, 4 DNQ's, Left First: 25%

2008: 14th-478 (-2225), 3/13, Average Qualifying Spot: 13.4, 1 DNQ, Left First: 37.5%

2006: 20th-159 (-1522), 1/4, Average Qualifying Spot: 10.2, 1 DNQ, Left First: 20%

2002: Finished 4th In The Division 4 Top Alcohol Dragster Points, 39th Nationally

2001: Finished 3rd In The Division 4 Top Alcohol Dragster Points, 20th Nationally

2000: Finished 2nd In The Division 4 Top Alcohol Dragster Points, 6th Nationally

1999: Finished 2nd in The Division 4 Top Alcohol Dragster Points

Scotty Cannon Date Of Birth: July 13, 1962 From: Lyman, SC

Pro Debut: TF: 2007 FC: 1999 Starts: 105 TF: 1 FC: 104

Consecutive Qualified Starts: 3 TF: 0 FC: 3

Win Percentage In Final Round: 0% IHRA: 65.2% TF: 66% PM: 65.1%

Average Career Qualifying Spot: 8.97 TF: 13 FC: 8.93

AT THE TREE:

Career Holeshot Win/Loss Record: FC: 2/12

Career Left Firsts/Left On: 37/117 = 24% TF: 1/0 = 100% FC: 36/117 = 23.5%

STATS:

Championships: 0 IHRA: PM: 6

Career Best E.T./Speed: 1320ft.: TF: 4.557/326.40 FC: 4.783/325.73

Career Wins: 0 IHRA: 30 TF: 2 PM: 28

Career Finals: 3 FC: 3 IHRA: 46 TF: 3 PM: 43

Last Final: FC: 2002 Madison Most Successful Event: Denver: 7/5, 1 Final

TF: Chicago: 0/1 FC: Denver: 7/5, 1 Final

Elimination Round Win/Loss Record: 60/105 = 36.3% TF: 0/1 = 0% FC: 60/104 = 36.5%

Career # 1 Qualifiers: FC: 2

Career Provisional # 1 Qualifiers: FC: 4

Top Five Point Finishes: 0 IHRA: 8 TF: 1 PM: 7

Top Ten Point Finishes: FC: 2 IHRA: 10 TF: 1 PM: 9

Career Best Points Finish: Countdown: 27th-61 (-3125)

Pre-Countdown (2006 And Before): 6th-1230 (-762)

YEARLY CAREER SUMMARY:

2007: 27th-61 (-3125), 0/1, Average Qualifying Spot: 13, 3 DNQ's, Left First: 100%

2003: 14th-772 (-996), 4/21, Average Qualifying Spot: 11, 2 DNQ's, Left First: 22.7%

2002: 8th-1121 (-655), 17/23, 2 Finals, Average Qualifying Spot: 6.82, Qualified # 1 Twice, Including 2 Consecutive, Left First: 26.3%, Lost 4 Rounds On A Holeshot

2001: 12th-861 (-1139), 6/22, Average Qualifying Spot: 8.95, 2 DNQ's, Left First: 25.9%

2000: 6th-1114 (-878), 22/20, 1 Final, Average Qualifying Spot: 8.7, 3 DNQ's, Left First: 25.6%

1999: 11/18, Average Qualifying Spot: 9.27, 4 DNQ's, 1 By 4 Thousandths, Left First: 14.8%, Lost 5 Rounds On A Holeshot, Won Auto Club Road To The Future Award

Andy Carter Date Of Birth: N/A From: Clermont, FL
Formally: London, England

Pro Debut: 2009 Starts: 2 Consecutive Qualified Starts: 0

Average Career Qualifying Spot: 14.5

AT THE TREE:

Career Left Firsts/Left On: 1/1 = 50%

STATS:

Championships: 0 FIA: TF: 3 Career Best E.T./Speed: 1000ft.: 3.947/301.81

Most Successful Event: Phoenix: 0/1 Elimination Round Win/Loss Record: 0/2 = 0%

Career Best Points Finish: Countdown: 12th-460 (-2224)

YEARLY CAREER SUMMARY:

2010: 34th-41 (-2643), 0/1, Average Qualifying Spot: 16, 1 DNQ, Left First: 100%

2009: 41st-31 (-2540), My Points Do Not Match NHRA—Unknown Reason, 0/1, Average Qualifying Spot: 13, Left First: 0%

2008: Won FIA Top-Fuel Championship

2004: Won FIA Top-Fuel Championship

2001: Won FIA Top-Fuel Championship

Steve Chrisman Date Of Birth: July 23, 1954 From: Anaheim, CA
Sponsor: Nitrofish Crew Chief: Kevin Meredyk Owner: Steve Chrisman
Chassis: '00 McKinney Engine: TFX 500
Pro Debut: 1983 Starts: 1997-2012: 33 Consecutive Qualified Starts: 1
Average Career Qualifying Spot: 1997-2012: 14.7

AT THE TREE: 1997-2012:

Career Holeshot Win/Loss Record: 0/1 Career Left Firsts/Left On: 3/32 = 8.5%

STATS:

Career Best E.T./Speed: 1000ft.: 3.994/291.95 1320ft.: 4.872/300.86
Most Successful Event: 1997-2012: Phoenix: 1/2
Elimination Round Win/Loss Record: 1997-2012: 2/32 = 5.71%
Career Best Points Finish: Countdown: 14th-297 (-2274)
Pre-Countdown (2006 And Before): 26th-92 (-1902)

YEARLY CAREER SUMMARY:

2012: 19th-41 (-496), 0/1, Average Qualifying Spot: 15, 1 DNQ, Left First: 0%

2011: 20th-185 (-2442), 0/5, Average Qualifying Spot: 14.8, 3 DNQ's, Left First: 40%

2010: 16th-324 (-2360), 1/9, Average Qualifying Spot: 14, 2 DNQ's, Left First: 0%

2009: 14th-297 (-2274), 1/8, Won First Career Round, Average Qualifying Spot: 14.3, 3 DNQ's, Left First: 11.1%

2008: 18th-185 (-2518), 0/5, Average Qualifying Spot: 15.8, 3 DNQ's, Left First: 0%

2007: 25th-81 (-3105), 0/1, Average Qualifying Spot: 13, 5 DNQ's, Left First: 0%

2006: 27th-61 (-1620), 0/1, Average Qualifying Spot: 16, 3 DNQ's, Left First: 0%

2005: 32nd-50 (-1931), 5 DNQ's

2004: 26th-92 (-1902), 0/2, Average Qualifying Spot: 16, 3 DNQ's, Left First: 0%

2003: 34th-51 (-1943), 0/1, Average Qualifying Spot: 16, 2 DNQ's, Left First: 0%

Gary Clapshaw Date Of Birth: December 27, 1950 From: Las Vegas, NV

Pro Debut: FC: 1995? TF: 2001 Starts: 1997-2011: 8 Consecutive Qualified Starts: 4

Win Percentage In Final Round: 50% FC: 50%

Average Career Qualifying Spot: 1997-2011: 13.6

AT THE TREE: 1997-1999:

Career Left Firsts/Left On: 2/7 = 22.2%

STATS:

Career Best E.T./Speed: 1320ft.: 4.684/312.42 FC: 5.076/295.27

Career Wins: 1 FC: 1

Career Finals: 2 TF: 1 FC: 2

Last Win: FC: 1995 Memphis

Last Final: TF: 2001 Las Vegas-2 FC: 1995 Memphis

Most Successful Event: TF: Indianapolis: 3/1, 1 Final FC: Memphis: 1 Wins, 1 Final

Elimination Round Win/Loss Record: 1997-2011: 3/8 = 27.2%

Top Ten Point Finishes: 1 FC: 1 IHRA: TF: 3

Career Best Points Finish: TF: 21st-194 (-1696) FC: 8th-831 (-859)

YEARLY CAREER SUMMARY:

2002: 38th-31 (-1920), 0/1, Average Qualifying Spot: 14, Left First: 0%

2001: 30th-94 (-2008), 0/3, Average Qualifying Spot: 12.6, Left First: 0%

2000: 21st-194 (-1696), 3/4, 1 Final, Average Qualifying Spot: 14.2, Left First: 33.3%

1995: 8th-831 (-859), 1 Win, 1 Final

Andrew Cowin Date Of Birth: N/A From: Australia

Pro Debut: 1999 Starts: 61 Consecutive Qualified Starts: 2

Win Percentage In Final Round: 0% IHRA: TF: 50% Average Career Qualifying Spot: 9.36

AT THE TREE:

Career Holeshot Win/Loss Record: 1/2 Career Left Firsts/Left On: 38/51 = 42.6%

STATS:

U.S. Nationals Wins/Finals: 0/1

Career Best E.T./Speed: 1320ft.: 4.490/328.38

Career Wins: 0 IHRA: TF: 1

Career Finals: 3 TF: 3 IHRA: TF: 2

Last Final: 2002 Madison

Most Successful Event: Indianapolis: 6/4, 1 Final, 1 DNQ

Elimination Round Win/Loss Record: 37/61 = 37.7%

Career # 1 Qualifiers: 4 IHRA: TF: 2

Career Provisional # 1 Qualifiers: 3

Top Ten Point Finishes: 1 IHRA: TF: 1

Career Best Points Finish: 8th-1133 (-818)

YEARLY CAREER SUMMARY:

2006: 24th-123 (-1558), 0/3, Average Qualifying Spot: 14, 3 DNQ's, 1 By 8 Thousandths, Left First: 50%

2005: 27th-99 (-1882), 2/3, Average Qualifying Spot: 13.3, Left First: 50%

2004: 23rd-159 (-1830), 2/4, Average Qualifying Spot: 14, 1 DNQ, Left First: 40%

2003: 34th-51 (-1943), 0/1, Average Qualifying Spot: 15, 2 DNQ's, Left First: 0%

2002: 8th-1132 (-819), 18/23, 1 Final, Average Qualifying Spot: 7, Qualified # 1 Four Times, Left First: 50%

2001: 11th-604 (-1498), 6/15, 1 Final, Average Qualifying Spot: 8.06, Left First: 70%

2000: 16th-295 (-1595), 5/6, Average Qualifying Spot: 9.16, 2 DNQ's, Left First: 30%

1999: 4/6, 1 Final, Average Qualifying Spot: 13.3, 2 DNQ's, Left First: 33.3%

Del Cox Jr. Date Of Birth: January 12, 1963 From: Downey, CA

Pro Debut: 2009 Starts: 6 Consecutive Qualified Starts: 1

Win Percentage In Final Round: 0% IHRA: TF: 70% Average Career Qualifying Spot: 13.6

AT THE TREE:

Career Left Firsts/Left On: 3/2 = 60%

STATS:

Championships: 0 IHRA: TF: 1
Career Best E.T./Speed: 1000ft.: 3.936/306.46
Career Wins: 0 IHRA: TF: 7
Career Finals: 0 IHRA: TF: 10
Most Successful Event: Houston: 0/2
Elimination Round Win/Loss Record: 0/6 = 0%
Career # 1 Qualifiers: 0 IHRA: TF: 3
Top Five Point Finishes: 0 IHRA: TF: 2
Top Ten Point Finishes: 0 IHRA: TF: 2
Career Best Points Finish: Countdown: 27th-134 (-2437)

YEARLY CAREER SUMMARY:

2010: 36th-31 (-2637), 0/1, Average Qualifying Spot: 16, Left First: 0%

2009: 27th-134 (-2437), 0/5, Average Qualifying Spot: 13.2, 2 DNQ's, Left First: 60%, Won IHRA Top-Fuel Championship

2007: Division 7 Top Dragster Champion

2006: Finished 5th In The Division 7 Top Comp Points,

2005: Finished 14th In The Division 7 Super Eliminator Points

2004: Finished 2nd In The Division 7 Super Elimination Points

2003: Finished 4th In The Division 7 Super Eliminator Points

Tim Cullinan Date Of Birth: December 26, 1961

From: Chicago, IL Pro Debut: 2002

Starts: 8 Consecutive Qualified Starts: 0 Average Career Qualifying Spot: 13.3

AT THE TREE:

Career Left Firsts/Left On: 5/4 = 55.5%

STATS:

Career Best E.T./Speed: 1000ft.: 3.988/301.87 1320ft.: 4.669/315.42

Career Wins: 0 IDBA: 1 FB: 1

Career Finals: 0 IHRA: TF: 3

Most Successful Event: Chicago: 1/3, 2 DNQ's

Elimination Round Win/Loss Record: 4/8 = 33.3%

Top Five Point Finishes: 0 IHRA: TF: 1 IDBA: 1 PS: FB: 1

Top Ten Point Finishes: 0 IHRA: TF: 1 IDBA: 1 PS: FB: 1

Career Best Points Finish: Countdown: 29th-113 (-2458)

Pre-Countdown (2006 And Before): 25th-134 (-1847)

YEARLY CAREER SUMMARY:

2010: 29th-61 (-2623), 0/1, Average Qualifying Spot: 16, 3 DNQ's, Left First: 100%

2009: 29th-113 (-2458), 1/2, Average Qualifying Spot: 13, 3 DNQ's, Left First: 0%

2005: 25th-134 (-1847), 1/3, Average Qualifying Spot: 13, 2 DNQ's, 1 By 2 Thousandths, Left First: 66.6%

2004: 28th-62 (-1932), 1/1, Average Qualifying Spot: 11, 1 DNQ, Left First: 50%

2003: 34th-51 (-1943), 1/1, Average Qualifying Spot: 15, Left First: 100%

2002: 50th-10 (-1941), 1 DNQ

1992: Won A Race And Finished In The Top Ten In The International Drag Bike Association And Pro Star Racing A Funny Bike

Pat Dakin Date Of Birth: N/A From: Dayton, OH

Sponsor: Commercial Metal Fabrications Crew Chief: N/A Owner: Pat Dakin

Chassis: '09 McKinney Engine: TFX 500

Pro Debut: 1971 Starts: 1997-2012: 38 Consecutive Qualified Starts: 1

Win Percentage In Final Round: 33.3% IHRA: TF: 46.1%

Average Career Qualifying Spot: 12.6

AT THE TREE: 1997-2012:

Career Holeshot Win/Loss Record: 1/0 Career Left Firsts/Left On: 23/16 = 58.9%

STATS:

Championships: 0 IHRA: TF: 1

Career Best E.T./Speed: 1000ft.: 3.864/313.95 1320ft.: 4.691/310.13

Career Wins: 2 IHRA: TF: 6

Career Finals: 6 IHRA: TF: 7

Last Win: 1973 Montreal

Last Final: 1998 Atlanta

Most Successful Event: 1997-2012: Atlanta: 4/3, 1 Final

Elimination Round Win/Loss Record: 1997-2012: 9/38 = 19.1%

Top Five Point Finishes: 1974-2011:1 IHRA: TF: 3

Top Ten Point Finishes: 1974-2011: 2 IHRA: TF: 6

Career Best Points Finish: Countdown: 14th-354 (-2330)

Pre-Countdown (2006 And Before): 2nd-8640 (-3299)

YEARLY CAREER SUMMARY:

2012: 19th-41 (-496), 0/1, Average Qualifying Spot: 16, 1 DNQ, Left First: 0%

2011: 22nd-174 (-2453), 0/4, Average Qualifying Spot: 15, 8 DNQ's, Left First: 0%

2010: 14th-354 (-2330), 3/9, Average Qualifying Spot: 12, 1 DNQ, Left First: 66.6%

2009: 25th-161 (-2410), 0/5, Average Qualifying Spot: 10.6, Left First: 40%

2008: 28th-62 (-2641), 0/2, Average Qualifying Spot: 15.5, Left First:100%

1998: 6/8, 1 Final, Average Qualifying Spot: 12.6, 2 DNQ's, Left First: 76.9%

1997: 0/9, Average Qualifying Spot: 12.3, 3 DNQ's, Left First: 62.5%

1994: 1 Final

1977: 2nd-8640 (-3299), 2 Finals

1974: 10th-2848 (-4732)

1973: 1 Win, 1 Final

1970: 1 Win, 1 Final

Larry Dixon Date Of Birth: October 23, 1966 From: Indianapolis, IN Pro Debut: 1995 Starts: 377 Consecutive Qualified Starts: 68
Win Percentage In Final Round: 57.4% Average Career Qualifying Spot: 1997-2011: 4.56

AT THE TREE: 1997-2011:

Career Holeshot Win/Loss Record: 17/33 Career Left Firsts/Left On: 424/388 = 52.2%

Career Final Rounds Won/Lost On A Holeshot: 1/2

STATS:

Championships: 3 U.S. Nationals Wins/Finals: 4/7

Career Best E.T./Speed: 1000ft.: 3.769/324.98 1320ft.: 4.481/332.75

Career Wins: 62

Career Finals: 108

Last Win: 2011 Phoenix Last Final: 2011 Phoenix

Most Successful Event:

Englishtown: 46/11, 6 Wins, Including 2 Consecutive Twice, 10 Finals, Including 6 Consecutive

Elimination Round Win/Loss Record: 637/314 = 66.9%

Career # 1 Qualifiers: 55

Career Provisional # 1 Qualifiers: 1997-2011: 49

Top Five Point Finishes: 12, 5 Consecutive

Top Ten Point Finishes: 17 Consecutive

Career Best Points Finish: Countdown: 1st-2684

Pre-Countdown (2006 And Before): 1st-1994

Best Points Finish If Countdown Never Was: 1st/4th

YEARLY CAREER SUMMARY:

2011: 4th-2540 (-87), 38/20, 2 Wins, 4 Finals, Including 2 Consecutive, Average Qualifying Spot: 3.77, Qualified # 1 Three Times, Left First: 46.4%

2010: 1st-2684, Won By 102 Points, 62/11, 12 Wins, Including 3 Consecutive, 12 Finals, Average Qualifying Spot: 2.52, Qualified # 1 Eight Times, Left First: 39.3%, Won A Round On A Holeshot When Opponent Ran Identical E.T. And Speed

2009: 2nd-2569 (-2), 47/18, 5 Wins, Including 2 Consecutive, 9 Finals, Including 3 Consecutive, Average Qualifying Spot: 2.56, Qualified # 1 Nine Times, Including Five Consecutive, 1 DNQ, Left First: 49.1%, Lost 5 Rounds On Holeshots, Lost Championship By Smallest Points Difference In Class History Under The Countdown Points Format

2008: 2nd-2445 (-258), 36/22, 2 Wins, 6 Finals, Including 2 Consecutive, Average Qualifying Spot: 5.33, Qualified # 1 Four Times, Including 3 Consecutive, Left First: 69%

2007: 4th-3135 (-51), 35/20, 3 Wins, Including 2 Consecutive, 6 Finals, Average Qualifying Spot: 6.78, Qualified # 1 Once, Left First: 68.5%

2006: 7th-1151 (-530), 20/23, 1 Final, Average Qualifying Spot: 7.45, Left First: 47.5%

2005: 2nd-1566 (-415), 38/20, 3 Wins, 7 Finals, Including 2 Consecutive, Average Qualifying Spot: 4.43, Qualified # 1 Three Times, Left First: 53.4%

2004: 6th-1242 (-752), 26/20, 2 Wins, 3 Finals, Average Qualifying Spot: 7.31, Qualified # 1 Four Times, 1 DNQ, Left First: 52.1%, Lost 4 Rounds On Holeshots

2003: 1st-1994, Won By 330 Points, 59/15, 8 Wins, 13 Finals, Including 5 Consecutive, Appeared In 8 Of The First 11 Finals Of The Season, Average Qualifying Spot: 3.26, Qualified # 1 Four Times, Left First: 44.2%, Swept The Western Swing; Won The Weather Delayed '02 $100,000 Shootout

2002: 1st-1951, Won By 193 Points, 57/13, 9 Wins, 14 Finals, Including 6 Consecutive, Appeared In 10 Of The First 11 Finals Of The Season, Average Qualifying Spot: 2.72, Qualified # 1 Seven Times, 1 DNQ, Left First: 67.7%

2001: 2nd-2007 (-95), 57/18, 6 Wins, Including 2 Consecutive, 9 Finals, Average Qualifying Spot: 3.04, Qualified # 1 Four Times, Left First: 52.7%, Won $100,000 Shootout

2000: 3rd-1603 (-287), 42/21, 2 Wins, Including 2 Consecutive, 6 Finals, Average Qualifying Spot: 6, Qualified # 1 Once, Left First: 49.1% Never Lost In Round One

1999: 8th-1210 (-278), 23/19, 2 Wins, 4 Finals, Average Qualifying Spot: 6.23, Qualified # 1 Three Times, Including 3 Consecutive, 1 DNQ, Left First: 40.5%, First Driver To Break The 4.4 Second Barrier With A 4.486 At Houston-1, Possibly The Sports Last Great E.T. Barrier, Dale Armstrong Was The Crew Chief

1998: 7th-1093 (-688), 19/20, 1 Win, 2 Finals, Average Qualifying Spot: 7.47, Qualified # 1 Once, 2 DNQ's, Left First: 54%, Won Pomona-1 Joining His Dad (1970) On The Event Winners List

1997: 7th-1071 (-766), 18/22, 3 Finals, Average Qualifying Spot: 7.77, Qualified # 1 Once, 1 DNQ, Left First: 46.1%

1996: 4th-1193 (-222), 28/18, 1 Win, 2 Finals

1995: 3rd-1318 (-257), 32/15, 4 Wins, 6 Finals, Including 2 Consecutive, Qualified # 1 Twice, Won The U.S. Nationals, Won Auto Club Road To The Future Award, Won $100,000 Shootout

Mike Dunn Date Of Birth: September 28, 1956 From: Wrightsville, PA RETIRED

Pro Debut: FC: 1977 TF: 1992 Starts: 1997-2011: 92 Consecutive Qualified Starts: 30

Win Percentage In Final Round: 55% TF: 44% FC: 76.9% IHRA: FC: 50%

Average Career Qualifying Spot: 1997-2011: 6.03

AT THE TREE: 1997-2011:

Career Holeshot Win/Loss Record: 5/8 Career Left Firsts/Left On: 90/95 = 48.6%

STATS:

U.S. Nationals Wins/Finals: 1/3 TF: 0/1 FC: 1/2

Career Best E.T./Speed: TF: 1320ft.: 4.494/331.61 FC: 5.194/276.66

Career Wins: 22 TF: 12 FC: 10 IHRA: FC: 1

Career Finals: 40 TF: 27 FC: 13 IHRA: FC: 2

Last Win: 2001 Atlanta

Last Final: 2001 Pomona-2

Most Successful Event: 1997-2011: Gainesville: 10/3, 1 Win, 1 Final

Elimination Round Win/Loss Record: 1997-2011: 114/70 = 61.9%

Career # 1 Qualifiers: 16 TF: 14 FC: 2

Career Provisional # 1 Qualifiers: 1997-2011: 9

Top Five Point Finishes: 6 TF: 5 FC: 1

Top Ten Point Finishes: 12 TF: 8 FC: 4

Career Best Points Finish: 4th-1593 (-508)

YEARLY CAREER SUMMARY:

2001: 4th-1594 (-508), 37/22, 2 Wins, 5 Finals, Average Qualifying Spot: 3.83, Qualified # 1 Five Times, Including 2 Consecutive Twice, Left First: 53.8%, First Driver To Break The 4.4 Barrier Under The 90% Nitro Rule

2000: 23rd-167 (-1723), 3/3, Average Qualifying Spot: 5.33, Qualified # 1 Twice, Including 2 Consecutive, Left First: 50%

1999: 4th-1326 (-162), 29/17, 4 Wins, 4 Finals, Average Qualifying Spot: 6.52, Qualified # 1 Three Times, 1 DNQ, Left First: 57.1%

1998: 5th-1344 (-437), 30/22, 4 Finals, Average Qualifying Spot: 6.5, Qualified # 1 Three Times, 1 DNQ, Left First: 38%, Lost 3 Consecutive Finals To The Same Opponent

1997: 8th-1044 (-793), 15/22, 1 Final, Average Qualifying Spot: 8.31, 1 DNQ, Left First: 45.7%

1996: 7th-1017 (-398), 1 Win, 3 Finals

1995: 4th-1255 (-320), 3 Wins, 5 Finals, Qualified # 1 Once

1994: 7th-8638 (-4962), 1 Final

1993: 4th-10064 (-2734), 2 Wins, 4 Finals

1991: 3rd-12100 (-3438), 3 Wins, Including 2 Consecutive, 3 Finals, Qualified # 1 Once

1990: 1 Win, 2 Finals

1989: 10th-7676 (-8462), 2 Wins, 2 Finals, Qualified # 1 Once

1988: 7th-7312 (-5050), 2 Wins, 2 Finals, Including 2 Consecutive

1987: 10th-4902 (-7786), 1 Final

1986: 1 Win, 1 Final

1982: 1 Final

1981: 1 Win, 1 Final

Urs Erbacher Date Of Birth: October 25, 1961 From: Arlesheim, Switzerland

Pro Debut: 2007 Starts: 12 Consecutive Qualified Starts: 2 Average Career Qualifying Spot: 13

AT THE TREE:

Career Left Firsts/Left On: 5/8 = 38.4%

STATS:

Championships: 0 FIA: TF: 4 Top Methanol: 3
Career Best E.T./Speed: 1000ft.: 3.887/316.67 1320ft.: 4.571/326.98

Most Successful Event: Pomona-2: 2/2, 1 DNQ

Elimination Round Win/Loss Record: 3/12 = 20%

Career Best Points Finish: Countdown: 19th-196 (-2375)

YEARLY CAREER SUMMARY:

2011: Won FIA Top-Fuel Championship

2010: Won FIA Top-Fuel Championship

2009: 18th-196 (-2375), 0/6, Average Qualifying Spot: 11.5, 1 DNQ, Left First: 60%

2008: 19th-180 (-22523), 3/5, Average Qualifying Spot: 14.4, 1 DNQ By A Thousandth, Left First: 28.5%

2007: 28th-41 (-3145), 0/1, Average Qualifying Spot: 15, 1 DNQ, Left First: 0%, Won FIA Top-Fuel Championship

2005: Won FIA Top Methanol Funny Car Championship

2004: Won FIA Top Methanol Funny Car Championship

2003: Won FIA Top Methanol Funny Car Championship

Steve Faria Date Of Birth: N/A From: Tulare, CA

Sponsor: System 1 Filtration Crew Chief: Steve Faria Owner: Steve Faria

Chassis: '99 N/A Engine: TFX 496

Pro Debut: 2009 Starts: 6 Consecutive Qualified Starts: 2

Win Percentage In Final Round: 50% TAD: 50% Average Career Qualifying Spot: 15.5

AT THE TREE:

Career Left Firsts/Left On: 3/3 = 50%

STATS:

Career Best E.T./Speed: 1000ft.: 4.159/268.92

Career Wins: 3 TAD: 3

Career Finals: 6 TAD: 6

Most Successful Event: Pomona-1: 0/3, 1 DNQ

Elimination Round Win/Loss Record: 0/6 = 0%

Career Best Points Finish: Countdown: 16th-623 (-2563)

Pre-Countdown (2006 And Before): 21st-157 (-1524)

YEARLY CAREER SUMMARY:

2012: 17th-62 (-475), 0/2, Average Qualifying Spot: 15.5, Left First: 0%

2011: 32nd-51 (-2576), 0/1, Average Qualifying Spot: 15, 2 DNQ's, Left First: 100%

2010: 27th-92 (-2592), 0/2, Average Qualifying Spot: 15.5, 3 DNQ's, Left First: 50%

2009: 37th-50 (-2521), 0/1, Average Qualifying Spot: 16, 2 DNQ's, Left First: 100%

2000: Finished 3rd In The Division 7 Top Alcohol Dragster Points, 16th Nationally

Fred Farndon Date Of Birth: September 4, 1938 From: Edmond, OK

Formally: Toronto, Canada

Pro Debut: 1960's? Starts: 1997-2011: 1 Consecutive Qualified Starts: 0

Average Career Qualifying Spot: 1997-2011: 16

AT THE TREE: 1997-2011:

Career Left Firsts/Left On: 0/1 = 0%

Patrick J. Keenan

STATS: 1997-2011:

Career Best E.T./Speed: 1000ft.: 4.046/288.15 1320ft.: 5.335/272.72

Most Successful Event: Englishtown: 0/1

Elimination Round Win/Loss Record: 0/1 = 0%

Top Ten Point Finishes: 0 IHRA: TF: 1

Career Best Points Finish: Countdown: 19th-196 (-2375)

Pre-Countdown (2006 And Before): 54th-10 (-1941)

YEARLY CAREER SUMMARY:

2011: 28th-71 (-2556), 0/1, Average Qualifying Spot: 16, 4 DNQ's, Left First: 0%

2010: 40th-20 (-2664), 2 DNQ's

2002: 50th-10 (-1941), 1 DNQ

1998: 0/0, 1 DNQ

1997: 0/0, 1 DNQ

Doug Foley Date Of Birth: June 3, 1964 From: Sewell, NJ

Pro Debut: 2005 Starts: 37 Consecutive Qualified Starts: 6

Win Percentage In Final Round: 0% IHRA: 46.1% Average Career Qualifying Spot: 11.6

AT THE TREE:

Career Holeshot Win/Loss Record: 0/3 Career Left Firsts/Left On: 15/33 = 31.2%

STATS:

Career Best E.T./Speed: 1000ft.: 3.821/314.24 1320ft.: 4.527/331.20

Career Wins: 0 IHRA: TF: 6

Career Finals: 4 TAD: 4 IHRA: TF: 13

Most Successful Event: Reading: 3/5

Elimination Round Win/Loss Record: 18/37= 32.7%

Career Provisional # 1 Qualifiers: 1 TAD: 1

Top Five Point Finishes: 0 IHRA: TF: 3

Top Ten Point Finishes: 1 TAD: 1 IHRA: TF: 4

Career Best Points Finish: Countdown: 16th-623 (-2563)

Pre-Countdown (2006 And Before): 21st-157 (-1524)

YEARLY CAREER SUMMARY:

2011: 21st-182 (-2445), 1/5, Average Qualifying Spot: 10, Left First: 25%

2010: 21st-232 (-2452), 3/5, Average Qualifying Spot: 10.6, 1 DNQ, Left First: 28.5%

2009: 30th-103 (-2468), 2/2, Average Qualifying Spot: 11.5, Left First: 0%

2008: 20th-164 (-2539), 0/5, Average Qualifying Spot: 9.6, Left First: 25%

2007: 16th-623 (-2563), 11/12, Average Qualifying Spot: 12, 2 DNQ's, Left First: 33.3%

2006: 21st-157 (-1524), 0/5, Average Qualifying Spot: 13.8, Left First: 33.3%

2005: 26th-113 (-1868), 1/3, Average Qualifying Spot: 14.3, Left First: 75%

2003: Finished 2nd In The Division 1 Top Alcohol Dragster Points, 9th Nationally

2002: Finished 7th In The Division 1 Top Alcohol Dragster Points, 43rd Nationally

2000: Division 3 Super Comp Champion, Finished 6th In The Division 1 Top Alcohol Dragster Points, 30th Nationally

1999: Finished 2nd In The Division 2 Top Alcohol Dragster Points

1998: Division 5 Super Gas Champion

Rod Fuller Date Of Birth: April 20, 1971 From: Las Vegas, NV

Pro Debut: 1995 Starts: 108 Consecutive Qualified Starts: 104? (Only 2005-2012 Data)

Win Percentage In Final Round: 55.5% TF: 38.8% Sportsman: 72.2%

Average Career Qualifying Spot: 2005-2012: 6.2

AT THE TREE: 2005-2012:

Career Holeshot Win/Loss Record: 7/5 Career Left Firsts/Left On: 98/110 = 47.1%

STATS:

Career Best E.T./Speed: 1000ft.: 3.785/325.85 1320ft.: 4.464/331.61

Career Wins: 20 TF: 7 Sportsman: 13

Career Finals: 36 TF: 18 Sportsman: 18

Last Win: 2008 Madison Last Final: 2008 Pomona-2

Most Successful Event: Phoenix: TF Only: 10/2, 2 Wins, 2 Finals

Bonus For Phoenix: 2006-2007 Won TF, Won Super Gas In 2004, Won 17 Consecutive Rounds

Elimination Round Win/Loss Record: 127/101 = 55.7%

Career # 1 Qualifiers: 6

Career Provisional # 1 Qualifiers: 9

Top Five Point Finishes: 3 TF: 2 SC: 1

Top Ten Point Finishes: 5 TF: 4 SC: 1

Career Best Points Finish: Countdown: 2nd-3167 (-19)

Pre-Countdown (2006 And Before): 5th-1384 (-297)

Best/Worst Points Finish If Countdown Never Was: 1st/5th

YEARLY CAREER SUMMARY:

2012: 24th-31 (-506), 0/1, Average Qualifying Spot: 16, Left First: 0%

2011: 13th-454 (-2173), 6/10, Average Qualifying Spot: 7.3, Left First: 40%

2010: 22nd-204 (-2480), 3/4, Average Qualifying Spot: 7.75, Left First: 57.1%

2009: 21st-192 (-2379), 3/4, Average Qualifying Spot: 8.25, Left First: 66.6%

2008: 6th-2368 (-335), 29/23, 1 Win, 4 Finals, Including 2 Consecutive, Average Qualifying Spot: 7.78, Qualified # 1 Once, Left First: 42%

2007: 2nd-3167 (-19), 40/20, 3 Wins, 6 Finals, Average Qualifying Spot: 4.13, Qualified # 1 Three Times, Left First: 44.8%, Doubled Up At Vegas-2, Won Shootout And The Race Netting $150,000

2006: 5th-1384 (-297), 31/21, 2 Wins, 5 Finals, Including 2 Consecutive, Average Qualifying Spot: 5.34, Qualified # 1 Twice, Left First: 57.4%

2005: 10th-801 (-1180), 15/14, 1 Win, 3 Finals, Including 2 Consecutive, Average Qualifying Spot: 7.33, Left First: 50%, Ran 15 Of 23 Events And Still Finished In The Top Ten With A 64 Point Lead Over 11th Placed Driver, Who Ran 23 Events.

2004: Finished 2nd In The Division 6 Super Comp Points, 12th Nationally

2002: Finished 9th In The Division 5 Super Comp Points, 62nd Nationally, 2nd In Super Gas, 14th Nationally

2001: Finished 163rd In The Super Comp National Points

2000: Division 3 Super Comp Champion, 3rd Nationally
1999: Finished 6th In The Division 5 Super Gas Points
1998: Division 5 Super Gas Champion
1996: 30th, 3 DNQ's
1995: 26th, 2 DNQ's

Don Garlits Date Of Birth: January 14, 1932 From: Ocala, FL
Pro Debut: TF: 1955 Starts: 1997-2011: 2 Consecutive Qualified Starts: 0
Win Percentage In Final Round: 81.3% IHRA: TF: 78.1%
Average Career Qualifying Spot: 1997-2011: 15.5

AT THE TREE: 1997-2011:

Career Left Firsts/Left On: 1/1 = 50%

STATS:

Championships: 3 IHRA: 4 AHRA: 10 U.S. Nationals Wins/Finals: 8/11
Career Best E.T./Speed: 1320ft: 4.720/323.04
Career Wins: 35 IHRA: TF: 25, 84 Outside Of NHRA/IHRA, Specifics To Many Sanctioning Bodies Unknown
Career Finals: 43 IHRA: TF: 32, At Least 69 Outside Of NHRA/IHRA, Specifics To Many Sanctioning Bodies Unknown
Last Win: 1987 Pomona-1
Last Final: 1987 Pomona-1
Most Successful Event: 1997-2011: Atlanta: 0/1
Elimination Round Win/Loss Record: 1997-2011: TF: 0/2 = 0%

Career # 1 Qualifiers: 1974-2011: 11

Top Five Point Finishes: 1974-2011: 5 IHRA: TF: 6

Top Ten Point Finishes: 1974-2011: 8 IHRA: TF: 7

Career Best Points Finish: 1st-12078

YEARLY CAREER SUMMARY:

2003: 33rd-61 (-1933), 0/1, Average Qualifying Spot: 16, 3 DNQ's, Left First: 100%

2002: 40th-30 (-1921), 3 DNQ's, 1 By 3 Thousandths

2001: 33rd-41 (-2061), 0/1, Average Qualifying Spot: 15, 1 DNQ, Left First: 50%, # 1 On The Top 50 NHRA Drivers List

1987: 1 Win, 2 Finals

1986: 1st-11936, 5 Wins, 6 Finals, Including 2 Consecutive, Qualified # 1 Three Times

1985: 1st-12078, 6 Wins, 6 Finals, Including 2 Consecutive Three Times, Qualified # 1 Twice,

1984: 8th-4030 (-6616), 2 Wins, Including 2 Consecutive, 2 Finals

1980: 8th-3367 (-4747)

1979: 3rd-5955 (-1575), 3 Wins, 3 Finals, Including 2 Consecutive

1978: 2nd-10591 (-1615), 2 Wins, 2 Finals, Qualified # 1 Once

1977: 9th-6419 (-5520), 1 Win, 2 Finals, Qualified # 1 Twice

1975: 1st-9693, 4 Wins, 4 Finals, Including 2 Consecutive, 2 Consecutive Between Seasons. Qualified # 1 Three Times

1974: 1 Win, 1 Final

1973: 2 Wins, 3 Finals

1972: 1 Win, 1 Final

1971: 2 Wins, 4 Finals, Debuted First Successful Rear Engine Dragster And It Began The Trend For TF

1968: 2 Wins, 2 Finals
1967: 1 Win, 1 Final
1964: 1 Win, 1 Final
1963: 1 Win, 2 Finals
1962: 1 Final

David Grubnic Date Of Birth: August 6, 1962 From: Ypsilanti, MI Formally: Brisbane, Australia
Sponsor: Candlewood Suites Crew Chief: Connie Kalitta Owner: Connie Kalitta
Chassis: '06 Attic Engine: TFX 500
Pro Debut: 1995 Starts: 275 Consecutive Qualified Starts: 27
Win Percentage In Final Round: 13.3% Average Career Qualifying Spot: 8.89

AT THE TREE:

Career Holeshot Win/Loss Record: 5/9 Career Left Firsts/Left On: 168/253 = 39.9%

Career Final Rounds Won/Lost On A Holeshot: 0/1

STATS:

Career Best E.T./Speed: 1000ft.: 3.803/326.08 1320ft.: 4.448/333.58

Career Wins: 2

Career Finals: 15

Last Win: 2006 Gainesville

Last Final: 2011 Chicago

Most Successful Event: Seattle: 13/13, 2 Finals

Elimination Round Win/Loss Record: 175/272 = 39.1%

Career # 1 Qualifiers: 8

Career Provisional # 1 Qualifiers: 5

Top Five Point Finishes: 3

Top Ten Point Finishes: 8, 2 Consecutive

Career Best Points Finish: Countdown: 7th-2273 (-354)

Pre-Countdown (2006 And Before): 4th-1407 (-574)

Best/Worst Points Finish If Countdown Never Was: 10th/11th

YEARLY CAREER SUMMARY:

2012: 9th-259 (-278), 2/6, Average Qualifying Spot: 9.33, Left First: 44.4%

2011: 7th-2273 (-354), 10/21, 1 Final, Average Qualifying Spot: 10.4, 1 DNQ, Left First: 31%

2010: 9th-2288 (-396), 10/23, Average Qualifying Spot: 8.39, Left First: 28.1%

2009: 22nd-178 (-2393), 1/5, Average Qualifying Spot: 12.2, Left First: 16.6%

2008: 10th-2194 (-509), 10/23, 1 Final, Average Qualifying Spot: 7.43, Qualified # 1 Once, 1 DNQ, Left First: 40.6%

2007: 11th-1023 (-2163), 15/22, Average Qualifying Spot: 10.1, 1 DNQ, Left First: 35.2%

2006: 6th-1285 (-396), 26/22, 1 Win, 3 Finals, Average Qualifying Spot: 7.6, Left First: 38.2%

2005: 4th-1407 (-574), 32/22, 1 Win, 3 Finals, Average Qualifying Spot: 7.86, Qualified # 1 Once, Left First: 28.5%

2004: 5th-1368 (-626), 28/23, 5 Finals, Including 3 Consecutive, Average Qualifying Spot: 4.73, Qualified # 1 Five Times, Including 2 Consecutive, Left First: 52%, Won $100,000 Shootout

2003: 16th-496 (-1498), 2/14, Average Qualifying Spot: 11, 1 DNQ, Left First: 66.6%

2002: 11th-747 (-1204), 7/19, Average Qualifying Spot: 9.26, Left First: 46.1%

2001: 9th-843 (-1259), 10/20, Average Qualifying Spot: 8.8, Left First: 33.3%

2000: 10th-861 (-1029), 9/22, Average Qualifying Spot: 9.86, 1 DNQ, Left First: 48.1%

1999: 14th-N/A (-N/A), 4/13, Average Qualifying Spot: 11, Qualified # 1 Once, 5 DNQ's, Left First: 35.2%

1998: 13th-N/A (-N/A), 9/12, 1 Final, Average Qualifying Spot: 8.41, 2 DNQ's, Left First: 64.7%

1997: 19th, 0/6, Average Qualifying Spot: 14.8, 4 DNQ's, Left First: 20%

1995: 38th, 1 DNQ

Michael Gunderson Date Of Birth: N/A From: Middleburg, FL

Pro Debut: 2006 Starts: 5 Consecutive Qualified Starts: 2

Win Percentage In Final Round: 58.3% TAD: 58.3% Average Career Qualifying Spot: 14.8

AT THE TREE:

Career Left Firsts/Left On: 3/3 = 50%

STATS:

Career Best E.T./Speed: 1000ft.: 4.079/290.63 1320ft.: 4.635/326.16

Career Wins: 7 TAD: 7

Career Finals: 12 TAD: 12

Most Successful Event: Gainesville: 1/3, DNQ

Elimination Round Win/Loss Record: 1/5 = 16.6%

Career # 1 Qualifiers: 5 TAD: 5

Career Provisional # 1 Qualifiers: 5 TAD: 5

Top Ten Point Finishes: 2 TAD: 2

Career Best Points Finish: Countdown: 29th-31 (-3155)

Pre-Countdown (2006 And Before): 29th-51 (-1630)

YEARLY CAREER SUMMARY:

2009: 35th-62 (-2509), 0/2, Average Qualifying Spot: 15, Left First: 100%

2008: 30th-51 (-2652), 1/1, Average Qualifying Spot: 15, Left First: 0%

2007: 29th-31 (-3155), 0/1, Average Qualifying Spot: 13, Left First: 0%

2006: 29th-51 (-1630), 0/1, Average Qualifying Spot: 16, Left First: 100%

2004: Finished 2nd In The Division 2 Top Alcohol Dragster Points, 18th Nationally

2003: Finished 5th In The Division 2 Top Alcohol Dragster Points, 18th Nationally

2001: Division 2 Top Alcohol Dragster Champion, 15th Nationally

2000: Division 2 Top Alcohol Dragster Champion, 10th Nationally

1999: Division 2 Top Alcohol Dragster Champion

1998: Finished 4th In The Top Alcohol Dragster National Points

Damien Harris From: Australia Pro Debut: 2011 Starts: 0

STATS:

Career Best E.T./Speed: 1000ft.: 4.006/287.05 Most Successful Event: Pomona-2: 1 DNQ

Career Best Points Finish: Countdown: 41st-10 (-2617)

YEARLY CAREER SUMMARY:

2012: 32nd-5 (-532), 1 DNQ

2011: 41st-10 (-2617), 1 DNQ

Joe Hartley Date Of Birth: September 4, 1976 From: Portland, OR
Pro Debut: 2000 Starts: 49 Consecutive Qualified Starts: 0
Average Career Qualifying Spot: 12.2

AT THE TREE:

Career Left Firsts/Left On: 28/38 = 42.4%

STATS:

Career Best E.T./Speed: 1000ft.: 3.903/309.06 1320ft.: 4.518/330.88

Career Finals: 1 Last Final: 2007 Houston

Most Successful Event: Houston: 6/3, 1 Final, 1 DNQ

Elimination Round Win/Loss Record: 17/49 = 25.7%

Career # 1 Qualifiers: 1

Career Provisional # 1 Qualifiers: 1

Career Best Points Finish: Countdown: 11th-689 (-1882)

Pre-Countdown (2006 And Before): 17th-266 (-1624)

YEARLY CAREER SUMMARY:

2009: 11th-689 (-1882), 7/17, Average Qualifying Spot: 11.2, 1 DNQ, Left First: 12.5%, Qualified # 2 At Pomona-1 With A 3.748, Timing Error, Should have been About A 3.888 Qualifying # 4

2008: 23rd-115 (-2588), 1/3, Average Qualifying Spot: 13.3, Left First: 66.6%

2007: 17th-349 (-2837), 5/6, 1 Final, Average Qualifying Spot: 8.83, Qualified # 1 Once, 5 DNQ's, Left First: 83.3%

2006: 22nd-133 (-1548), 0/3, Average Qualifying Spot: 15.6, 4 DNQ's, 1 By 5 Thousandths, Left First: 100%

2005: 23rd-173 (-1808), 1/3, Average Qualifying Spot: 14.6, 7 DNQ's, 1 By 4 Thousandths, Left First: 25%

2004: 24th-133 (-1861), 0/2, Average Qualifying Spot: 12.5, 7 DNQ's, Left First: 100%

2003: 27th-101 (-1893), 0/1, Average Qualifying Spot: 16, 7 DNQ's, Left First: 100%

2002: 26th-142 (-1809), 1/2, Average Qualifying Spot: 14, 6 DNQ's, Left First: 66.6%

2001: 18th-252 (-1850), 0/7, Average Qualifying Spot: 12, 3 DNQ's, Left First: 57.1%

2000: 17th-246 (-1644), 2/5, Average Qualifying Spot: 14, 7 DNQ's, Left First: 57.1%

Rhonda Hartman-Smith Date Of Birth: September 18, 1974 From: Anderson, SC

Pro Debut: 1997 Starts: 113 Consecutive Qualified Starts: 1

Win Percentage In Final Round: 0% IHRA: TF: 42.8% Average Career Qualifying Spot: 10.6

AT THE TREE:

Career Holeshot Win/Loss Record: 4/1 Career Left Firsts/Left On: 71/77 = 47.9%

STATS:

Career Best E.T./Speed: 1000ft.: 3.888/313.15 1320ft.: 4.523/325.92

Career Wins: 0 IHRA: TF: 3 CIFCA: 1
Career Finals: 0 IHRA: TF: 7 CIFCA: N/A
Most Successful Event: Las Vegas-1: 4/3
Elimination Round Win/Loss Record: 49/113 = 30.2%
Top Five Point Finishes: 0 IHRA: TF: 3 CIFCA: 1
Top Ten Point Finishes: 4 IHRA: TF: 5 CIFCA: 1
Career Best Points Finish: Countdown: 31st-53 (-2631)
Pre-Countdown (2006 And Before): 9th-997 (-954)

YEARLY CAREER SUMMARY:

2010: 31st-53 (-2631), 1/1, Average Qualifying Spot: 8, Left First: 0%

2006: 32nd-20 (-1661), 2 DNQ's

2004: 9th-840 (-1154), 10/19, Average Qualifying Spot: 12.1, 4 DNQ's, Left First: 48.1%

2003: 10th-870 (-1124), 11/19, Average Qualifying Spot: 10.9, 4 DNQ's, Left First: 51.7%

2002: 9th-997 (-954), 13/22, Average Qualifying Spot: 7.9, 1 DNQ, Left First: 48.2%

2001: 10th-822 (-1280), 5/22, Average Qualifying Spot: 10.6, 2 DNQ's, Left First: 61.5%

2000: 12th-743 (-1147), 5/20, Average Qualifying Spot: 12.4, 3 DNQ's, Left First: 42.8%

1999: 1 DNQ

1998: 0/2, Average Qualifying Spot: 14.5, 1 DNQ, Left First: 100%

1997: 4/8, Average Qualifying Spot: 12.8, 9 DNQ's, Left First: 16.6%

Doug Herbert Date Of Birth: October 5, 1967 From: Lincolnton, NC
Sponsor: Doug Herbert Performance Crew Chief: Scott Gaddy
   Owner: Doug Herbert
Chassis: '08 McKinney Engine: BAE 500
Pro Debut: 1991 Starts: 304 Consecutive Qualified Starts: 7
Win Percentage In Final Round: 37% IHRA: 42.5% Average Career
   Qualifying Spot: 8.95

AT THE TREE: 1997-2011:

Career Holeshot Win/Loss Record: 11/7 Career Left Firsts/Left On: 232/196 = 54.2%

Career Final Rounds Won/Lost On A Holeshot: 1/1

STATS:

Championships: 0 IHRA: TF: 4

Career Best E.T./Speed: 1000ft.: 3.789/317.27 1320ft.: 4.441/330.63

Career Wins: 10 IHRA: TF: 20

Career Finals: 27 IHRA: TF: 47

Last Win: 2008 Norwalk

Last Final: 2008 Memphis

Most Successful Event: Active Track: Houston: 15/12, 1 Win, 1 Final

Ex-Track Since 2006: Columbus: 17/11, 2 Wins, 3 Finals

Elimination Round Win/Loss Record: 249/294 = 45.8%

Career # 1 Qualifiers: 4

Career Provisional # 1 Qualifiers: 3

Top Five Point Finishes: 0 IHRA: TF: 7

Top Ten Point Finishes: 11 IHRA: 8

Career Best Points Finish: Countdown: 6th-2292 (-894)

Pre-Countdown (2006 And Before): 6th-1353 (-628)

Best/Worst Points Finish If Countdown Never Was: 8th/9th

YEARLY CAREER SUMMARY:

2012: 28th-10 (-527), 1 DNQ

2011: 33rd-31 (-2596), 0/1, Average Qualifying Spot: 15, Left First: 0%

2010: 25th-136 (-2548), 2/3, Average Qualifying Spot: 11.3, Left First: 80%

2009: 33rd-90 (-2481), 1/2, Average Qualifying Spot: 6.5, Left First: 33.3%

2008: 8th-2307 (-396), 22/22, 1 Win, 2 Finals, Average Qualifying Spot: 8, 1 DNQ, Left First: 73.1%, Won The Last Quarter Mile National Event

2007: 6th-2292 (-894), 21/18, 1 Win, 4 Finals, Average Qualifying Spot: 8.95, Qualified # 1 Once, 4 DNQ's, Left First: 68.4%

2006: 13th-865 (-816), 8/22, Average Qualifying Spot: 11, 1 DNQ, Left First: 56.6%

2005: 6th-1353 (-628), 29/23, 4 Finals, Including 2 Consecutive, Average Qualifying Spot: 7.17, Qualified # 1 Once, Left First: 39.1%

2004: 8th-1098 (-896), 17/22, 1 Win, 1 Final, Average Qualifying Spot: 7.95, Left First: 41.6%

2003: 9th-912 (-1082), 13/19, 1 Final, Average Qualifying Spot: 8.31, 4 DNQ's, Left First: 64.5%

2002: 7th-1333 (-618), 28/22, 1 Win, 3 Finals, Average Qualifying Spot: 7.26, Qualified # 1 Twice, Left First: 40.4%, Went 14 Races Without Losing In Round One

2001: 7th-1206 (-896), 21/23, 1 Win, 1 Final, Average Qualifying Spot: 7.16, Left First: 56%

2000: 9th-963 (-927), 14/22, Average Qualifying Spot: 8.31, 1 DNQ, Left First: 69.6%

1999: 7th-1259 (-229), 28/17, 4 Wins, Including 2 Consecutive, 6 Finals, Average Qualifying Spot: 8.66, 1 DNQ, Left First: 62.2%, Won 4 Rounds On Holeshots, Selected No Bull Driver At Houston-1, Won Event Netting $100,000, Had Very Violent Engine Explosion At Pomona-2, Many Consider This To Have Introduced The 90% Nitro Rule Following The Race

1998: 7/20, Average Qualifying Spot: 10.7, 3 DNQ's, Left First: 29.6%

1997: 3/13, Average Qualifying Spot: 14.6, 6 DNQ's, Left First: 26.6%

1996: 0/3, Average Qualifying Spot: 14.3, Won IHRA Top Fuel Championship

1995: 0/1, Average Qualifying Spot: 15, 3 DNQ's, Won IHRA Top Fuel Championship

1994: 4 DNQ's, Won IHRA Top Fuel Championship

1993: 9th-8424 (-4374), 18/14, 1 Win, 3 Finals, Average Qualifying Spot: 9.33, 3 DNQ's

1992: 9th-9000 (-3232), 16/18, 2 Finals, Average Qualifying Spot: 7.27, Won IHRA Top Fuel Championship

1991: 0/9, Average Qualifying Spot: 12.4, 7 DNQ's

Eddie Hill Date Of Birth: March 6, 1936 From: Witchita Falls, TX RETIRED

Pro Debut: 1961 Starts: 1997-2011: 62 Consecutive Qualified Starts: 16

Win Percentage In Final Round: 39.3% IHRA: TF: 42.8%

Average Career Qualifying Spot: 1997-2011: 7.66

AT THE TREE: 1997-1999:

Career Holeshot Win/Loss Record: 0/7 Career Left Firsts/Left On: 19/68 = 21.8%

STATS:

Championships: 1 AHRA: TF: 1 ADBA: 5 SDBA: 7 NDBA: 4

Career Best E.T./Speed: 1320ft.: 4.520/323.74

Career Wins: 13 IHRA: TF: 3

Career Finals: 33 IHRA: TF: 7

Last Win: 1996 Denver

Last Final: 1999 Brainerd

Most Successful Event: 1997-2011: Brainerd: 5/3, 1 Final

Elimination Round Win/Loss Record: 1997-2011: 32/62 = 34%

Career # 1 Qualifiers: 18

Career Provisional # 1 Qualifiers: 1997-2011: 1

Top Five Point Finishes: 5 IHRA: TF: 1

Top Ten Point Finishes: 9 IHRA: TF: 3

Career Best Points Finish: 1st-12798

YEARLY CAREER SUMMARY:
(MISSING 1 FINAL, UNKNOWN):

2001: # 14 On The Top 50 NHRA Drivers List

1999: 14/20, 1 Final, Average Qualifying Spot: 6.05, Qualified # 1 Once, 1 DNQ, Left First: 25.8%, Oldest Top-Fuel Driver To Go To A Final Round And Qualify # 1 At 63

1998: 9/22, Average Qualifying Spot: 7, Left First: 20.6%

1997: 9/20, Average Qualifying Spot: 10, Qualified # 1 Once, 2 DNQ's, Left First: 18.5%

1996: 10th-915 (-500), 1 Win, 2 Finals, Qualified # 1 Once

1995: 6th-983 (-592), 1 Win, 2 Finals, Qualified # 1 Twice

1994: Qualified # 1 Twice, 2 Finals

1993: 1st-12798, 6 Wins, 7 Finals, Including 2 Consecutive, Qualified # 1 Once, Oldest Championship Winning Top-Fuel Driver At 57

1992: 4th-11712 (-520), 1 Win, 6 Finals, Qualified # 1 Four Times

1991: 6th-8636 (-5752), Qualified # 1 Twice

1990: 6th-9642 (-6416), 2 Finals

1989: 5th-9606 (-5346), 3 Finals

1988: 3rd-12768 (-1336), 4 Wins, 5 Finals, Including 2 Consecutive Twice, Qualified # 1 Four Times, Broke The 4 Second Barrier With A 4.990/288.55 At Dallas, Fuzzy Carter Was The Crew Chief

1987: 4th-7818 (-5334), 2 Finals

1986: 1 Final

Kevin Jones Date Of Birth: N/A From: Berea, KY

Pro Debut: 2009 Starts: 1 Consecutive Qualified Starts: 1

Win Percentage In Final Round: 0% IHRA: TF: 100% Average Career Qualifying Spot: 16

AT THE TREE:

Career Left Firsts/Left On: 0/1 = 0%

STATS:

Career Best E.T./Speed: 1000ft.: 4.226/211.66

Career Wins: 0 IHRA: TF: 2
Career Finals: 0 IHRA: TF: 2
Most Successful Event: Madison: 0/1
Elimination Round Win/Loss Record: 0/1 = 0%
Career # 1 Qualifiers: 0 IHRA: TF: 1
Top Ten Point Finishes: 0 IHRA: TF: 1
Career Best Points Finish: Countdown: 41st-31 (-2540)

YEARLY CAREER SUMMARY:

2009: 41st-31 (-2530), 0/1, Average Qualifying Spot: 16, Left First: 0%

Lex Joon Date Of Birth: N/A From: Netherlands Pro Debut: 2009 Starts: 0

STATS:

Championships: 0 FIA: TF: 1
Career Best E.T./Speed: 1000ft.: 3.933/293.98
Most Successful Event: Las Vegas-2: 1 DNQ
Career Best Points Finish: Countdown: 42nd-10 (-2674)

YEARLY CAREER SUMMARY:

2010: 42nd-10 (-2674), 1 DNQ
2009: 46th-20 (-2551), 2 DNQ's

Connie Kalitta Date Of Birth: February 24, 1938 From: Ypsilanti, MI
RETIRED

Pro Debut: TF: 1963 FC: 1972? Starts: 1997-2011: 19 Consecutive Qualified Starts: 8

Win Percentage In Final Round: 45.4% TF: 45.4% IHRA: TF: 50%

Average Career Qualifying Spot: 1997-2011: 10.1

AT THE TREE: 1997-2011:

Career Left Firsts/Left On: 11/15 = 42.3%

STATS:

Championships: 0 IHRA: TF: 2 U.S. Nationals Wins/Finals: 1/3 TF: 1/3

Career Best E.T./Speed: TF: 1320ft.: 4.584/314.61 FC: 7.465/216.00

Career Wins: 10 TF: 10 IHRA: TF: 5

Career Finals: 22 TF: 22 IHRA: TF: 10

Last Win: 1994 Indianapolis

Last Final: 1996 Reading

Most Successful Event: 1997-2011: Phoenix: 2/2

Elimination Round Win/Loss Record: 1997-2011: 7/19 = 26.9%

Career # 1 Qualifiers: 1979-2011: 3 TF: 3

Career Provisional # 1 Qualifiers: 1997-2011: 1

Top Five Point Finishes: 5 TF: 5 IHRA: TF: 4

Top Ten Point Finishes: 9 TF: 9 IHRA: TF: 7

Career Best Points Finish: 3rd-8366 (-3712)

Patrick J. Keenan

YEARLY CAREER SUMMARY: MISSING EXACT FINAL ROUND DETAILS:

1999: 0/8, Average Qualifying Spot: 12.6, Left First: 25%

1998: 2/6, Average Qualifying Spot: 11.1, 2 DNQ's, Left First: 37.5%

1997: 5/5, Average Qualifying Spot: 4.8, Qualified # 1 Once, Left First: 60%

1996: 9th-983 (-432), 2 Finals

1994: 4th-10582 (-3018), 3 Wins, Including 2 Consecutive, 3 Finals

1992: 1 Final

1986: 5th-7346 (-4590), 1 Win, 2 Finals

1985: 3rd-8366 (-3712), 2 Wins, Including 2 Consecutive, 3 Finals, Qualified # 1 Once

1984: 3rd-7602 (-3044), 1 Win, 2 Finals

1983: 7th-5066 (-5864), 1 Final

1982: 3rd-6457 (-1445), 2 Wins, 3 Finals, Won IHRA Top-Fuel Championship

1981: 10th-3737 (-3409)

1980: 6th-4684 (-3430), 1 Final, Qualified # 1 Once

1979: 1 Final, Won IHRA Top-Fuel Championship

1967: 1 Win, 1 Final

Doug Kalitta Date Of Birth: August 20, 1964 From: Ypsilanti, MI

Sponsor: Kalitta Air Crew Chief: Jim Oberhofer Owner: Connie Kalitta

Chassis: '06 Attac Engine: TFX 496

Pro Debut: 1998 Starts: 321 Consecutive Qualified Starts: 29

Win Percentage In Final Round: 50% Average Career Qualifying Spot: 6.34

AT THE TREE:

Career Holeshot Win/Loss Record: 23/13 Career Left Firsts/Left On: 349/303 = 53.5%

Career Final Rounds Won/Lost On A Holeshot: 6/2

STATS:

Championships: 0 USAC (Sprint Car): 1 U.S. Nationals Wins/Finals: 0/2

Career Best E.T./Speed: 1000ft.: 3.789/322.50 1320ft.: 4.428/335.57

Career Wins: 32

Career Finals: 64 IHRA: FC: 1

Last Win: 2010 Denver

Last Final: 2010 Concord

Most Successful Event: Sonoma: 29/9, 5 Wins, Including 3 Consecutive, 6 Finals

Elimination Round Win/Loss Record: 424/288 = 59.5%

Career # 1 Qualifiers: 29

Career Provisional # 1 Qualifiers: 33

Top Five Point Finishes: 8

Top Ten Point Finishes: 14 Consecutive

Career Best Points Finish: Countdown: 6th-2371 (-313)

Pre-Countdown (2006 And Before): 2nd—1668 (-326)

Best/Worst Points Finish If Countdown Never Was: 5th/9th

YEARLY CAREER SUMMARY:

2012: 7th-313 (-224), 6/6, Average Qualifying Spot: 60/6 = 10, Left First: 5/7 = 41.6%

2011: 8th-2239 (-388), 17/22, Average Qualifying Spot: 7.68, Left First: 37.8%

2010: 6th-2371 (-313), 36/21, 1 Win, 6 Finals, Including 2 Consecutive, Average Qualifying Spot: 5.18, Qualified # 1 Twice, 1 DNQ, Left First: 48.1%

2009: 8th-2325 (-246), 18/22, 1 Win, 3 Finals, Average Qualifying Spot: 9.47, 1 DNQ, Left First: 31.5%

2008: 9th-2209 (-494), 14/23, 1 Final, Average Qualifying Spot: 9.47, 1 DNQ, Left First: 51.5%

2007: 10th-1045 (-2141), 17/20, 1 Win, 2 Finals, Average Qualifying Spot: 9.95, 2 DNQ's, Left First: 68.7%

2006: 2nd-1667 (-14), 43/18, 5 Wins, Including 2 Consecutive Twice, 5 Finals, Average Qualifying Spot: 4.56, Qualified # 1 Twice, Left First: 70.4%, Won 7 Rounds On A Holeshot

2005: 3rd-1538 (-443), 37/18, 5 Wins, 7 Finals, Including 3 Consecutive, Average Qualifying Spot: 5.13, Qualified # 1 Three Times, Left First: 60.8%, Won 2 Final Rounds On A Holeshot

2004: 2nd-1668 (-326), 42/19, 4 Wins, 8 Finals, Including 2 Consecutive Twice, Average Qualifying Spot: 3.43, Qualified # 1 Seven Times, Left First: 51.7%,

2003: 2nd-1664 (-330), 42/19, 4 Wins, 8 Finals, Including 3 Consecutive, Average Qualifying Spot: 3.52, Qualified # 1 Nine Times, Including 5 Consecutive, Left First: 54.7%, Ran The Quickest Quarter Mile E.T. Ever (Not Nationally Backed, Missed Required 1% By A Thousandth Of A Second, Ran 4.478), 4.428 second performance at Chicago-1, Jim Oberhofer Was The Crew Chief, Won Shootout Netting $100,000, Won Brainerd By Winning Semi-Final And Final On A Holeshot

2002: 4th-1425 (-526), 31/20, 3 Wins, Including 2 Consecutive, 4 Finals, Average Qualifying Spot: 4.69, Qualified # 1 Three Times, Left First: 64.5%

2001: 3rd-1598 (-504), 39/21, 3 Wins, 6 Finals, Average Qualifying Spot: 5.25, Qualified # 1 Once, Left First: 58.9%

2000: 5th-1413 (-477), 34/19, 3 Wins, 6 Finals, Including 3 Consecutive, Average Qualifying Spot: 6.5, Qualified # 1 Once, 1 DNQ, Left First: 48.9%

1999: 5th-1307 (-181), 28/21, 1 Win, 6 Finals, Including 3 Consecutive, Average Qualifying Spot: 6.5, Qualified # 1 Once, Left First: 48.8%

1998: 6th-1098 (-683), 20/20, 1 Win, 2 Finals, Average Qualifying Spot: 6.95, 1 DNQ, Left First: 41.6%, Won $100,000 Shootout, Won Automobile Club Of Southern California Road To The Future Award

Brady Kalivoda Date Of Birth: March 23, 1973 From: Seattle, WA
Sponsor: Warrior Racing Crew Chief: Bob Peck Owner: Mike Dakin
Chassis: '09 McKinney Engine: TFX 500
Pro Debut: 2001 Starts: 26 Consecutive Qualified Starts: 2
Average Career Qualifying Spot: 10.8

AT THE TREE:

Career Left Firsts/Left On: 17/8 = 68%

STATS:

Career Best E.T./Speed: 1000ft.: 3.919/308.64 1320ft.: 4.490/329.42
Most Successful Event: Atlanta: 1/1
Elimination Round Win/Loss Record: 2/26 = 7.1%
Career Best Points Finish: Countdown: 22nd-119 (-3067)
Pre-Countdown (2006 And Before): 17th-445 (-1549)

YEARLY CAREER SUMMARY:

2012: 19th-41 (-496), 0/1, Average Qualifying Spot: 16, 1 DNQ, Left First: 0%

2011: 33rd-31 (-2596), 0/1, Average Qualifying Spot: 13, Left First: 0%

2007: 22nd-119 (-3067), 1/3, Average Qualifying Spot: 6.33, 1 DNQ, Left First: 75%

2005: 33rd-32 (-1949), 0/1, Average Qualifying Spot: 12, Left First: 100%

2004: 17th-445 (-1549), 0/14, Average Qualifying Spot: 11.5, Left First: 92.8%

2003: 43rd-10 (-1984), 1 DNQ

2002: 35th-53 (-1898), 1/1, Average Qualifying Spot: 8, Left First: 0%

2001: 26th-175 (-1927), 0/5, Average Qualifying Spot: 14.6, 2 DNQ's, Left First: 0/2

Chris Karamesines Date Of Birth: November 11, 1928 From: Chicago, IL

Sponsor: Lucas Oil Crew Chief: Tim Finley Owner: Chris Karamesines

Chassis: '09 McKinney Engine: TFX 500

Pro Debut: 1964 Starts: 1997-2011: 37 Consecutive Qualified Starts: 0

Win Percentage In Final Round: 0% Average Career Qualifying Spot: 1997-2011: 13.6

AT THE TREE: 1997-2011:

Career Left Firsts/Left On: 5/20 = 20%

STATS:

Championships: 0 AHRA: TF: 1

Career Best E.T./Speed: 1000ft.: 3.897/310.63 1320ft.: 4.677/312.78

Career Wins: 0 IHRA, AHRA, ADRA: Around 10 Combined

Career Finals: 3 TF: 3 IHRA, AHRA, ADRA: Around 10 Combined

Last Final: 1990 Seattle Most Successful Event: 1997-2011: Bristol: 1/2, 1 DNQ

Elimination Round Win/Loss Record: 1997-2011: 1/37 = 2.63%

Top Ten Point Finishes: 0 IHRA: TF: 4

Career Best Points Finish: Countdown: 18th-196 (-2375)

Pre-Countdown (2006 And Before): 11th

YEARLY CAREER SUMMARY:

2012: 26th-20 (-517), 2 DNQ's

2011: 19th-224 (-2403), 1/4, Average Qualifying Spot: 14.2, 9 DNQ's, Left First: 0%, Won First Elimination Round Since 1990

2010: 19th-247 (-2437), 0/6, Average Qualifying Spot: 13.5, 6 DNQ's Left First: 20%

2009: 18th-196 (-2375), 0/4, Average Qualifying Spot: 13.2, 7 DNQ's, Left First: 0%

2007: 34th-10 (-3176), 1 DNQ

2005: 36th-30 (-1951), 3 DNQ's

2004: 30th-60 (-1934), 6 DNQ's

2003: 24th-155 (-1839), 0/3, Average Qualifying Spot: 13, 6 DNQ's, Left First: 0%

2002: 15th-362 (-1589), 0/9, Average Qualifying Spot: 13.4, 8 DNQ's, Left First: 40%

2001: 17th-320 (-1782), 0/9, Average Qualifying Spot: 13.6, 4 DNQ's, Left First: 40%, # 30 On The Top 50 NHRA Drivers List

2000: 30th-92 (-1798), 0/2, Average Qualifying Spot: 16, 3 DNQ's, Left First: 0%

1999: 1 DNQ

1990: 11th, 2 Finals

1965: 1 Final

Bobby Lagana Jr. Date Of Birth: 1978 From: Scarsdale, NY

Pro Debut: 2000 Starts: 27 Consecutive Qualified Starts: 4

Win Percentage In Final Round: 0% IHRA: TF: 60.5% Average Career Qualifying Spot: 10.5

AT THE TREE:

Career Left Firsts/Left On: 14/17 = 45.1%

STATS:

Championships: 0 IHRA: TF: 2

Career Best E.T./Speed: 1000ft.: 3.884/309.42 1320ft.: 4.645/319.14

Career Wins: 0 IHRA: TF: 23

Career Finals: 0 IHRA: TF: 38

Most Successful Event: Gainesville: 2/2

Elimination Round Win/Loss Record: 6/27 = 18.1%

Top Five Point Finishes: 0 IHRA: TF: 8

Top Ten Point Finishes: 0 IHRA: TF: 12

Career Best Points Finish: Countdown: 23rd-174 (-2397)

Pre-Countdown (2006 And Before): 19th-257 (-1724)

YEARLY CAREER SUMMARY:

2011: Won IHRA Top-Fuel Championship

2010: 26th-126 (-2558), 0/4, Average Qualifying Spot: 13, Left First: 66.6%, Won IHRA Top-Fuel Championship

2009: 23rd-174 (-2397), 4/3, Average Qualifying Spot: 13.3, Left First: 42.8%

2007: 31st-30 (-3156), 3 DNQ's

2006: 30th-41 (-1640), 0/1, Average Qualifying Spot: 15, 1 DNQ, Left First: 100%

2005: 19th-257 (-1724), 0/6, Average Qualifying Spot: 14.8, 7 DNQ's, Left First: 60%

2004: 27th-82 (-1912), 1/2, Average Qualifying Spot: 15.5, Left First: 0%

2002: 32nd-71 (-1880), 0/1, Average Qualifying Spot: 13, Left First: 0%

2001: 25th-185 (-1917), 1/4, Average Qualifying Spot: 14.2, 4 DNQ's, Left First: 20%

2000: 20th-207 (-1683), 0/6, Average Qualifying Spot: 14.5, 3 DNQ's, Left First: 66.6%

Dom Lagana Date Of Birth: August 13, 1985 From: Scarsdale, NY
 Sponsor: Service Central Crew Chief: Bobby Lagana Jr. Owner: Bobby Lagana
  Chassis: '09 Hadman Engine: BAE 496
  Pro Debut: 2009 Starts: 14 Consecutive Qualified Starts: 1
  Average Career Qualifying Spot: 14.1

AT THE TREE:

Career Left Firsts/Left On: 6/9 = 40%

STATS:

Career Best E.T./Speed: 1000ft.: 3.862/319.60

Career Finals: 1 Last Final: 2010 Vegas-2 Most Successful Event: Las Vegas-2: 3/2, 1 Final

Elimination Round Win/Loss Record: 3/14 = 17.6%

Top Ten Point Finishes: 0 IHRA: TF: 1

Career Best Points Finish: Countdown: 17th-290 (-2337)

YEARLY CAREER SUMMARY:

2012: 19th-41 (-496), Average Qualifying Spot: 15, 1 DNQ, Left First: 0%

2011: 17th-285 (-2342), 0/9, Average Qualifying Spot: 14.3, 2 DNQ's, Left First: 42.8%

2010: 23rd-186 (-2498), 3/4, 1 Final, Average Qualifying Spot: 13.5, Left First: 42.8%

2009: 48th-10 (-2561), 1 DNQ

Austin Lambright Date Of Birth: June 8, 1987 From: Elkhart, IN

Pro Debut: 2011 Starts: 1 Consecutive Qualified Starts: 0 Average Career Qualifying Spot: 16

AT THE TREE:

Career Left Firsts/Left On: 0/1 = 0%

STATS:

Career Best E.T./Speed: 1000ft.: 4.043/292.96

Most Successful Event: Bristol: 0/1

Elimination Round Win/Loss Record: 0/1 = 0%
Career Best Points Finish: Countdown: 35th-31 (-2596)

YEARLY CAREER SUMMARY:

2011: 35th-31 (-2596), 0/1, Average Qualifying Spot: 16, Left First: 0%

Shawn Langdon Date Of Birth: September 3, 1982 From: Danville, IN

Sponsor: Al-Anabi Crew Chief: Brian Husen/Nick Peters Owner: Alan Johnson

Chassis: '11 Hadman Engine: TFX 500

Pro Debut: 2009 Starts: 72 Consecutive Qualified Starts: 6

Win Percentage In Final Round: 53.8% Sportsman: 77.7%

Average Career Qualifying Spot: 7.95

AT THE TREE:

Career Holeshot Win/Loss Record: 11/2 Career Left Firsts/Left On: 91/40 = 69.4%

STATS:

Championships: 3 Super Comp: 2 Jr. Dragster: 1

Career Best E.T./Speed: 1000ft.: 3.754/325.06

Career Wins: 7 Sportsman: 7

Career Finals: 13 TF: 4 Sportsman: 9

Last Final: 2011 Pomona-1 Most Successful Event: Dallas: 5/3, 1 Final

Elimination Round Win/Loss Record: 65/72 = 47.4%

Career # 1 Qualifiers: 3 TF: 1 TAD: 2

Career Provisional # 1 Qualifiers: 2 TF: 1 TAD: 1

Top Five Point Finishes: 3 TF: 1 SC: 2

Top Ten Point Finishes: 6 TF: 3 Consecutive SC: 2 SG: 1

Career Best Points Finish: Countdown: 5th-2431 (-253)

Best/Worst Points Finish If Countdown Never Was: 7th/9th

YEARLY CAREER SUMMARY:

2012: 5th-348 (-189), 7/6, Average Qualifying Spot: 5.16, Left First: 6/7 = 46.1%

2011: 9th-2208 (-419), 13/20, 1 Final, Including 2 Consecutive, Average Qualifying Spot: 9.85, 2 DNQ's, Left First: 38.7%

2010: 5th-2431 (-253), 22/23, 2 Finals, Average Qualifying Spot: 8.21, Left First: 85.7%, Won 5 Rounds On A Holeshot

2009: 9th-2299 (-272), 24/23, 1 Final, Average Qualifying Spot: 6.78, Qualified # 1 Once, 1 DNQ, Left First: 82.2%, Won 4 Rounds On A Holeshot

2008: Won Super Comp National Championship, Division 3 Super Comp Champion, 3rd In The Division 7 Super Gas Points, 8th Nationally

2007: Won Super Comp National Championship, Division 3 Super Comp Champion, 10th In The Division 7 Top Alcohol Dragster Points, 46th Nationally

2006: Finished 9th In The Division 7 Super Comp Points, 28th Nationally, Won Super Comp At JEGS Allstars Event

2005: Finished 16th In The Division 7 Super Gas Points, 14th Nationally, 37th In Super Comp, 88th Nationally, Won Super Comp At JEGS Allstars Event

2003: Finished 6th In The Division 7 Super Comp Points, 19th Nationally

2002: Finished 14th In The Division 7 Super Comp Points, 35th Nationally

1999: Won Division 7 Junior Dragster Championship

1997: Won National Championship in NHRA Jr. Drag Racing League 14 Year Old bracket

Arley Langlo Date Of Birth: N/A From: Goleta, CA Pro Debut: N/A Starts: 0

STATS:

Career Best E.T./Speed: 1000ft.: 4.904/166.72 1320ft.: 5.043/261.17
Most Successful Event: Phoenix, Seattle, Sonoma: 1 DNQ
Career Best Points Finish: Countdown: 33rd-20 (-2683)
Pre-Countdown (2006 And Before): 35th-10 (-1671)

YEARLY CAREER SUMMARY:

2009: 48th-10 (-2561), 1 DNQ

2008: 33rd-20 (-2683), 2 DNQ's

2007: 34th-10 (-3176), 1 DNQ

2002: 43rd-20 (-1931), 2 DNQ's

2001: 42nd-30 (-2072), 3 DNQ's

2000: 36th-30 (-1860), 3 DNQ's

1999: 1 DNQ

Bruce Litton Date Of Birth: December 6, 1955 From: Indianapolis, IN

Sponsor: Lucas Oil Crew Chief: Mike Wolfarth Owner: Bruce Litton Chassis: '10 Hadman Engine: TFX 500

Patrick J. Keenan

Pro Debut: 1997 Starts: 56 Consecutive Qualified Starts: 0

Win Percentage In Final Round: 0% IHRA: TF: 33.7% Average Career Qualifying Spot: 12.7

AT THE TREE:

Career Holeshot Win/Loss Record: 1/0 Career Left Firsts/Left On: 35/30 = 53.8%

STATS:

Championships: 0 IHRA: 4 TF: 1 Q8: 3

Career Best E.T./Speed: 1000ft.: 3.888/315.71 1320ft.: 4.575/329.18

Career Wins: 0 IHRA: 25

Career Finals: 0 IHRA: 74

Most Successful Event: Gainesville: 3/8, 1 DNQ

Elimination Round Win/Loss Record: 12/56 = 17.6%

Top Five Point Finishes: 0 IHRA: TF: 14

Top Ten Point Finishes: 0 IHRA: TF: 16

Career Best Points Finish: Countdown: 20th-185 (-3001)

Pre-Countdown (2006 And Before): 14th-378 (-1724)

YEARLY CAREER SUMMARY:

* 2011-2009 Results For This Driver As Opposed To What The NHRA Officially Counts, Since He Competed In The IHRA Full-Time, It Violated NHRA's 2009-Present Rule That Teams In TF, FC May Run Outside Of NHRA National Events, (Various Events, Testing) No More Than 4 Days Once A Season Begins. *

2012: 28th-10 (-527), 1 DNQ

2011: 27th-82 (-2545), 0/2, Average Qualifying Spot: 16, 2 DNQ's, Left First: 0%

2010: 36th-31 (-2653), 0/1, Average Qualifying Spot: 16, Left First: 100%

2009: 41st-31 (-2540), 0/1, Average Qualifying Spot: 14, Left First: 0%

2008: 25th-113 (-2590), 2/2, Average Qualifying Spot: 13.5, 1 DNQ, Left First: 25%

2007: 20th-185 (-3001), 3/4, Average Qualifying Spot:12.5, Left First: 71.4%, Won IHRA Top-Fuel Championship

2006: 26th-92 (-1589), 0/2, Average Qualifying Spot: 16, 3 DNQ's, Left First: 100%

2005: 21st-186 (-1795), 0/5, Average Qualifying Spot: 14.4, 3 DNQ's, 1 By 5 Thousandths, Left First: 75%

2004: 21st-219 (-1775), 1/7, Average Qualifying Spot: 12.8, Left First: 57.1%

2003: 19th-248 (-1746), 1/7, Average Qualifying Spot: 13.4, 1 DNQ, Left First: 62.5%

2002: 19th-271 (-1680), 1/8, Average Qualifying Spot: 13.3, Left First: 11.1%

2001: 14th-378 (-1724), 4/10, Average Qualifying Spot: 10.8, Left First: 53.8%

2000: 18th-220 (-1650), 0/7, Average Qualifying Spot: 12.8, Left First: 85.7%

1999: 3 DNQ's

1998: 1 DNQ

1997: 1 DNQ

1995: Won IHRA Quick 8 Competition Championship

1994: Won IHRA Quick 8 Competition Championship

1993: Won IHRA Quick 8 Competition Championship

Morgan Lucas Date Of Birth: November 27, 1983 From: Brownsburg, IN
Sponsor: Geico Powersports Crew Chief: Aaron Brooks/Rod Centorbi
Owner: Morgan Lucas Chassis: '04 Hadman Engine: TFX 500
Pro Debut: 2004 Starts: 162 Consecutive Qualified Starts: 7
Win Percentage In Final Round: 68% TF: 54.5% TAD: 78.5%
Average Career Qualifying Spot: 8.85

AT THE TREE:

Career Holeshot Win/Loss Record: 9/6 Career Left Firsts/Left On: 165/116 = 58.7%

STATS:

U.S. Nationals Wins/Finals: 1/1 TAD: 1/1

Career Best E.T./Speed: 1000ft.: 3.743/327.74 1320ft.: 4.474/333.33

Career Wins: 17 TF: 6 TAD: 11

Career Finals: 25 TF: 11 TAD: 14

Last Win: 2012 Houston

Last Final: 2012 Houston

Most Successful Event: Brainerd: 10/7, 1 Win, 1 Final

Elimination Round Win/Loss Record: 144/156 = 48%

Career # 1 Qualifiers: 20 TF: 8 TAD: 12

Career Provisional # 1 Qualifiers: 17 TF: 7 TAD: 10

Top Five Point Finishes: 2 TF: 1 TAD: 2

Top Ten Point Finishes: 6, 3 Consecutive TF: 4 TAD: 3

Career Best Points Finish: Countdown: 7th-2353 (-218)

Pre-Countdown (2006 And Before): 5th-1357 (-624)

Best/Worst Points Finish If Countdown Never Was: 7th/11th

YEARLY CAREER SUMMARY:

2012: 3rd-505 (-32), 13/4, 2 Wins, 2 Finals, Average Qualifying Spot: 4.33, Qualified # 1 Four Times, Including 2 Consecutive, Left First: 76.4%

2011: 10th-2138 (-489), 11/18, 1 Win, 1 Final, Average Qualifying Spot: 10.7, 3 DNQ's, Left First: 50%,

2010: 10th-2252 (-432), 13/22, Average Qualifying Spot: 9.9, 1 DNQ, Left First: 53.1%

2009: 7th-2353 (-218), 27/21, 3 Wins, 3 Finals, Average Qualifying Spot: 6.62, Qualified # 1 Twice, Left First: 60.8%

2008: 12th-966 (-1737), 12/22, Average Qualifying Spot: 10.9, 2 DNQ's, 1 By 7 Thousandths, Left First: 65.6%, Finished 5th In The Divisional 2 Top Alcohol Dragster Points, 36th Nationally

2007: 15th-790 (-2396), 10/16, Average Qualifying Spot: 9.81, 7 DNQ's, Left First: 60%, Division 2 Top Alcohol Dragster Champion, 3rd Nationally

2006: 11th-1026 (-655), 17/22, Average Qualifying Spot: 11.1, 1 DNQ, Left First: 54%, Finished 12th In The Division 7 Top Alcohol Dragster Points, 31st Nationally

2005: 5th-1357 (-624), 29/23, 3 Finals, Including 2 Consecutive, Average Qualifying Spot: 5.04, Qualified # 1 Twice, Left First: 55.5%

2004: 16th-502 (-1492), 12/8, 2 Finals, Average Qualifying Spot: 8.62, Left First: 63.1%, Finished 3rd In The Division 7 Top Alcohol Dragster Points, 8th Nationally

2003: Won Division 7 Top Alcohol Dragster Championship, 2nd Nationally

2002: Finished 5th In The Division 7 Top Alcohol Dragster Points, 18th Nationally

Bonus Fact: Tuned His Top-Fuel Dragster In The Countdown Of 2011

Ike Maier Date Of Birth: N/A From: Ontario, Canada
Pro Debut: 2011 Starts: 2 Consecutive Qualified Starts: 0
Average Career Qualifying Spot: 13

AT THE TREE:

Career Left Firsts/Left On: 0/2 = 0%

STATS:

Career Best E.T./Speed: 1000ft.: 3.931/307.93

Career Finals: 0 IHRA: PM: 1 Most Successful Event: Atlanta/ Norwalk: 0/1

Elimination Round Win/Loss Record: 0/2 = 0%

Top Ten Point Finishes: 0 PM: 1

Career Best Points Finish: Countdown: 27th-78 (-2549)

YEARLY CAREER SUMMARY:

2012: 28th-10 (-527), 1 DNQ

2011: 27th-78 (-2549), 0/2, Average Qualifying Spot: 13, 3 DNQ's, Left First: 0%

Mark Mariani Date Of Birth: N/A From: Australia

Pro Debut: 2010 Starts: 1 Consecutive Qualified Starts: 1

Average Career Qualifying Spot: 15

AT THE TREE:

Career Left Firsts/Left On: 1/1 = 50%

STATS:

Career Best E.T./Speed: 1000ft.: 3.930/307.44

Most Successful Event: Las Vegas-2: 1/1

Elimination Round Win/Loss Record: 1/1 = 50%

Career Best Points Finish: Countdown: 29th-61 (-2623)

YEARLY CAREER SUMMARY:

2010: 29th-61 (-2623), 1/1, Average Qualifying Spot: 15, 1 DNQ, Left First: 50%

Spencer Massey Date Of Birth: September 13, 1982 From: Fort Worth, TX

Sponsor: Fram Crew Chief: Todd Okuhara/Phil Schuler Owner: Don Schumacher

Chassis: '11 DSR Engine: TFX 498

Pro Debut: 2008 Starts: 52 Consecutive Qualified Starts: 8

Win Percentage In Final Round: 52.1% TF: 56.2% TAD: 42.8% IHRA: TF: 55.5%

Average Career Qualifying Spot: 5.05

AT THE TREE:

Career Holeshot Win/Loss Record: 8/1 Career Left Firsts/Left On: 105/20 = 84%

Career Final Rounds Won/Lost On A Holeshot: 2/0

STATS:

Championships: 0 IHRA: TF: 1

Career Best E.T./Speed: 1000ft.: 3.745/332.18 1320ft.: 4.630/315.27

Career Wins: 12 TF: 9 TAD: 3 IHRA: TF: 5

Career Finals: 23 TF: 16 TAD: 7 IHRA: TF: 9

Last Win: 2012 Concord

Last Final: 2012 Concord

Most Successful Event: Reading/Las Vegas-2: 7/1, 1 Win, 2 Finals

Elimination Round Win/Loss Record: 92/43 = 68.1%

Career # 1 Qualifiers: 6 TF: 3 TAD: 3

Career Provisional # 1 Qualifiers: 6 TF: 3 TAD: 3

Top Five Point Finishes: 2 TF: 1 TAD: 1 IHRA: TF: 2

Top Ten Point Finishes: 5 TF: 2 TAD: 3 IHRA: TF: 2

Career Best Points Finish: Countdown: 2nd-2579 (-48)

Best/Worst Points Finish If Countdown Never Was: 3rd/6th

YEARLY CAREER SUMMARY:

2012: 2nd-523 (-14), 14/3, 3 Wins, Including 2 Consecutive, 3 Finals, Average Qualifying Spot: 4.16, Left First: 76.4%, Holds The National Speed Record, 332.18, Todd Okuhara And Phil Schuler Were The Crew Chiefs

2011: 2nd-2569 (-58), 45/17, 4 Wins, Including 2 Consecutive, 8 Finals, Including 3 Consecutive, Average Qualifying Spot: 3.85, Qualified # 1 Twice, 1 DNQ, Left First: 84.2%

2010: 36th-31 (-2653), 0/1, Average Qualifying Spot: 15, Left First: 0%

2009: 6th-2437 (-134), 33/21, 2 Wins, 5 Finals, Including 2 Consecutive, Average Qualifying Spot: 5.69, Qualified # 1 Once, 1 DNQ, Left First: 89.7%,Won Auto Club Road to the Future Award

2008: 31st-32 (-2671), 0/1, Average Qualifying Spot: 11, Left First: 0%, Finished 2nd In The Division 4 Top Alcohol Dragster Points, 9th Nationally, Won IHRA Top-Fuel Championship

2007: Finished 3rd In The Division 4 Top Alcohol Dragster Points, 7th Nationally

2006: Division 4 Top Alcohol Dragster Championship; Finished 3rd Nationally

Cory McClenathan Date Of Birth: January 30, 1963 From: La Habra, CA

Sponsor: Uplift Cranes Crew Chief: Keith Stewart Owner: Santo Rapisarda

Chassis: '11 Hadman Engine: TFX 498

Pro Debut: 1991 Starts: 403 Consecutive Qualified Starts: 0

Win Percentage In Final Round: 53.5% TF: 52.3% TAD: 66.6% IHRA: TF: 50%

Average Career Qualifying Spot: 1997-2011: 4.85

AT THE TREE: 1997-2011:

Career Holeshot Win/Loss Record: 18/24 Career Left Firsts/Left On: 237/347 = 40.5%

Career Final Rounds Won/Lost On A Holeshot: 2/3

STATS:

U.S. Nationals Wins/Finals: 2/4

Career Best E.T./Speed: 1000ft.: 3.752/324.75 1320ft.: 4.463/334.07

Career Wins: 38 TF: 34 TAD: 4 IHRA: TF: 1

Career Finals: 71 TF: 65 TAD: 6 IHRA: TF: 2

Last Win: 2010 Seattle

Last Final: 2010 Reading

Most Successful Event: 1997-2011: Houston: 24/12, 1 Win, 4 Finals

Elimination Round Win/Loss Record: 512/369 = 58.1%

Career # 1 Qualifiers: 38

Career Provisional # 1 Qualifiers: 1997-2011: 30

Top Five Point Finishes: 11

Top Ten Point Finishes: 18

Career Best Points Finish: Countdown: 3rd-2551 (-133)

Pre-Countdown (2006 And Before): 2nd-1640 (-141)

Best/Worst Points Finish If Countdown Never Was: 3rd/5th

YEARLY CAREER SUMMARY:

2012: 15th-92 (-445), 0/2, Average Qualifying Spot: 14, 3 DNQ's, Left First: 0%

2011: 24th-138 (-2489), 0/4, Average Qualifying Spot: 11.7, 2 DNQ's, 1 By A Hundredth, Left First: 25%

2010: 3rd-2551 (-133), 45/20, 3 Wins, 8 Finals, Including 2 Consecutive Twice, Average Qualifying Spot: 3.39, Qualified # 1 Five Times, Left First: 30.6%, Lost 4 Rounds On A Holeshot, Went 16 Races Without Losing In The First Round Between 2009 And 2010 Seasons

2009: 4th-2490 (-81), 35/23, 1 Win, 4 Finals, Including 2 Consecutive, Average Qualifying Spot: 5.5, Qualified # 1 Once, Left First: 23.6%, Lost 5 Rounds On A Holeshot

2008: 3rd-2406 (-247), 32/23, 1 Win, 3 Finals, Average Qualifying Spot: 6, Qualified # 1 Twice, Left First: 29.1%, Lost 4 Rounds On A Holeshot

2007: 12th-971 (-2215), 13/23, 1 Final, Average Qualifying Spot: 11, Left First: 47.2%

2006: 10th-1036 (-645), 15/21, 1 Win, 2 Finals, Average Qualifying Spot: 8.54, Qualified # 1 Once, 1 DNQ, 1 By A Thousandth, Left First: 42.8%

2005: 9th-1096 (-855), 16/23, 1 Final, Average Qualifying Spot: 6.6, Left First: 58.3%

2004: 7th-1152 (-842), 20/21, 1 Win, 2 Finals, Average Qualifying Spot: 7.09, Qualified # 1 Twice, 1 DNQ, Left First: 48.6%

2003: 5th-1150 (-844), 20/23, 2 Finals, Average Qualifying Spot: 7.17, Left First: 40.4%

2002: 5th-1425 (-526), 33/22, 1 Win, 4 Finals, Average Qualifying Spot: 5.13, Qualified # 1 Once, Left First: 50%, Lost 4 Rounds On A Holeshot

2001: 44th-10 (-2092), 1 DNQ

2000: 7th-1249 (-641), 25/20, 2 Wins, Including 2 Consecutive, 2 Finals, Average Qualifying Spot: 4.77, Qualified # 1 Twice, 1 DNQ, Left First: 39%

1999: 9th-1149 (-339), 21/20, 2 Wins, 2 Finals, Average Qualifying Spot: 7.95, Left First: 61.5%

1998: 2nd-1640 (-141), 44/17, 6 Wins, Including 3 Consecutive, 8 Finals, Average Qualifying Spot: 5.39, Qualified # 1 Twice, Left First: 47.3%

1997: 2nd-1660 (-177), 44/17, 6 Wins, Including 4 Consecutive, 8 Finals, Including 6 Consecutive, Average Qualifying Spot: 4.13,

Qualified # 1 Three Times, Left First: 46.5%, Swept The Western Swing

1996: 3rd-1194 (-221), 27/16, 3 Wins, 4 Finals, Qualified # 1 Once

1995: 2nd-1360 (-215), 35/16, 3 Wins, Including 2 Consecutive, 4 Finals, Qualified # 1 Once

1994: 3rd-10294 (-3306), 24/16, 2 Wins, 4 Finals, Qualified # 1 Six Times, Including 2 Consecutive Twice, Including 3 Consecutive Between Seasons

1993: 6th-9066 (-3732), 19/14, 3 Finals, Qualified # 1 Seven Times, Including 2 Consecutive

1992: 2nd-12140 (-92), 31/15, 2 Wins, 3 Finals, Qualified # 1 Four Times, Including 2 Consecutive

1991: 10th-6918 (-7470), 13/13

Ed McCulloch Date Of Birth: N/A From: Indianapolis, IN RETIRED

Pro Debut: TF: 1992 FC: 1971

Win Percentage In Final Round: 44% TF: 57.1% FC: 41.8% IHRA: FC: 72.7%

STATS:

Championships: 0 IHRA: FC: 1 U.S. Nationals Wins/Finals: 6/7 TF: 1/1 FC: 5/6

Career Best E.T./Speed: TF: 1320ft.: 4.795/304.05 FC: 5.132/280.89

Career Wins: 22 TF: 4 FC: 18 IHRA: FC: 8

Career Finals: 50 TF: 7 FC: 43 IHRA: FC: 11

Last Win: TF: 1993 Houston FC: 1990 Pomona

Last Final: TF: 1993 Gainesville FC: 1991 Pomona

Most Successful Event: 1997-2011: 1997 Rockingham

Career # 1 Qualifiers: 15 TF: 3 FC: 12

Top Five Point Finishes: 8 TF: 1 FC: 1975-2011: 7, 5 Consecutive IHRA: FC: 3

Top Ten Point Finishes: 12 TF: 1 FC: 1975-2011: 11, 7 Consecutive IHRA: FC: 4

Career Best Points Finish: TF: 5th-11536 (-696) FC: 2nd-15198 (-436)

YEARLY CAREER SUMMARY:

1997: 1 DNQ

1993: 8th-8652 (-4146), 1 Win, 2 Final, Qualified # 1 Once

1992: 5th-11536 (-696), 3 Wins, Including 2 Consecutive, 5 Finals, Qualified # 1 Twice, Including 2 Consecutive

1991: 4th-11364 (-4174), 4 Finals, Qualified # 1 Twice

1990: 2nd-15128 (-436), 5 Wins, Including 2 Consecutive, 9 Finals, Qualified # 1 Once

1989: 5th-12088 (-4050), 2 Wins, 4 Finals, Qualified # 1 Twice

1988: 5th-9554 (-2808), 2 Wins, 4 Finals, Qualified # 1 Four Times, Including 2 Consecutive, Won IHRA Funny Car Championship

1987: 3rd-9718 (-2970), 1 Win, 3 Finals, Qualified # 1 Once

1986: 6th-7720 (-5066), 2 Wins, Including 2 Consecutive, 3 Finals,

1985: 7th-6588 (-6064), 1 Final

1984: 1 Final, Qualified # 1 Twice

1980: 5th-4924 (-3524), 1 Win, 1 Final

1978: 9th-5787 (-7926), 1 Final

1976: 3rd-4727 (-6544), 3 Finals

1975: 7th-3699 (-6915)

1974: 1 Final

1973: 1 Final
1972: 4 Wins, 5 Finals
1971: 1 Win, 1 Final
1970: 1 Final

Terry McMillen Date Of Birth: August 30, 1954 From: Elkhart, IN
Sponsor: Amalie Oil Crew Chief: Richard Hartman Tuning Consultant: Lee Beard
Owner: Terry McMillen Chassis: '11 McKinney Engine: TFX 500
Pro Debut: 2007 Starts: 52 Consecutive Qualified Starts: 6
Win Percentage In Final Round: 0% IHRA: 25% TF: 37.5%
Average Career Qualifying Spot: 11.8

AT THE TREE:

Career Holeshot Win/Loss Record: 1/1 Career Left Firsts/Left On: 26/46 = 36.1%

STATS:

Career Best E.T./Speed: 1000ft.: 3.856/321.50 1320ft.: 4.674/315.86
Career Wins: 0 IHRA: TF: 3
Career Finals: 0 IHRA: 12 TF: 8 AFC: 4
Most Successful Event: Topeka/Sonoma: 2/2
Elimination Round Win/Loss Record: 12/52 = 18.7%
Top Five Point Finishes: 0 IHRA: 4 TF: 2 AFC: 2
Top Ten Point Finishes: 0 IHRA: 9 TF: 3 AFC: 6
Career Best Points Finish: Countdown: 11th-768 (-1916)

YEARLY CAREER SUMMARY:

* 2009 Results For This Driver As Opposed To What The NHRA Officially Counts, Since He Competed In The IHRA Full-Time, It Violated NHRA's 2009-Present Rule That Teams In TF, FC May Run Outside Of NHRA National Events, (Various Events, Testing) No More Than 4 Days Once A Season Begins. *

2012: 12th-209 (-328), 1/6, Average Qualifying Spot: 13, Left First: 57.1%

2011: 12th-717 (-1910), 6/19, Average Qualifying Spot: 10.8, 3 DNQ's, Left First: 29.1%

2010: 11th-768 (-1916), 4/21, Average Qualifying Spot: 11.8, 2 DNQ's, Left First: 41.6%

2009: 26th-145 (-2477), 1/4, Average Qualifying Spot: 13.7, Left First: 80%

2008: 29th-62 (-2641), 0/2, Average Qualifying Spot: 14, Left First: 50%

2003: Finished 23rd In Division 3 The Top Alcohol Funny Car Points, 110th Nationally

Clay Millican Date Of Birth: February 9, 1966 From: Drummonds, TN

Sponsor: Parts Plus Crew Chief: Justin Crosslin/Mike Domagala

Tuning Consultant: Lance Larsen

Owner: Mark Pickens Chassis: '12 Hadman Engine: BAE 496

Pro Debut: 1998 Starts: 116 Consecutive Qualified Starts: 10

Win Percentage In Final Round: 0% IHRA: TF: 85% Average Career Qualifying Spot: 9.36

AT THE TREE:

Career Holeshot Win/Loss Record: 10/2 Career Left Firsts/Left On: 134/45 = 74.8%

STATS:

Championships: 0 IHRA: TF: 6

Career Best E.T./Speed: 1000ft.: 3.818/318.92 1320ft.: 4.479/330.39

Career Wins: 0 IHRA: TF: 51

Career Finals: 4 IHRA: TF: 60

Last Final: 2009 Topeka Most Successful Event: Topeka: 7/4, 1 Final

Elimination Round Win/Loss Record: 70/116 = 37.6%

Career Provisional # 1 Qualifiers: 3

Top Five Point Finishes: 0 IHRA: TF: 7

Top Ten Point Finishes: 1 IHRA: TF: 8

Career Best Points Finish: Countdown: 10th-2093 (-478)

Pre-Countdown (2006 And Before): 14th-649 (-1345)

Best/Worst Points Finish If Countdown Never Was: 10th

YEARLY CAREER SUMMARY:

2012: 10th-258 (-279), 4/6, Average Qualifying Spot: 9.66, Left First: 66.6%

2011: 16th-310 (-2312), 1/9, Average Qualifying Spot: 10.8, 1 DNQ, Left First: 69.2%

2010: 28th-67 (-2617), 0/2, Average Qualifying Spot: 8.5, Left First: 50%

2009: 10th-2093 (-478), 9/19, 1 Final, Average Qualifying Spot: 9.63, Left First: 61.5%

2008: 16th-332 (-2371), 4/8, Average Qualifying Spot: 12.1, Left First: 75%

2007: 14th-826 (-2360), 7/20, Average Qualifying Spot: 9.6, 3 DNQ's, 1 By 2 Thousandths, Left First: 88.8%

2006: 16th-428 (-1253), 6/8, Average Qualifying Spot: 10.6, 5 DNQ's, Left First: 78.5%, Won IHRA Top-Fuel Championship

2005: 16th-446 (-1535), 6/10, Average Qualifying Spot: 9.5, Left First: 100%, Won IHRA Top-Fuel Championship

2004: 14th-592 (-1402), 13/10, 3 Finals, Including 3 Consecutive, Average Qualifying Spot: 7.5, Left First: 77.2%, Won IHRA Top-Fuel Championship

2003: 14th-649 (-1325), 12/13, Average Qualifying Spot: 7.3, Left First: 81.8%, Won IHRA Top-Fuel Championship

2002: 18th-289 (-1662), 4/6, Average Qualifying Spot: 7.66, Left First: 44.4%, Won IHRA Top-Fuel Championship

2001: 24th-193 (-1909), 4/4, Average Qualifying Spot: 7.75, Left First: 50%, Won IHRA Top-Fuel Championship

2000: 39th-10 (-1880), 1 DNQ

1999: 29th, 0/1, Average Qualifying Spot: 14, 1 DNQ, Left First: 0%

1998: 44th, 1 DNQ

Shirley Muldowney Date Of Birth: June 19, 1940 From: Armada, MI RETIRED

Pro Debut: FC: 1971 TF: 1974

Starts: 1997-2011: 13 Consecutive Qualified Starts: 3

Win Percentage In Final Round: 66.6% IHRA: 27.2% TF: 30% FC: 0%

Average Career Qualifying Spot: 1997-2011: 11.5

AT THE TREE: 1997-2011:

Career Holeshot Win/Loss Record: 1/1 Career Left Firsts/Left On: 10/8 = 55.5%

STATS:

Championships: 3 U.S. Nationals Wins/Finals: TF: 1/2

Career Best E.T./Speed: 1320ft.: TF: 4.578/327.66 FC: 6.630/225.00

Career Wins: 18 IHRA: TF: 3

Career Finals: 27 IHRA: 11 TF: 10 FC: 1

Last Win: 1989 Phoenix

Last Final: 1989 Phoenix

Most Successful Event: 1997-2011: Columbus/Chicago-2: 2/1

Elimination Round Win/Loss Record: 1997-2011: 8/13 = 38%

Career # 1 Qualifiers: 1997-2011: 13

Top Five Point Finishes: 6 IHRA: TF: 2

Top Ten Point Finishes: 11 IHRA: TF: 4

Career Best Points Finish:: 1st-11939

YEARLY CAREER SUMMARY:

2003: 20th-228 (-1766), 3/5, Average Qualifying Spot: 12.2, 1 DNQ, Left First: 71.4%

2002: 20th-260 (-1691), 5/5, Average Qualifying Spot: 10.2, Left First: 44.4%

2001: 36th-32 (-2070), 0/1, Average Qualifying Spot: 12, Left First: 0%, # 5 On The Top 50 NHRA Drivers List

2000: 33rd-53 (-1837), 0/2, Average Qualifying Spot: 13, Left First: 50%

1997: 1 DNQ

1990: 10th-7348 (-8710)

1989: 9th-7708 (-7244), 1 Win, 3 Finals, Qualified # 1 Three Times, Including 2 Consecutive

1988: 9th-5792 (-8312)

1987: 8th-5714 (-7438)

1986: 10th-5526 (-6410)

1983: 4th-8550 (-2380), 2 Wins, 3 Finals

1982: 1st-7902, 4 Wins, 7 Finals, Including 2 Consecutive, Qualified # 1 Twice

1981: 5th-5317 (-1829), 2 Wins, 2 Finals, Including 2 Consecutive

1980: 1st-8114, 4 Wins, Including 2 Consecutive, 4 Finals,

1979: 4th-5243 (-2287), 1 Final, Qualified # 1 Twice, Including 2 Consecutive Between Seasons

1977: 1st-11939, 3 Wins, 3 Finals Qualified # 1 Four Times, Including 3 Consecutive, The First Woman In NHRA History To Win A Championship

1976: 1 Win, 1 Final, Qualified # 1 Twice

1975: 1 Final

Keith Murt Date Of Birth: 1957 From: Paducah, KY

Sponsor: Murtco Inc. Crew Chief: Jim Dupey Owner: Mitch King

Chassis: '11 McKinney Engine: BAE 500

Pro Debut: 2011 Starts: 1 Consecutive Qualified Starts: 0

Average Career Qualifying Spot: 15

AT THE TREE:

Career Left Firsts/Left On: 0/0 = 0%

STATS:

Career Best E.T./Speed: 1000ft.: 3.914/312.64

Most Successful Event: Pomona-2: 0/1

Elimination Round Win/Loss Record: 0/1 = 0%

Career Best Points Finish: Countdown: 28th-71 (-2556)

YEARLY CAREER SUMMARY:

2012: 26th-20 (-517), 2 DNQ's

2011: 28th-71 (-2556), 0/1, Average Qualifying Spot: 15, 4 DNQ's, Left First: 0%

Thomas Nataas Date Of Birth: N/A From: Norway

Sponsor: Andersen Racing Crew Chief And Owner: Karsten And Per Andersen

Chassis: N/A Engine: N/A

Pro Debut: 2009 Starts: 2 Consecutive Qualified Starts: 0

Average Career Qualifying Spot: 7.5

AT THE TREE:

Career Left Firsts/Left On: 0/2 = 0%

STATS:

Career Best E.T./Speed: 1000ft.: 3.844/310.34

Most Successful Event: Pomona-1: 0/1

Elimination Round Win/Loss Record: 0/2 = 0%

Career Best Points Finish: Countdown: 35th-34 (-2650)

YEARLY CAREER SUMMARY:

2011: 39th-20 (-2607), 2 DNQ's

2010: 35th-34 (-2650), 0/1, Average Qualifying Spot: 7, Left First: 0%

2009: 38th-44 (-2527), 0/1, Average Qualifying Spot: 8, 1 DNQ, Left First: 0%

Stig Neergaard Date Of Birth: N/A From: Denmark

Sponsor: Persaker Racing Crew Chief: John Smith Owner: Stig Neergaard

Chassis: N/A Engine: N/A

Pro Debut: 2009 Starts: 1 Consecutive Qualified Starts: 0

Average Career Qualifying Spot: 14

AT THE TREE:

Career Left Firsts/Left On: 0/1= 0%

STATS:

Career Best E.T./Speed: 1000ft.: 3.963/307.02

Most Successful Event: Las Vegas-2: 0/1, DNQ

Elimination Round Win/Loss Record: 0/1 = 0%

Career Best Points Finish: Countdown: 12th-460 (-2224)

YEARLY CAREER SUMMARY:

2011: 41st-10 (-2617), 1 DNQ

2010: 40th-10 (-2664), 1 DNQ

2009: 39th-41 (-2530), 0/1, Average Qualifying Spot: 14, 1 DNQ, Left First: 0%

Luigi Novelli Date Of Birth: December 20, 1942 From: Crete, IL

Sponsor: National Machine Repair Crew Chief: Buzz Ols Owner: Luigi Novelli

Chassis: '11 McKinney Engine: TFX 498

Pro Debut: 1960's? Starts: 1997-2011: 38 Consecutive Qualified Starts: 0

Average Career Qualifying Spot: 1997-2011: 14.1

AT THE TREE: 1997-2011:

Career Left Firsts/Left On: 15/21= 41.6%

STATS:

Championships: 0 UDRA: TF: 2

Career Best E.T./Speed: 1000ft.: 3.946/307.44 1320ft.: 4.598/326.32

Career Finals: 0 IHRA: TF: 1 Most Successful Event: 1997-2011: Brainerd: 1/7, 7 DNQ's

Ex-Track Since 2006: Columbus: 1/5, DNQ

Elimination Round Win/Loss Record: 1997-2011: 3/38 = 7.31%

Top Ten Point Finishes: 0 IHRA: TF: 2

Career Best Points Finish: Countdown: 24th-154 (-2530)

Pre-Countdown (2006 And Before): 22nd-207 (-1895)

YEARLY CAREER SUMMARY:

2011: 25th-118 (-2509), 0/3, Average Qualifying Spot: 14, 3 DNQ's, Left First: 33.3%

2010: 24th-154 (-2530), 0/4, Average Qualifying Spot: 15.2, 3 DNQ's, Left First: 50%

2009: 34th-71 (-2500), 0/1, Average Qualifying Spot: 16, 4 DNQ's, Left First: 0%

2008: 21st-123 (-2580), 0/3, Average Qualifying Spot: 14.6, 3 DNQ's, Left First: 50%

2007: 23rd-96 (-3090), 0/2, Average Qualifying Spot: 7.5, 4 DNQ's, Left First: 0%

2006: 23rd-132 (-1549), 1/2, Average Qualifying Spot: 15, 5 DNQ's, Left First: 66.6%

2005: 24th-142 (-1839), 0/2, Average Qualifying Spot: 14, 8 DNQ's, Left First: 50%

2004: 25th-101 (-1893), 0/1, Average Qualifying Spot: 15, 7 DNQ's, Left First: 100%

2003: 23rd-164 (-1830), 0/4, Average Qualifying Spot: 14.7, 4 DNQ's, Left First: 66.6%

2002: 24th-175 (1776), 1/4, Average Qualifying Spot: 14.5, 3 DNQ's, Left First: 25%

2001: 22nd-207 (-1895), 1/5, Average Qualifying Spot: 13.4, 4 DNQ's, Left First: 0%

2000: 25th-155 (-1735), 0/5, Average Qualifying Spot: 13.8, 2 DNQ's, Left First: 60%

1999: 5 DNQ's

1998: 0/2, Average Qualifying Spot: 16, 4 DNQ's, Left First: 100%

1997: 4 DNQ's

Yuichi Oyama Date Of Birth: N/A From: N/A, Japan

Pro Debut: 2002 Starts: 8 Consecutive Qualified Starts: 8

Average Career Qualifying Spot: 11.1

AT THE TREE:

Career Holeshot Win/Loss Record: 0/1 Career Left Firsts/Left On: 3/9 = 25%

Career Final Rounds Won/Lost On A Holeshot: 0/1

STATS:

Career Best E.T./Speed: 1320ft.: 4.674/318.24

Career Finals: 1 Last Final: 2002 Pomona-2

Most Successful Event: Pomona-2: 3/1, 1 Final

Elimination Round Win/Loss Record: 6/8 = 42.8%

Career Best Points Finish: 14th—367 (-1584)

YEARLY CAREER SUMMARY:

2002: 14th-367 (-1584), 6/8, 1 Final, Average Qualifying Spot: 11.1, Left First: 25%

Scott Palmer Date Of Birth: September 11, 1963 From: Branson, MO

Sponsor: Farmer's Insurance Crew Chief: Scott Palmer Owner: Scott Palmer

Chassis: '09 McKinney Engine: BAE 500

Pro Debut: 2002 Starts: 38 Consecutive Qualified Starts: 1

Average Career Qualifying Spot: 13.7

AT THE TREE:

Career Left Firsts/Left On: 25/14 = 64.1%

STATS:

Career Best E.T./Speed: 1000ft.: 3.947/296.70 1320ft.: 4.572/328.70

Career Finals: 0 IHRA: TF: 1 Most Successful Event: Bristol: 2/3, 3 DNQ's

Elimination Round Win/Loss Record: 5/38 = 11.6%

Top Five Point Finishes: 0 IHRA: TF: 7

Top Ten Point Finishes: 0 IHRA: TF: 1

Career Best Points Finish: Countdown: 19th-247 (-2437)

Pre-Countdown (2006 And Before): 18th-287 (-1694)

YEARLY CAREER SUMMARY:

2011: 23rd-159 (-2468), 0/4, Average Qualifying Spot: 14.5, 5 DNQ's, Left First: 33.3%

2010: 19th-247 (-2437), 0/7, Average Qualifying Spot: 14.4, 3 DNQ's, Left First: 71.4%

2009: 20th-195 (-2376), 0/4, Average Qualifying Spot: 13.5, 5 DNQ's, Left First: 0%

2008: 32nd-31 (-2672), 0/1, Average Qualifying Spot: 16, Left First: 100%

2007: 21st-148 (-3038), 0/4, Average Qualifying Spot: 12, 2 DNQ's, Left First: 75%

2006: 18th-236 (-1445), 1/3, Average Qualifying Spot: 11.6, 12 DNQ's, 1 By 4 Thousandths, Left First: 50%

2005: 18th-287 (-1694), 3/6, Average Qualifying Spot: 14.6, 4 DNQ's, Left First: 100%

2004: 20th-223 (-1771), 0/6, Average Qualifying Spot: 14, 5 DNQ's, Left First: 60%

2003: 22nd-194 (-1800), 1/3, Average Qualifying Spot: 13, 8 DNQ's, Left First: 75%

2002: 37th-40 (-1911), 4 DNQ's, 1 By 8 Thousandths, 1 By 4 Thousandths, Finished 10th In The Division 5 Top Alcohol Funny Car Points, 60th Nationally

2001: Finished 7th In The Division 5 Top Alcohol Funny Car Points, 32nd Nationally

Rob Passey Date Of Birth: N/A From: Salt Lake City, UT

Sponsor: MSP Motorsports Crew Chief: N/A Owner: N/A

Chassis: '00 McKinney Engine: TFX 500

Pro Debut: 2001 Starts: 7 Consecutive Qualified Starts: 0

Average Career Qualifying Spot: 15.2

AT THE TREE:

Career Left Firsts/Left On: 1/6 = 14.2%

STATS:

Career Best E.T./Speed: 1000ft.: 4.423/260.66 1320ft.: 5.154/263.77

Most Successful Event: Denver: 0/4, 4 DNQ's

Elimination Round Win/Loss Record: 0/7 = 0%

Career Best Points Finish: Countdown: 33rd-51 (-2633)

Pre-Countdown (2006 And Before): 33rd-51 (-1943)

YEARLY CAREER SUMMARY:

2012: 28th-10 (-527), 1 DNQ

2011: 40th-20 (-2607), 2 DNQ's

2010: 33rd-51 (-2633), 0/1, Average Qualifying Spot: 16, 2 DNQ's, Left First: 0%

2009: 36th-61 (-2510), 0/1, Average Qualifying Spot: 16, 3 DNQ's, Left First: 0%

2008: 36th-10 (-2693), 1 DNQ

2007: 32nd-30 (-3156), 3 DNQ's

2006: 34th-20 (-1666), 2 DNQ's

2005: 34th-31 (-1950), 0/1, Average Qualifying Spot: 16, Left First: 0%

2004: 31st-51 (-1943), 0/1, Average Qualifying Spot: 14, 2 DNQ's, Left First: 0%

2002: 43rd-20 (-1931), 2 DNQ's

2001: 28th-153 (-1949), 0/3, Average Qualifying Spot: 15, 6 DNQ's, Left First: 33.3%

Todd Paton Date Of Birth: December 13, 1969 From: Aliso Viejo, CA

Formally: Ontario, Canada

Sponsor: Tim Horton's Crew Chief: N/A Owner: N/A

Chassis: '08 McKinney Engine: TFX 500

Pro Debut: FC: 1999 TF: 2004 Starts: 28 TF: 5 FC: 23 Consecutive Qualified Starts: 0

Win Percentage In Final Round: 50% TAFC: 50% IHRA: 50% TF: 0% AFC: 58.3%

Average Career Qualifying Spot: 9.78 TF: 15 FC: 8.65

AT THE TREE: 1997-2011:

Career Left Firsts/Left On: 16/20 = 44.4% TF: 1/3 = 25% FC: 15/17 = 46.8%

STATS:

Championships: 0 IHRA: AFC: 2 U.S. Nationals: 1/1 TAFC: 1/1

Career Best E.T./Speed: 1000ft.: TF: 3.949/294.05 1320ft.: TF: 4.896/276.75 FC: 4.876/315.42

Career Wins: 4 TAFC: 4 IHRA: 7 AFC: 7

Career Finals: 8 TAFC: 8 IHRA: 14 TF: 3 AFC: 12

Most Successful Event: Atlanta: 3/3, 1 DNQ TF: Reading: 0/1 FC: Atlanta: 3/2

Elimination Round Win/Loss Record: 10/28 = 26.3% TF: 0/5 = 0% FC: 10/23 = 30.3%

Career # 1 Qualifiers: 6 FC: 1 TAFC: 5 IHRA: TF: 1

Career Provisional # 1 Qualifiers: 5 FC: 1 TAFC: 4

Top Five Point Finishes: 0 IHRA: 6 TF: 2 AFC: 4

Top Ten Point Finishes: 0 IHRA: 10 TF: 6 AFC: 4

Career Best Points Finish: Countdown: 26th-83 (-2620)

Pre-Countdown (2006 And Before): TF: 33rd-51 (-1943) FC: 16th-439 (-1553)

YEARLY CAREER SUMMARY:

2011: 43rd-10 (-2617), 1 DNQ

2010: 38th-31 (-2653), 0/1, Average Qualifying Spot: 16, Left First: 100%

2009: 51st-10 (-2561), 1 DNQ

2008: 26th-83 (-2620), 0/3, Average Qualifying Spot: 15, Left First: 0%

2004: 31st-51 (-1943), 0/1, Average Qualifying Spot: 14, Left First: 0%

2003: 30th-10 (-1758), 1 DNQ

2002: 17th-587 (-1189), 4/14, Average Qualifying Spot: 14.2, 7 DNQ's, Left First: 47%

2000: 16th-429 (-1563), 6/9, Average Qualifying Spot: 7.77, Qualified # 1 Once, 2 DNQ's, Left First: 46.6%

1999: Finished 2nd In The Division 2 Top Alcohol Funny Car Points

Joran Persaker Date Of Birth: N/A From: Sweden Pro Debut: 2010 Starts: 0

STATS:

Career Best E.T./Speed: 1000ft.: 4.113/225.67
Most Successful Event: Pomona-2: 1 DNQ
Career Best Points Finish: Countdown: 42nd-10 (-2674)

YEARLY CAREER SUMMARY:

2010: 42nd-10 (-2674), 1 DNQ

Rit Pustari Date Of Birth: N/A From: Norwalk, CT
Sponsor: Surf Rodz Crew Chief: Jimmy Walsh Owner: Rit Pustari
Chassis: '04 McKinney Engine: BAE 500
Pro Debut: 1997 Starts: 11 Consecutive Qualified Starts: 0
Average Career Qualifying Spot: 14.6

AT THE TREE:

Career Left Firsts/Left On: 3/6 = 33.3%

STATS:

Career Best E.T./Speed: 1000ft.: 4.312/273.05 1320ft.: 4.562/327.98

Most Successful Event: Englishtown: 1/7, 2 DNQ

Elimination Round Win/Loss Record: 1/11 = 8.3%

Career Best Points Finish: Countdown: 26th-62 (-3124)

Pre-Countdown (2006 And Before): 29th-93 (-1797)

YEARLY CAREER SUMMARY:

2011: 44th-10 (-2617), 1 DNQ

2009: 43rd-31 (-2540), 0/1, Average Qualifying Spot: 15, Left First: 0%

2007: 26th-62 (-3124), 0/2, Average Qualifying Spot: 14, Left First: 100%

2006: 31st-41 (-1640), 0/1, Average Qualifying Spot: 16, 1 DNQ, Left First: 100%

2005: 31st-52 (-1929), 0/1, Average Qualifying Spot: 11, 2 DNQ's, 1 By 4 Thousandths, 1 By 23.72 MPH, Left First: 0%

2004: 31st-51 (-1943), 1/1, Average Qualifying Spot: 15, Left First: 50%

2003: 31st-81 (-1913), 0/1, Average Qualifying Spot: 16, 5 DNQ's, Left First: 0%

2001: 33rd-41 (-2061), 0/1, Average Qualifying Spot: 16, 1 DNQ, Left First: 0%

2000: 29th-93 (-1797), 0/3, Average Qualifying Spot: 14.6, Left First: 0%

1998: 3 DNQ's

1997: 1 DNQ

Paul Romine Date Of Birth: August 8, 1947 From: Indianapolis, IN
Pro Debut: 1970's Starts: 57 Consecutive Qualified Starts: 18
Win Percentage In Final Round: 0% IHRA: TF: 43.4% PFC: 50%
Average Career Qualifying Spot: 11.8

AT THE TREE: 1997-2011:

Career Holeshot Win/Loss Record: 5/0 Career Left Firsts/Left On: 51/21 = 70.8%

STATS:

Championships: 0 IHRA: TF: 3 Career Best E.T./Speed: 1320ft.: 4.509/320.28

Career Wins: 0 IHRA: 11 TF: 10 PFC: 1

Career Finals: 1 IHRA: 25 TF: 23 PFC: 2

Last Final: 1998 Rockingham Most Successful Event: Denver: 3/4

Elimination Round Win/Loss Record: 22/57 = 27.8%

Top Five Point Finishes: 0 IHRA: TF: 6

Top Ten Point Finishes: 0 IHRA: TF: 7

Career Best Points Finish: 11th-806 (-1188)

YEARLY CAREER SUMMARY:

2003: 11th-806 (-1188), 7/22, Average Qualifying Spot: 10.5, 1 DNQ, Left First: 73%

2002: 16th-325 (-1626), 3/8, Average Qualifying Spot: 11.3, 1 DNQ, Left First: 80%

2001: 21st-209 (-1893), 2/6, Average Qualifying Spot: 12.7, Left First: 62.5%

2000: 20th-208 (-1682), 0/6, Average Qualifying Spot: 13.6, 2 DNQ's, Left First: 33.3%

1999: 4/8, Average Qualifying Spot: 13.5, 2 DNQ's, Left First: 83.3%

1998: 6/5, 1 Final, Average Qualifying Spot: 11.8, 3 DNQ's, Left First: 62.5%

1997: 0/2, Average Qualifying Spot: 6, Left First: 100%

Darrell Russell Date Of Birth: September 20, 1976 From: Hockley, TX

Died In 2004—Racing Accident Pro Debut: 2001 Starts: 82 Consecutive Qualified Starts: 81

Win Percentage In Final Round: 46.6% TF: 35.2% TAD: 61.5%

Average Career Qualifying Spot: 6.9

AT THE TREE:

Career Holeshot Win/Loss Record: 3/3 Career Left Firsts/Left On: 86/83 = 50.8%

Career Final Rounds Won/Lost On A Holeshot: 1/0

STATS:

U.S. Nationals Wins/Finals: 1/1 TAD: 1/1 Career Best E.T./Speed: 1320ft.: 4.511/329.91

Career Wins: 14 TF: 6 TAD: 8

Career Finals: 30 TF: 17 TAD: 13

Last Win: 2004 Columbus

Last Final: 2011 Columbus

Most Successful Event: Columbus: 11/3, 1 Win, 3 Finals
Elimination Round Win/Loss Record: 106/76 = 58.2%
Career # 1 Qualifiers: 2
Career Provisional # 1 Qualifiers: 2
Top Five Point Finishes: 1
Top Ten Point Finishes: 3 TF: 3 TAD: 1
Career Best Points Finish: 4th-1301 (-693)

YEARLY CAREER SUMMARY:

2004: 12th-695 (-1299), 14/11, 1 Win, 2 Finals, Average Qualifying Spot: 5.27, Qualified # 1 Once, Left First: 44%

2003: 4th-1301 (-693), 27/23, 3 Finals, Average Qualifying Spot: 7.52, Left First: 45.6%

2002: 6th-1343 (-608), 29/20, 3 Wins, Including 2 Consecutive, 5 Finals, Average Qualifying Spot: 7.73, Qualified # 1 Once, Left First: 68.1%

2001: 6th-1505 (-597), 36/22, 2 Wins, 7 Finals, Including 2 Consecutive, Average Qualifying Spot: 6.54, Left First: 44.4%, Became The Second Driver Ever To Win In First Career Start And Reach The Final Round In First 2 Events

1999: Division 4 Top Alcohol Dragster Champion

1998: Division 4 Top Alcohol Dragster Champion, Finished 3rd Nationally

1997: Division 4 Top Alcohol Dragster Champion

1996: Division 4 Top Alcohol Dragster Champion

1994: Division 4 Top Alcohol Dragster Champion

Mike Salinas Date Of Birth: 1961 From: San Jose, CA

Sponsor: Scrappers Racing Crew Chief: Wayne Dupey Owner: Mike Salinas

Chassis: '10 Hadman Engine: TFX 500

Pro Debut: 2011 Starts: 0

STATS:

Career Best E.T./Speed: 1000ft.: 3.965/310.27

Career Best Points Finish: Countdown: 38th-30 (-2597)

YEARLY CAREER SUMMARY:

2011: 38th-30 (-2597), 3 DNQ's

Terry Sainty Date Of Birth: N/A From: Phoenix, AZ

Formally: Australia

Pro Debut: 2011 Starts: 1 Consecutive Qualified Starts: 0 Average Career Qualifying Spot: 14

AT THE TREE:

Career Left Firsts/Left On: 0/1 = 0%

STATS:

Career Best E.T./Speed: 1000ft.: 3.966/309.27

Most Successful Event: Topeka: 0/1

Elimination Round Win/Loss Record: 0/1 = 0%

Career Best Points Finish: Countdown: 30th-67 (-2560)

YEARLY CAREER SUMMARY:

2011: 30th-67 (-2560), 0/1, Average Qualifying Spot: 14, 4 DNQ's, Left First: 0%

Tony Schumacher Date Of Birth: December 25, 1969 From: Long Grove, IL

Sponsor: U.S. Army Crew Chief: Mike Green Assistant Crew Chief: Neal Strausbaugh

Owner: Don Schumacher Chassis: '11 DSR Engine: TFX 496

Pro Debut: 1996 Starts: 335 Consecutive Qualified Starts: 206, The Most In TF

Win Percentage In Final Round: 59.2% Average Career Qualifying Spot: 1997-2012: 5.02

AT THE TREE: 1997-2012:

Career Holeshot Win/Loss Record: 16/20 Career Left Firsts/Left On: 387/416 = 48.1%

Career Final Rounds Won/Lost On A Holeshot: 5/3

STATS:

Championships: 7 TF: 7, Holds Record For The Most Championships Won In Top-Fuel As Well As Winning 6 Consecutive Championships

U.S. Nationals Wins/Finals: 8/8, Including 4 Consecutive Wins And 8 Consecutive Finals, Tied For The Most Wins In Top-Fuel With Don Garlits

Career Best E.T./Speed: 1000ft.: 3.753/330.23 1320ft.: 4.428/337.58

Career Wins: 67, The Most Wins Of Any Top-Fuel Driver In NHRA History

Career Finals: 113, The Most Final Rounds Of Any Top-Fuel Driver In NHRA History

Last Win: 2010 Las Vegas-2

Last Final: 2012 Concord

Most Successful Event: Indianapolis: 43/7, 8 Wins, 10 Finals, 1 DNQ

Elimination Round Win/Loss Record: 599/268 = 69%

Career # 1 Qualifiers: 67, The Most Of Any Top-Fuel Driver In NHRA History

Career Provisional # 1 Qualifiers: 1997-2011: 72

Top Five Point Finishes: 10 Consecutive

Top Ten Point Finishes: 13 Consecutive

Career Best Points Finish: Countdown: 1st-2703 Pre-Countdown (2006 And Before): 1st-1994

Best/Worst Points Finish If Countdown Never Was: 1st/5th

YEARLY CAREER SUMMARY:

2012: 4th-500 (-37), 12/6, 3 Finals, Average Qualifying Spot: 4.5, Left First: 44.4%, Broke The 330 MPH Barrier At 1000ft, 330.23, Happens To Be Same Speed He Broke The 330 MPH Barrier At 1320ft. With, Mike Green Was The Crew Chief

2011: 5th-2467 (-160), 37/22, 7 Finals, Including 4 Consecutive, Average Qualifying Spot: 3.68, Qualified # 1 Six Times, Including 2 Consecutive, Left First: 57.8%, Went 21 Races Without Losing In Round One Between 2011, 2010 Seasons

2010: 2nd-2582 (-102), 48/17, 6 Wins, 8 Finals, Including 2 Consecutive, Average Qualifying Spot: 4.04, Qualified # 1 Three Times, Including 2 Consecutive, Left First: 47.4%, Went 19 Races Without Losing In Round One Between 2010, 2009 Seasons, Broke A Streak Of Winning 6 Consecutive Championships

2009: 1st-2571, 47/19, 5 Wins, Including 2 Consecutive, 7 Finals, Including 2 Consecutive Twice, Average Qualifying Spot: 3.91, Qualified # 1 Twice, Left First: 35%, Won A Round On A Holeshot When Opponent Ran Identical E.T. And Speed, Went 35 Races Without Losing In Round One Between 2009, 2008, 2007 Seasons

2008: 1st-2703, 76/9, 15 Wins, Including 7 Consecutive, 18 Finals, Including 11 Consecutive, Average Qualifying Spot: 3.87, Qualified # 1 Nine Times, Including 3 Consecutive, Left First: 57.5%, Won 31 Consecutive Rounds Of Racing Before A Round Loss, Never Lost Round 1, Elimination Round Winning Percentage: 89.4%, Won 79.1% Of All Possible Rounds (76/96), Appeared In 88.5% Of All Possible Rounds (85/96), Swept the Western Swing, Won Driver Of The Year Award For All Of Motorsports, Won The First 7 Events In The 1000 Foot Era, Went To 11 Finals Of The First 12 Finals In The 1000 Foot Era, Lost 4 Rounds, Including 2 Finals, On A Holeshot

2007: 1st-3186, 32/17, 6 Wins, Including 2 Consecutive, 6 Finals, Average Qualifying Spot: 3.43, Qualified # 1 Twelve Times, 2 Consecutive Three Times, 3 Consecutive Once, Left First: 31.1%

2006: 1st-1681, 41/18, 5 Wins, 8 Finals, Including 5 Consecutive, Average Qualifying Spot: 2.6, Qualified # 1 Thirteen Times, Including 5 Consecutive, Left First: 40%, Overcame A Record 336 Point Deficit To Win The Championship, Won The Championship On What Is Referred To As "The Run" On Which He Had To Win The Race And Set A National Record And Against All Odds He Did With A 4.428 At Pomona-2, The Last National E.T. Record Set At 1320 Feet, Alan Johnson Was The Crew Chief

2005: 1st-1981, 56/14, 9 Wins, Including 5 Consecutive, 12 Finals, Including 7 Consecutive, Average Qualifying Spot: 2.91, Qualified # 1 Eleven Times, Including 6 Consecutive, Left First: 55.5%, Ran The Fastest Speed Ever, 337.58 At Brainerd (Missed Backing By 4.05 MPH), Holds The National Speed Record with 336.15 At Columbus, The Last National Speed Record Set At 1320 Feet,

Alan Johnson Was The Crew Chief, Won 20 Consecutive Rounds Of Racing, Won $100,000 Shootout

2004: 1st-1994, 60/13, 10 Wins, 13 Finals, Including 4 Consecutive, Average Qualifying Spot: 4, Qualified # 1 Twice, Left First: 53.6%

2003: 3rd-1523 (-471), 36/18, 4 Wins, 6 Finals, Including 3 Consecutive, Average Qualifying Spot: 4.72, Qualified # 1 Five Times, Including 4 Consecutive, 1 DNQ, Left First: 48.9%

2002: 3rd-1428 (-523), 32/21, 2 Wins, 5 Finals, Including 2 Consecutive, Average Qualifying Spot: 5.82, Qualified # 1 Once, Left First: 52.9%

2001: 8th-1153 (-949), 18/24, 1 Final, Average Qualifying Spot: 7.83, Left First: 26.1%

2000: 2nd-1624 (-266), 45/17, 4 Wins, Including 2 Consecutive, 10 Finals, Including 3 Consecutive, Average Qualifying Spot: 4.61, Qualified # 1 Three Times, Left First: 42.8%, Worst Accident Of His Career At Memphis And Missed 2 Events Due To Injuries

1999: 1st-1488, 37/21, 1 Win, 5 Finals, Average Qualifying Spot: 6.36, Left First: 41.5%, The First Driver To Break The 330 MPH Barrier, Possibly The Last Great Speed Barrier, At Phoenix Running 330.23, Dan Olson Was The Crew Chief

1998: 15th, 7/11, 1 Final, Average Qualifying Spot: 12.9, 2 DNQ's, Left First: 76.4%

1997: 19th, 11/17, 2 Finals, Average Qualifying Spot: 11.4, 5 DNQ's, 1 By 3 Thousandths, Left First: 74%

1996: 13th, 4/4, 1 Final

Ron Smith Date Of Birth: N/A From: Kapowsin, WA

Sponsor: Foster Machine Services Crew Chief: Gus Foster Owner: Ron Smith

Chassis: '98 Hadman Engine: TFX 498

Pro Debut: 1972? Starts: 1997-2011: 8 Consecutive Qualified Starts: 3

Average Career Qualifying Spot: 15.1

AT THE TREE: 1997-2011:

Career Left Firsts/Left On: 1/7 = 12.5%

STATS: 1997-2011:

Career Best E.T./Speed: 1000ft.: 4.320/267.53 1320ft.: 4.939/296.83

Most Successful Event: Seattle: 0/7, 6 DNQ's

Elimination Round Win/Loss Record: 0/8 = 0%

Career Best Points Finish: Countdown: 33rd-31 (-2596)

Pre-Countdown (2006 And Before): 36th-30 (-1860)

YEARLY CAREER SUMMARY:

2011: 33rd-31 (-2596), 0/1, Average Qualifying Spot: 15, Left First: 0%

2010: 36th-31 (-2653), 0/1, Average Qualifying Spot: 13, Left First: 100%

2009: 41st-31 (-2540), 0/1, Average Qualifying Spot: 14, Left First: 0%

2008: 35th-10 (-2693), 1 DNQ

2005: 39th-10 (-1971), 1 DNQ

2004: 43rd-10 (-1984), 1 DNQ

2003: 38th-31 (-1963), 0/1, Average Qualifying Spot: 15, Left First: 0%

2002: 38th-31 (-1920), 0/1, Average Qualifying Spot: 16, Left First: 0%

Patrick J. Keenan

2001: 37th-31 (-2071), 0/1, Average Qualifying Spot: 16, Left First: 0%

2000: 36th-30 (-1860), 3 DNQ's

1999: 1 DNQ

1998: 0/2, Average Qualifying Spot: 16, Left First: 0%

1997: 2 DNQ's

Mike Strasburg Date Of Birth: August 15, 1959 From: Lehi, UT

Sponsor: Procomp Electronics Crew Chief: Jeff Strasburg Owner: Allen Strasburg

Chassis: '08 Hadman Engine: TFX 500

Pro Debut: 2002 Starts: 48 Consecutive Qualified Starts: 2

Average Career Qualifying Spot: 13.9

AT THE TREE:

Career Left Firsts/Left On: 19/31 = 38%

STATS:

Career Best E.T./Speed: 1000ft: 3.922/311.49 1320ft.: 4.518/330.15

Career Finals: 1 TAD: 1 IHRA: TF: 1 Most Successful Event: Denver: 3/8

Elimination Round Win/Loss Record: 9/48 = 15.7%

Top Five Point Finishes: 0 IHRA: TF: 2

Top Ten Point Finishes: 1 TAD: 1 IHRA: TF: 2

Career Best Points Finish: Countdown: 15th-289 (-2282)

Pre-Countdown (2006 And Before): 19th-267 (-1727)

YEARLY CAREER SUMMARY:

2012: 24th-31 (-506), 0/1, Average Qualifying Spot: 15, Left First: 0%

2011: 30th-67 (-2560), 0/2, Average Qualifying Spot: 15, 2 DNQ's, Including 1 By 3 Thousandths, Left First: 0%

2010: 17th-294 (-2390), 1/8, Average Qualifying Spot: 13.2, 2 DNQ's, Left First: 22.2%

2009: 15th-267 (-2304), 3/7, Average Qualifying Spot: 13.5, 1 DNQ, Left First: 37.5%

2008: 27th-71 (-2632), 1/1, Average Qualifying Spot: 14, 2 DNQ's, Including 1 By 9 Thousandths, Left First: 50%

2007: 19th-206 (-2980), 1/4, Average Qualifying Spot: 12, 6 DNQ's, Left First: 25%

2006: 19th-225 (-1456), 1/5, Average Qualifying Spot: 14.8, 5 DNQ's, Left First: 20%

2005: 22nd-174 (-1807), 1/3, Average Qualifying Spot: 14.3, 6 DNQ's, Left First: 66.6%

2004: 19th-267 (-1727), 0/7, Average Qualifying Spot: 14.5, 5 DNQ's, Left First: 85.7%

2003: 21st-217 (-1777), 0/6, Average Qualifying Spot: 14.6, 3 DNQ's, Left First: 40%

2002: 25th-155 (-1796), 1/4, Average Qualifying Spot: 13.5, 1 DNQ, Left First: 25%

2001: Finished 2nd In The Division 7 Top Alcohol Dragster Points, 10th Nationally

2000: Finished 2nd In The Division 7 Top Alcohol Dragster Points, 15th Nationally

1999: Finished 7th In The Division 5 Top Alcohol Dragster Points

J.R.Todd Date Of Birth: December 16, 1981 From: Indianapolis, IN

Sponsor: Total Equipment Crew Chief: Kurt Elliot Owner: Bob Vandergriff Jr.

Chassis: '10 Hadman Engine: TFX 500

Pro Debut: 2006 Starts: 67 Consecutive Qualified Starts: 24

Win Percentage In Final Round: 75% Average Career Qualifying Spot: 8.25

AT THE TREE:

Career Holeshot Win/Loss Record: 10/4 Career Left Firsts/Left On: 68/44 = 60.7%

Career Final Rounds Won/Lost On A Holeshot: 1/0

STATS:

Career Best E.T./Speed: 1000ft.: 3.811/317.94 1320ft.: 4.473/334.24

Career Wins: 6

Career Finals: 8 IHRA: TF: 2

Last Win: 2008 Dallas

Last Final: 2008 Dallas

Most Successful Event: Sonoma: 7/3, 1 Win, 1 Final

Elimination Round Win/Loss Record: 64/61 = 51.2%

Career # 1 Qualifiers: 3 TF: 3 IHRA: TF: 1

Career Provisional # 1 Qualifiers: 7 IHRA: TF: N/A

Top Ten Point Finishes: 2

Career Best Points Finish: Countdown: 7th-2273 (-913)

Pre-Countdown (2006 And Before): 8th-1105 (-576)

Best/Worst Points Finish If Countdown Never Was: 5th/10th

YEARLY CAREER SUMMARY:

2012: 23rd-32 (-505), Average Qualifying Spot: 11, Left First: 0%

2009: 24th-163 (-2408), 3/3, Average Qualifying Spot: 6.66, Qualified # 1 Once, Left First: 83.3%

2008: 11th-983 (-1720), 11/22, 1 Win, 1 Final, Average Qualifying Spot: 9.04, 1 DNQ, Left First: 70%

2007: 7th-2273 (-913), 25/20, 2 Wins, 3 Finals, Average Qualifying Spot: 8.09, Qualified # 1 Twice, 1 DNQ, Left First: 48.6%

2006: 8th-1105 (-576), 25/15, 3 Wins, 4 Finals, Average Qualifying Spot: 7.55, 1 DNQ, Left First: 63.1%, Won 5 Rounds On A Holeshot, Auto Club Road To The Future Award Winner

Steve Torrence Date Of Birth: April 17, 1983 From: Kilgore, TX

Sponsor: Capco Contractors Crew Chief: Richard Hogan Owner: Steve Torrence

Chassis: '12 Hadman Engine: TFX 500

Pro Debut: 2006 Starts: 52 Consecutive Qualified Starts: 9

Win Percentage In Final Round: 66.6% TAD: 66.6% Average Career Qualifying Spot: 8.15

AT THE TREE:

Career Holeshot Win/Loss Record: 6/5 Career Left Firsts/Left On: 50/32 = 60.9%

STATS:

Championships: 1 TAD: 1 U.S. Nationals Wins/Finals: 1/1 TAD: 1/1

Career Best E.T./Speed: 1000ft.: 3.772/322.88 1320ft.: 4.577/326.56

Career Wins: 4 TAD: 4

Career Finals: 6 TAD: 6

Most Successful Event: Phoenix: 5/3

Elimination Round Win/Loss Record: 30/52 = 36.5%

Career # 1 Qualifiers: 4 TF: 1 TAD: 3

Career Provisional # 1 Qualifiers: 5 TF: 1 TAD: 4

Top Five Point Finishes: 1 TAD: 1

Top Ten Point Finishes: 2 TF: 1 TAD: 1

Career Best Points Finish: Countdown: 8th-2289 (-395)

Pre-Countdown (2006 And Before): 25th-115 (-1566)

Best/Worst Points Finish If Countdown Never Was: 9th

YEARLY CAREER SUMMARY:

2012: 6th-343 (-194), 6/6, Average Qualifying Spot: 5.33, Left First: 66.6%

2011: 14th-343 (-2284), 4/8, Average Qualifying Spot: 10.8, 1 DNQ, Left First: 41.6%

2010: 8th-2289 (-395), 12/22, Average Qualifying Spot: 8.27, 1 DNQ, Left First: 73.5%

2009: 17th-198 (-2373), 3/4, Average Qualifying Spot: 8.5, Left First: 57.1%

2008: 15th-372 (-2331), 4/9, Average Qualifying Spot: 9.8, Left First: 38.4%

2006: 25th-115 (-1566), 1/3, Average Qualifying Spot: 11.6, Left First: 75%, Finished 3rd In The Division 4 Top Alcohol Dragster Points, 12th Nationally

2005: Won Top Alcohol Dragster National Championship; Division 4 Top Alcohol Dragster Champion

2004: Finished 11th In The Division 4 Super Comp Points, 70th Nationally

2002: Finished 17th In The Division 4 Super Comp Points, 121st Nationally

Bob Vandergriff Jr. Date Of Birth: February 7, 1965 From: Cumming, GA

Sponsor: C&J Energy Services Crew Chief: Rob Flynn Owner: Bob Vandergriff Jr.

Chassis: '08 Hadman Engine: TFX 500

Pro Debut: 1994 Starts: 234 Consecutive Qualified Starts: 17

Win Percentage In Final Round: 7.1% Average Career Qualifying Spot: 1997-2012: 9.52

AT THE TREE: 1997-2011:

Career Holeshot Win/Loss Record: 8/5 Career Left Firsts/Left On: 160/156 = 50.6%

STATS:

U.S. Nationals Wins/Finals: 0/1

Career Best E.T./Speed: 1000ft.: 3.795/326.24 1320ft.: 4.499/333.08

Career Wins: 1

Career Finals: 14

Last Win: 2011 Dallas

Last Final: 2011 Dallas

Most Successful Event: 1997-2011: Indianapolis: 10/9, 1 Final, 2 DNQ's

Elimination Round Win/Loss Record: 155/233 = 39.9%

Career # 1 Qualifiers: 2

Career Provisional # 1 Qualifiers: 4

Top Five Point Finishes: 1

Top Ten Point Finishes: 5

Career Best Points Finish: Countdown: 5th-2235 (-828)

Pre-Countdown (2006 And Before): 6th-1083 (-754)

Best/Worst Points Finish If Countdown Never Was: 8th

YEARLY CAREER SUMMARY:

2012: 8th-300 (-237), 4/6, Average Qualifying Spot: 8.33, Left First: 44.4%

2011: 11th-952 (-1675), 14/19, 1 Win, 2 Finals, Average Qualifying Spot: 10.2, 2 DNQ's, 1 By 2 Thousandths, Left First: 36.3%

2010: 13th-393 (-2229), 0/12, Average Qualifying Spot: 9.91, Left First: 50%

2009: 16th-202 (-2369), 2/5, Average Qualifying Spot: 9.6, Left First: 50%

2008: 13th-842 (-1861), 8/21, Average Qualifying Spot: 11, 3 DNQ's, 1 By 9 Thousandths, Left First: 52%

2007: 5th—2358 (-828), 25/22, 5 Finals, Average Qualifying Spot: 9.63, 1 DNQ, Left First: 48.8%

2006: 14th-753 (-928), 5/19, Average Qualifying Spot: 10.5, 3 DNQ's, 1 By 2 Thousandths, Left First: 63.6%

2004: 15th-544 (-1450), 9/11, 1 Final, Average Qualifying Spot: 10.1, 1 DNQ, Left First: 57.8%

2000: 8th-1001 (-889), 19/20, 1 Final, Average Qualifying Spot: 7.95, 1 DNQ, Left First: 52.7%, Went 12 Races Without Losing In Round 1

1999: 10th-1131 (-357), 22/20, 1 Final, Average Qualifying Spot: 7.65, Qualified # 1 Twice, 2 DNQ's, Left First: 45%

1998: 9th-993 (-788), 15/23, 1 Final, Average Qualifying Spot: 10, Left First: 47.2%

1997: 6th-1083 (-754), 19/22, 2 Finals, Average Qualifying Spot: 8.27, 1 DNQ, Left First: 62.8%

1996: 19th, 7/17, 1 Final

1995: 19th, 4/4

1994: 15th, 2/12

Scott Weis Date Of Birth: August 16, 1966 From: Ashland, VA

Pro Debut: TF: 2001 FC: 1999

Starts: 106 TF: 91 FC: 15 Consecutive Qualified Starts: 0 TF: 0 FC: 0

Win Percentage In Final Round: 0% IHRA: 42.8% TF: 100% AFC: 38.4%

Average Career Qualifying Spot: 12.7 TF: 12.6 FC: 13.2

AT THE TREE:

Career Holeshot Win/Loss Record: 2/1 TF: 2/1

Career Left Firsts/Left On: 55/59 = 48.2% TF: 49/53 = 48% FC: 6/6 = 50%

STATS:

Career Best E.T./Speed: 1000ft: 3.974/305.42 1320ft.: TF: 4.545/327.66 FC: 4.956/305.60

Career Wins: 0 IHRA: 6 TF: 1 AFC: 5

Career Finals: 0 IHRA: 14 TF: 1 AFC: 13

Last Final: 2003 Madison Most Successful Event: Madison: 5/6, 1 Final, 2 DNQ's

TF: Madison: 5/5, 1 Final, 2 DNQ's FC: Reading: 1/2

Elimination Round Win/Loss Record: 27/106 = 20.3% TF: 26/91 = 22.2% FC: 1/15 = 6.2%

Top Five Point Finishes: 0 IHRA: AFC: 6

Top Ten Point Finishes: 1 IHRA: AFC: 7

Career Best Points Finish: Countdown: 32nd-30 (-3156)

Pre-Countdown (2006 And Before): 10th-803 (-1191)

YEARLY CAREER SUMMARY:

2009: 40th-32 (-2539), 0/1, Average Qualifying Spot: 11, Left First: 0%

2007: 31st-30 (-3156), 3 DNQ's

2006: 17th-294 (-1387), 1/6, Average Qualifying Spot: 13.1, 10 DNQ's, Left First: 50%

2005: 11th-737 (-1244), 4/20, Average Qualifying Spot: 13.1, 3 DNQ's Left First: 40.9%

2004: 10th-803 (-1191), 7/20, Average Qualifying Spot: 12.3, 3 DNQ's, Left First: 39.1%

2003: 13th-713 (-1281), 7/16, 1 Final, Average Qualifying Spot: 11.1, 7 DNQ's, Left First: 61.1%

2002: 12th-696 (-1255), 3/19, Average Qualifying Spot: 13.1, 4 DNQ's, Including 1 By 5 Thousandths, Left First: 45%

2001: TF: 15th-362 (-1740), 4/9, Average Qualifying Spot: 13.6, Left First: 66.6% FC: 30th-20 (-1980), 2 DNQ's

2000: 19th-289 (-1764), 1/5, Average Qualifying Spot: 13, 8 DNQ's, Left First: 60%

1999: 0/9, Average Qualifying Spot: 13.7, 2 DNQ's, Left First: 42.8%

Hillary Will Date Of Birth: April 1, 1980 From: Eureka, CA

Sponsor: Dote Racing Crew Chief: Doug Kuch Owner: Dote Family

Chassis: '11 Hadman Engine: TFX 498

Pro Debut: 2006 Starts: 71 Consecutive Qualified Starts: 27

Win Percentage In Final Round: 28.5% TF: 25% TAD: 33.3% IHRA: TF: 100%

Average Career Qualifying Spot: 8.61

AT THE TREE:

Career Holeshot Win/Loss Record: 1/9 Career Left Firsts/Left On: 38/76 = 33.3%

STATS:

U.S. Nationals Wins/Finals: 0/1 TAD: 0/1

Career Best E.T./Speed: 1000ft.: 3.799/315.49 1320ft.: 4.502/334.65

Career Wins: 2 TF: 1 TAD: 1 IHRA: TF: 1

Career Finals: 7 TF: 4 TAD: 3 IHRA: TF: 1

Last Win: 2008 Topeka

Last Final: 2008 Virginia

Most Successful Event: Sonoma: 6/3, 1 Final Won At: Topeka: 4/3, 1 Win, 1 Final

Elimination Round Win/Loss Record: 50/70 = 41.6%

Career # 1 Qualifiers: 2 TAD: 2

Career Provisional # 1 Qualifiers: 2 TAD: 2

Top Five Point Finishes: 1 TF: 1

Top Ten Point Finishes: 2 TF: 1 TAD: 1

Career Best Points Finish: Countdown: 4th-2405 (-298)

Pre-Countdown (2006 And Before): 25th-115 (-1566)

Best/Worst Points Finish If Countdown Never Was: 6th

YEARLY CAREER SUMMARY:

2012: 16th-64 (-473), 0/2, Average Qualifying Spot: 20/2 = 10, Left First: 0%

2009: Finished 11th In The Division 7 Top Alcohol Dragster Points, 60th Nationally

2008: 4th-2405 (-298), 27/23, 1 Win, 3 Finals, Average Qualifying Spot: 6.33, Left First: 32.6%

2007: 13th-892 (-2294), 9/22, Average Qualifying Spot: 10.9, 1 DNQ, Left First: 39.2%, Lost 4 Rounds On A Holeshot

2006: 11th-1035 (-646), 14/23, 1 Final, Average Qualifying Spot: 8.65, Left First: 31.4%, Lost 5 Rounds On A Holeshot

2005: Finished 2nd In The Division 6 Top Alcohol Dragster Points, 6th Nationally

2004: Finished 12th In The Division 7 Top Alcohol Dragster Points, 57th Nationally

2003: Finished 73rd In The Division 7 Super Comp Points

Del Worsham Date Of Birth: February 11, 1970 From: Chino Hills, CA RETIRED

Pro Debut: FC: 1990 TF: 1993 Starts: 1997-2011: Career: 412 TF: 31 FC: 381

Consecutive Qualified Starts: 69 TF: 1997-2011: 22 FC: 47

Win Percentage In Final Round: 66% TF: 72.7% FC: 64.1% IHRA: 60% TF: 100% FC: 50%

Average Career Qualifying Spot: 1997-2011: 7.9 TF: 3.04 FC: 8.25

AT THE TREE: 1997-2011:

Career Holeshot Win/Loss Record: 20/15 TF: 2/2 FC: 18/13

Career Left Firsts/Left On: 341/279 = 55% TF: 36/28 = 56.2% FC: 305/251 = 54.8%

Career Final Rounds Won/Lost On A Holeshot: 2/3 TF: 0/2 FC: 2/1

STATS: 1997-2011:

Championships: 1 TF: 1 IHRA: FC: 1 U.S. Nationals Wins/Finals: 2/3 TF: 1/1 FC: 1/2

Career Best E.T./Speed: 1000ft.: TF: 3.735/327.90 FC: 4.038/313.15 1320ft.: TF: 4.857/300.20 FC: 4.712/331.36

Career Wins: 33 TF: 8 FC: 25 IHRA: 3 TF: 1 FC: 2

Career Finals: 50 TF: 11 FC: 39 IHRA: 5 TF: 1 FC: 4

Last Win: TF: 2011 Pomona-2 FC: 2009 Richmond

Last Final: TF: 2011 Pomona-2 FC: 2010 Englishtown

Most Successful Event: Houston: 30/12, 3 Wins, 4 Finals

TF: Tied With The 8 Events He Won: 4/0, 1 Win, 1 Final

FC: Englishtown: 25/13, 2 Wins, 4 Finals

Elimination Round Win/Loss Record: 440/379 = 53.7%

TF: 57/23 = 72.1% FC: 383/356 = 51.8%

Career # 1 Qualifiers: 12 TF: 7 FC: 5 IHRA: FC: 1

Career Provisional # 1 Qualifiers: 15 TF: 5 FC: 10

Top Five Point Finishes: 6 TF: 1 Consecutive FC: 5 IHRA: FC: 1

Top Ten Point Finishes: 15 TF: 1 FC: 14, 2 Consecutive IHRA: 2 TF: 1 FC: 1

Career Best Points Finish: Countdown: TF: 1st-2627 FC: 6th-2307 (-314)

Pre-Countdown (2006 And Before): TF: 19th FC: 2nd-1586 (-297)

Best/Worst Points Finish If Countdown Never Was: TF: 1st FC: 8th/9th

YEARLY CAREER SUMMARY:

2011: 1st-2627, 53/14, 8 Wins, Including 2 Consecutive 3 Times, 11 Finals, Average Qualifying Spot: 3.04, Qualified # 1 Seven Times, Left First: 56.2%, Holds The National E.T. Record For The Quickest Time At 1000ft. At Reading, 3.735, Brian Husen And Alan Johnson Were The Crew Chiefs

2010: 6th-2307 (-314), 21/23, 1 Final, Average Qualifying Spot: 6.95, Qualified # 1 Once, Left First: 36.5%, Lost 4 Rounds On A Holeshot

2009: 7th-2352 (-195), 25/21, 3 Wins, Including 2 Consecutive, 3 Finals, Average Qualifying Spot: 9.04, Left First: 68.8%

2008: 13th-862 (-1699), 11/16, 1 Win, 1 Final, Average Qualifying Spot: 6.88, 7 DNQ's, 1 By 3 Thousandths, Left First: 42.3%

2007: 9th-1050 (-2128), 18/21, 2 Finals, Average Qualifying Spot: 10.3, Qualified # 1 Once, 2 DNQ's, 1 By 2 Thousandths, Left First: 55.5%

2006: 11th-929 (-707), 12/20, Average Qualifying Spot: 9, 3 DNQ's, Left First: 54.8%

2005: 8th-1208 (-308), 22/21, 2 Wins, 2 Finals, Average Qualifying Spot: 7.39, Left First: 56%, Doubled Up U.S. Nationals Weekend Winning Shootout And Event Netting $150,000

2004: 2nd-1586 (-297), 41/18, 5 Wins, Including 2 Consecutive Twice, 6 Finals, Average Qualifying Spot: 7.52, Qualified # 1 Once, Left First: 57.8%

2003: 4th-1387 (-381), 31/20, 3 Wins, 5 Finals, Including 2 Consecutive, Average Qualifying Spot: 7.43, Left First: 44.6%

2002: 3rd-1439 (-337), 35/18, 4 Wins, 6 Finals, Including 2 Consecutive, Average Qualifying Spot: 8.13, 1 DNQ, Left First: 48%

2001: 3rd-1490 (-510), 35/20, 4 Wins, 5 Finals, Including 2 Consecutive, Average Qualifying Spot: 8.79, Qualified # 1 Once, Left First: 60.7%, Car Craft Magazine Funny Car Driver of the Year

2000: 8th-1056 (-936), 17/22, Average Qualifying Spot: 8.09, 1 DNQ, Left First: 68.4%

1999: 7th-928 (-1143), 12/20, 1 Win, 1 Final, Average Qualifying Spot: 10.5, 1 DNQ, Left First: 61.2%

1998: 10th-905 (-758), 13/19, 1 Final, Average Qualifying Spot: 10.3, 3 DNQ's, Left First: 60%, Worsham Family Won The Blaine Johnson Award

1997: 11th, 12/22, 1 Final, Average Qualifying Spot: 10, 1 DNQ's, Left First: 54.8%

1996: 7th-918 (-1105), 17/17, 2 DNQ's, Left First: N/A

1995: TF: 34th, 2 DNQ's FC: 16th, 3/10, 7 DNQ's,

1994: TF: 20th, 1/3, 9 DNQ's FC: 19th, 2/3, 2 DNQ's

1993: TF: 19th, 3/6, 2 DNQ's FC: 13th, 7/11, 1 Final, 1 DNQ

1992: 4th-10566 (-4680), 24/18, 3 Finals, Qualified # 1 Once, Won IHRA Funny Car Championship

1991: 6th-10532 (-5006), 25/15, 2 Wins, 2 Finals, 1 DNQ, Youngest Driver Ever To Win An Event In Funny Car, NHRA Rookie of the Year

1990: 35th, 0/1

T.J. Zizzo Date Of Birth: August 19, 1975 From: Lincolnshire, IL
Sponsor: Peak Crew Chief: Mike Kern Owner: Tony Zizzo

Chassis: '99 McKinney Engine: TFX 500

Pro Debut: 2003 Starts: 35 Consecutive Qualified Starts: 19

Win Percentage In Final Round: 0% IHRA: TF: 33.3% Average Career Qualifying Spot: 12.1

AT THE TREE:

Career Holeshot Win/Loss Record: 1/2 Career Left Firsts/Left On: 13/20 = 39.3%

STATS:

Championships: 0 UDRA: 1

Career Best E.T./Speed: 1000ft.: 3.851/319.98 1320ft.: 4.578/324.36

Career Wins: 0 IHRA: TF: 2

Career Finals: 0 IHRA: TF: 6

Most Successful Event: Indianapolis: 2/6, 1 DNQ

Elimination Round Win/Loss Record: 5/35 = 12.5%

Career # 1 Qualifiers: 0 IHRA: TF: 5

Top Five Point Finishes: 0 IHRA: TF: 1

Top Ten Point Finishes: 0 IHRA: TF: 2

Career Best Points Finish: Countdown: 18th-268 (-2416)

Pre-Countdown (2006 And Before): 20th-209 (-1772)

YEARLY CAREER SUMMARY:

2012: 17th-62 (-475), 0/2, Average Qualifying Spot: 29/2 = 14.5, Left First: 0/1 = 0%

2011: 18th-245 (-2382), 1/7, Average Qualifying Spot: 11.7, Left First: 0%

2010: 18th-268 (-2416), 2/7, Average Qualifying Spot: 9.28, Left First: 37.5%

2009: 26th-135 (-2436), 0/4, Average Qualifying Spot: 13.2, 1 DNQ, Left First: 100%

2008: 21st-123 (-2580), 1/3, Average Qualifying Spot: 14.6, 1 DNQ, Left First: 50%

2007: 29th-31 (-3155), 0/1, Average Qualifying Spot: 14, Left First: 0%

2005: 20th-209 (-1772), 0/6, Average Qualifying Spot: 12.6, 2 DNQ's, Left First: 40%

2004: 22nd-198 (-1796), 1/5, Average Qualifying Spot: 12.2, 2 DNQ's, Left First: 80%

2003: 43rd-10 (-1984), 1 DNQ

2000: Finished 10th In The Division 2 Top Alcohol Dragster Points, 74th Nationally, UDRA's Supercharged Alcohol Dragster Champion

FUNNY CAR:

Blake Alexander Date Of Birth: September 26, 1988 From: Wirtz, VA

Sponsor: Auto Service Plus Crew Chief: Paul Smith Owner: Paul Smith

Body: '10 Chevrolet Monte Carlo Engine: TFX 500

Pro Debut: 2011 Starts: 3 Consecutive Qualified Starts: 3 Average Career Qualifying Spot: 14

AT THE TREE:

Career Left Firsts/Left On: 0/3 = 0%

STATS:

Career Best E.T./Speed: 1000ft.: 4.168/302.55

Most Successful Event: All Starts

Elimination Round Win/Loss Record: 0/3 = 0%

Career Best Points Finish: Countdown: 29th-31 (-2509)

YEARLY CAREER SUMMARY:

2012: 19th-62 (-535), 0/2, Average Qualifying Spot: 14, Left First: 0%

2011: 29th-31 (-2509), 0/1, Average Qualifying Spot: 14, Left First: 0%, Finished 45th In The Top Alcohol Dragster National Points

2008: Finished 16th In The Division 2 Comp Eliminator Points, 140th Nationally

2007: Finished 28th In The Division 2 Comp Eliminator Points, 211th Nationally

2006: Finished 23rd In The Division 2 Comp Eliminator Points, 139th Nationally

Randy Anderson Date Of Birth: N/A From: Ontario, CA

Pro Debut: 1997 Starts: 41 Consecutive Qualified Starts: 2

Win Percentage In Final Round: 48.4% FC: 40% TAFC: 50%

Average Career Qualifying Spot: 8.56

AT THE TREE:

Career Holeshot Win/Loss Record: 1/0 Career Left Firsts/Left On: 32/33 = 49.2%

Career Final Rounds Won/Lost On A Holeshot: 1/0

STATS:

Championships: 2 TAFC: 2 U.S. Nationals Wins/Finals: 1/3 FC: 0/1 TAFC: 1/2

Career Best E.T./Speed: 1320ft.: 4.848/318.92

Career Wins: 16 FC: 2 TAFC: 14

Career Finals: 33 FC: 5 TAFC: 28

Most Successful Event: Atlanta: 4/1, 1 Win, 1 Final

Ex-Track Since 2001: Dallas-1: 4/1, 1 Win, 1 Final

Elimination Round Win/Loss Record: 34/39 = 46.5%

Career # 1 Qualifiers: 3

Career Provisional # 1 Qualifiers: 4

Top Ten Point Finishes: 1

Career Best Points Finish: 6th-1167 (-698)

YEARLY CAREER SUMMARY:

1999: 2/2, Average Qualifying Spot: 10.5, 1 DNQ, Left First: 50%

1998: 10/19, 1 Final, Average Qualifying Spot: 9.57, 3 DNQ's, Left First: 62.5%

1997: 6th-1167 (-698), 22/18, 2 Wins, 4 Finals, Average Qualifying Spot: 6.72, Qualified # 1 Three Times, Including 2 Consecutive, 2 DNQ's, Left First: 40.5%

Jeff Arend Date Of Birth: November 27, 1962 From: La Verne, CA

Formally: Toronto, Canada

Sponsor: DHL Crew Chief: Jon Oberhofer/Nick Boninfante Owner: Connie Kalitta

Body: '08 Toyota Solara Engine: AJ 500

Pro Debut: 1995 Starts: 151 Consecutive Qualified Starts: 6

Win Percentage In Final Round: 37.5% Average Career Qualifying Spot: 11.1

AT THE TREE: 1997-2011:

Career Holeshot Win/Loss Record: 4/7 Career Left Firsts/Left On: 116/69 = 62.7%

STATS:

Career Best E.T./Speed: 1000ft.: 4.048/316.01 1320ft.: 4.712/327.66

Career Wins: 3

Career Finals: 8

Last Win: 2011 Houston

Last Final: 2011 Chicago

Most Successful Event: 1997-2012: Houston: 9/7, 1 Win, 2 Finals, 1 DNQ

Elimination Round Win/Loss Record: 70/148 = 32.1%

Career # 1 Qualifiers: 2

Career Provisional # 1 Qualifiers: 1997-2011: 4

Top Ten Point Finishes: 1

Career Best Points Finish: Countdown: 8th-2302 (-237)

Pre-Countdown (2006 And Before): 16th-560 (-956)

Best/Worst Points Finish If Countdown Never Was: 9th

YEARLY CAREER SUMMARY:

2012: 10th-252 (-345), 3/6, Average Qualifying Spot: 11.3, Left First: 44.4%

2011: 8th-2303 (-237), 21/20, 1 Win, 2 Finals, Average Qualifying Spot: 11.2, 1 DNQ, Left First: 61.1%

2010: 12th-1034 (-1587), 14/23, 3 Finals, Average Qualifying Spot: 10, Left First: 57.1%

2009: 13th-845 (-1702), 8/22, 1 Win, 1 Final, Average Qualifying Spot: 12.9, 1 DNQ, Left First: 68.9%

2008: 22nd-188 (-2373), 0/6, Average Qualifying Spot: 12.8, 1 DNQ's, Left First: 33.3%

2007: 11th-934 (-2244), 10/22, Average Qualifying Spot: 9.63, Qualified # 1 Twice, 1 DNQ, Left First: 67.7%

2006: 22nd-93 (-1543), 0/2, Average Qualifying Spot: 12, 3 DNQ's, Left First: 0%

2005: 16th-560 (-956), 6/13, 1 Final, Average Qualifying Spot: 10, 2 DNQ's, Left First: 77.7%

2004: 16th-536 (-1347), 0/16, Average Qualifying Spot: 12.6, 3 DNQ's, Left First: 73.3%

2000: 38th-10 (-1982), 1 DNQ

1999: 36th, 0/1, Average Qualifying Spot: 10, Left First: 100%

1998: 36th, 0/1, Average Qualifying Spot: 14, Left First: 0%

1997: 31st, 0/2, Average Qualifying Spot: 5, 1 DNQ, Left First: 50%

1996: 18th, 5/5, 1 Win, 1 Final, 1 DNQ,

1995: 18th, 3/9, 1 DNQ

* Wins/Final Rounds And There Details May Not Be 100% Accurate For This Driver's Top Alcohol Career, But Very Close *

Tony Bartone Date Of Birth: June 6, 1956 From: Long Island City, NY

Pro Debut: 2001 Starts: 91 Consecutive Qualified Starts: 0

Win Percentage In Final Round: 57.3% FC: 50% TAD: 60%

TAFC: 57.5% IHRA: AFC: 100% Average Career Qualifying Spot: 11.4

AT THE TREE:

Career Holeshot Win/Loss Record: 1/3 Career Left Firsts/Left On: 34/87 = 28%

STATS:

Championships: 1 TAFC: 1 U.S. Nationals Wins/Finals: 2/5

TAFC: 2/5, Including 3 Consecutive Finals

Career Best E.T./Speed: 1000ft.: 4.092/303.37 1320ft.: 4.761/325.92

Career Wins: 39 FC: 1 TAD: 3 TAFC: 35 IHRA: AFC: 2

Career Finals: 68 FC: 2 TAD: 5 TAFC: 61 IHRA: AFC: 2

Last Win: 2008 Seattle

Last Final: 2008 Seattle

Most Successful Event: Seattle: 6/4, 1 Win, 1 Final

Elimination Round Win/Loss Record: 39/90 = 30.2%

Career # 1 Qualifiers: 1997-2012: 28 FC: 2 TAD: 2 TAFC: 24

Career Provisional # 1 Qualifiers: 1997-2012: 26 FC: 2 TAD: 2 TAFC: 22

Top Five Finishes: 1997-2012: 6 TAD: 1 TAFC: 5, 4 Consecutive

Top Ten Point Finishes: 1997-2012: 7 TAD: 1 TAFC: 6, 4 Consecutive

Career Best Points Finish: Countdown: 16th-738 (-2440)

Pre-Countdown (2006 And Before): 13th-905 (-611)

YEARLY CAREER SUMMARY:

2011: Division 4 Top Alcohol Funny Car Champion, Finished 2nd Nationally

2010: Division 4 Top Alcohol Funny Car Champion, Finished 4th Nationally

2009: Finished 4th In The Top Alcohol Funny Car National Points, 4th In The Division 7 Points

2008: 16th-615 (-1946), 6/10, 1 Win, 1 Final, Average Qualifying Spot: 9.81, Qualified # 1 Once, 13 DNQ's, Left First: 31.2%

2007: 16th-738 (-2440), 8/16, Average Qualifying Spot: 11.6, 7 DNQ's, Left First: 26%

2006: 14th-754 (-882), 9/17, Average Qualifying Spot: 12, Qualified # 1 Once, 6 DNQ's, Left First: 39.1%

2005: 13th-905 (-611), 12/20, 1 Final, Average Qualifying Spot: 11.5, 3 DNQ's, Left First: 25%

2004: 15th-632 (-1251), 3/16, Average Qualifying Spot: 13.2, 7 DNQ's, Left First: 23.5%

2003: 25th-32 (-1736), 0/1, Average Qualifying Spot: 12, Left First: 100%, Finished 2nd In The Division 2 Top Alcohol Dragster Points, 3rd Nationally

2002: Finished 7th In The Division 2 Top Alcohol Dragster Points, 18th Nationally

2001: 19th-368 (-1632), 1/10, Average Qualifying Spot: 9.2, Left First: 11.1%, 2 DNQ's, Finished 13th In The Division 1 Top Alcohol Dragster Points, 63rd Nationally

2000: Finished 2nd In The Division 4 Top Alcohol Funny Car Points; 4th Nationally

1999: Division 2 Top Alcohol Funny Car Champion

1998: Finished 8th In The Top Alcohol Funny Car National Points

1996: Top Alcohol Funny Car National Champion

1994: Division 2 Top Alcohol Funny Car Champion

1993: Division 2 Top Alcohol Funny Car Champion

1992: Division 2 Top Alcohol Funny Car Champion

Jack Beckman Date Of Birth: June 28, 1966 From: Norco, CA

Sponsor: Valvoline NextGen Crew Chief: Todd Smith Assistant Crew Chief: Terry Snyder

Owner: Don Schumacher Body: '12 Dodge Charger Engine: Dodge 496

Pro Debut: FC: 2006 TF: 2005 Starts: 133 FC: 121 TF: 12

Consecutive Qualified Starts: TF: 12 FC: 0

Win Percentage In Final Round: 45.1% FC: 44.4% SC: 50%

Average Career Qualifying Spot: 7.89 TF: 11.7 FC: 7.48

AT THE TREE:

Career Holeshot Win/Loss Record: FC: 9/10

Career Left Firsts/Left On: 143/138 = 50.8% TF: 6/9 = 40% FC: 137/129 = 51.5%

Career Final Rounds Won/Lost On A Holeshot: 0/1 FC: 0/1

STATS:

Championships: 1 SC: 1 U.S. Nationals Wins/Finals: 0/1

Career Best E.T./Speed: 1000ft.: 4.039/318.99 1320ft.: TF: 4.563/324.28 FC: 4.662/333.66

Career Wins: 14 FC: 12 SC: 2

Career Finals: 31 FC: 27 SC: 4

Last Win: 2011 Phoenix

Last Final: 2011 Phoenix

Most Successful Event: Phoenix: 15/3, 3 Wins, Including 2 Consecutive, 3 Finals

TF: Englishtown: 2/1 FC: Phoenix: 15/3, 3 Wins, Including 2 Consecutive, 3 Finals

Elimination Round Win/Loss Record: 175/121 = 59.1% TF: 4/12 = 25% FC: 171/109 = 61%

Career # 1 Qualifiers: 4 FC: 4

Career Provisional # 1 Qualifiers: FC: 3

Top Five Finishes: 6 FC: 5 Consecutive SC: 1

Top Ten Point Finishes: 6 FC: 5 Consecutive SC: 1

Career Best Points Finish: Countdown: 2nd-2458 (-72)

Pre-Countdown (2006 And Before): TF:15th-461 (-1520) FC: 19th-329 (-1307)

Best/Worst Points Finish If Countdown Never Was: 2nd/6th

YEARLY CAREER SUMMARY:

2012: 4th-343 (-254), 7/5, Average Qualifying Spot: 3.6, 1 DNQ, Left First: 54.5%

2011: 2nd-2458 (-72), 34/19, 3 Wins, 5 Finals, Average Qualifying Spot: 6.45, Qualified # 1 Once, Left First: 71.4%, Set The National Speed Record For 1000 Feet At Concord-2, 318.99, Rahn Tobler Was The Crew Chief

2010: 4th-2439 (-182), 36/22, 1 Win, 5 Finals, Average Qualifying Spot: 6.56, Qualified # 1 Once, Left First: 50%

2009: 5th-2406 (-141), 29/22, 2 Wins, 5 Finals, Average Qualifying Spot: 8.7, Qualified # 1 Once, Left First: 38.7%

2008: 3rd-2457 (-104), 33/18, 3 Wins, 7 Finals, Including 4 Consecutive, Average Qualifying Spot: 10.5, 3 DNQ's, Left First: 55.1%

2007: 5th-2358 (-82), 24/19, 2 Wins, 3 Finals, Average Qualifying Spot: 6.04, 2 DNQ's, Left First: 50%, Won $100,000 Shootout

2006: 19th-329 (-1307), 8/4, 1 Win, 2 Finals, Including 2 Consecutive, Average Qualifying Spot: 7.4, Qualified # 1 Once, Left Once: 16.6%, Set The Last National Speed Record At 1320 Feet, 333.66, Finished 95th In The Top Alcohol Dragster National Points

2005: 15th-461 (-1520), 4/12, Average Qualifying Spot: 11.7, Left First: 40%, Finished 16th In The Division 7 Top Alcohol Dragster Points, 79th Nationally

2004: Finished 13th In The Division 7 Top Alcohol Dragster Points, 88th Nationally, 2nd In Super Comp, 29th Nationally

2003: Won Super Comp National And Division 7 Championship, 15th In Top Alcohol Dragster, 104th Nationally

2002: Finished 13th In The Division 7 Top Alcohol Dragster Points, 97th Nationally, 9th In Super Comp, 44th Nationally

2001: Finished 38th In The Division 7 Super Comp Points, 77th Nationally

2000: Finished 5th In The Division 7 Super Comp Points, 64th Nationally

Kenny Bernstein Date Of Birth: September 6, 1944 From: Lake Forest, CA RETIRED

Pro Debut: FC: 1973 TF: 1990 Starts: 1997-2011: 169 FC: 17 TF: 152

Consecutive Qualified Starts: 1997-2011: TF: 91 FC: 1

Win Percentage In Final Round: 58.1% TF: 56.9% FC: 60% IHRA: 62.9% TF: 50% FC: 64%

Average Career Qualifying Spot: 1997-2011: 5.62 TF: 5.30 FC: 8.47

AT THE TREE: 1997-2011:

Career Holeshot Win/Loss Record: 13/8 TF: 9/7 FC: 4/1

Career Left Firsts/Left On: 204/172 = 54.2% TF: 184/165 = 52.7% FC: 20/7 = 74%

Career Final Rounds Won/Lost On A Holeshot: TF: 1/1

STATS:

Championships: 6 TF: 2 FC: 4 Consecutive IHRA: FC: 1

U.S. Nationals Wins/Finals: 3/3 TF: 1/1 FC: 2/2

Career Best E.T./Speed: 1320ft.: TF: 4.477/332.18 FC: 4.759/327.43

Career Wins: 71 TF: 41 FC: 30 IHRA: 17 TF: 1 FC: 16

Career Finals: 122 TF: 72 FC: 50 IHRA: 27 TF: 2 FC: 25

Last Win: TF: 2003 Pomona-2 FC:

Last Final: TF: 2003 Pomona-2 FC: 2007 Brainerd

Most Successful Event: 1997-2011:

Madison: 17/6, 1 Win, 4 Finals, Including 3 Consecutive, 1 DNQ

TF: Madison: 17/6, 1 Win, 4 Final, Including 3 Consecutive FC: Norwalk/Brainerd: 3/1, 1 Final

Elimination Round Win/Loss Record: 1997-2011: 269/143 = 65.2%

TF: 255/126 = 66.9% FC: 14/17 = 45.1%

Career # 1 Qualifiers: 66 TF: 28 FC: 38

Career Provisional # 1 Qualifiers: 1997-2011: TF: 26

Top Five Finishes: 17 TF: 8 FC: 9 IHRA: 8 TF: 1 FC: 7

Top Ten Point Finishes: 24 TF: 14 Consecutive FC: 10 IHRA: 11 TF: 1 FC: 10

Career Best Points Finish: Countdown: 14th-903 (-2275)

Pre-Countdown (2006 And Before): TF: 1st-2102 FC: 1st-12786

YEARLY CAREER SUMMARY: MISSING EXACT FINAL ROUND DETAILS:

2007: 14th-903 (-2275), 14/17, Average Qualifying Spot: 8.47, 6 DNQ's, 1 By 9 Thousandths, Left First: 74%, Won 4 Rounds On A Holeshot

2003: 6th-1111 (-883), 29/11, 4 Wins, Including 4 Consecutive, 4 Finals, Qualified # 1 Once, Average Qualifying Spot: 3.93, Left First: 40.5%, Took Over Driving For Injured Son, Brandon, In Topeka, FC Only Following Season

2002: 2nd-1758 (-193), 47/19, 4 Wins, 9 Finals, Average Qualifying Spot: 3.73, Qualified # 1 Four Times, Including 2 Consecutive, Left First: 46.7%

2001: 1st-2102, 61/16, 8 Wins, Including 3 Consecutive, Then 2 Consecutive, 12 Finals, Average Qualifying Spot: 2.87, Qualified # 1 Nine Times, Including 3 Consecutive, Then 2 Consecutive, Left First: 54.9%

2000: 6th-1275 (-615), 25/21, 1 Wins, 4 Finals, Average Qualifying Spot: 6.34, Qualified # 1 Twice, Including 2 Consecutive, Left First: 60%

1999: 6th-1260 (-228), 27/22, 2 Finals, Average Qualifying Spot: 6.66, 1 DNQ, Left First: 62.5%

1998: 4th-1385 (-396), 36/17, 5 Wins, Including 2 Consecutive, 8 Finals, Including 3 Consecutive, Then 2 Consecutive, Average Qualifying Spot: 6.45, Qualified # 1 Twice, 1 DNQ, Left First: 56.2%,

1997: 5th-1279 (-558), 30/20, 3 Wins, Including 2 Consecutive, 5 Finals, Including 2 Consecutive, Average Qualifying Spot: 7.13, Left First: 47.8%

1996: 1st-1415, 4 Wins, Qualified # 1 Four Times,

1995: 7th-949 (-626), 2 Finals, Qualified # 1 Twice,

1994: 6th-9646 (-3954), 1 Win, 2 Finals, Qualified # 1 Once,

1993: 3rd-11064 (-1734), 1 Win, 3 Finals, Won Shootout

1992: 3rd-11980 (-252), 4 Wins, 6 Finals, Qualified # 1 Three Times, Including 2 Consecutive, First Driver To Break The 300 MPH Barrier, 301.70, At Gainesville, Dale Armstrong Was The Crew Chief

1991: 2nd-13832 (-556), 6 Wins, 7 Finals, Including 2 Consecutive, Won Shootout

1990: 8th-9228 (-6830), 1 Final

1989: 3rd-12698, 3 Wins, Including 2 Consecutive, Qualified # 1 Three Times, TF Only Following Seasons

1988: 1st-12362, 3 Wins, Qualified # 1 Five Times, Including 2 Consecutive,

1987: 1st-12688, 7 Wins, Including 4 Consecutive, Then 2 Consecutive, 4 Consecutive Between Seasons, Qualified # 1 Seven Times,

1986: 1st-12786, 5 Wins, 3 Consecutive, Qualified # 1 Eight Times, Including 5 Consecutive Then 3 Consecutive, And 4 Consecutive Between Seasons

1985: 1st-12652, 6 Wins, Including 2 Consecutive Twice, Qualified # 1 Six Times, Including 2 Consecutive, Won Shootout

1984: 3rd-7872 (-1016), 1 Win, Qualified # 1 Twice

1983: 3rd-7108 (-2827), 2 Wins, Including 2 Consecutive, Qualified # 1 Once, Won Shootout

1982: 4th-6306 (-1140), 1 Win, Qualified # 1 Once

1981: 3rd-6070 (-1416), 1 Win, Qualified # 1 Twice

1980: Qualified # 1 Once

1979: 9th-4515 (-2508), 1 Win, Qualified # 1 Once, Won IHRA Funny-Car Championship

1978: Qualified # 1 Once

1973: 1 Final

Bob Bode Date Of Birth: September 7, 1951 From: Barrington, IL

Sponsor: Stupid Fast Apparel Crew Chief: Walt Przybyl Jr. Owner: Bob Bode

Body: '10 Chevrolet Impala Engine: BAE 500

Pro Debut: 2001 Starts: 65 Consecutive Qualified Starts: 6

Win Percentage In Final Round: 100% Average Career Qualifying Spot: 12.3

AT THE TREE:

Career Holeshot Win/Loss Record: 2/0 Career Left Firsts/Left On: 24/53 = 31.1%

STATS:

Championships: 0 APBA: 1

Career Best E.T./Speed: 1000ft.: 4.109/304.12 1320ft.: 4.802/316.82

Career Wins: 1

Career Finals: 1

Last Win: 2010 Brainerd

Last Final: 2010 Brainerd

Most Successful Event: Brainerd: 6/6, 1 Win, 1 Final, 3 DNQ's

Elimination Round Win/Loss Record: 18/64 = 21.9%

Career Provisional # 1 Qualifiers: 1

Career Best Points Finish: Countdown: 16th-481 (-2140)

Pre-Countdown (2006 And Before): 18th-485 (-1291)

YEARLY CAREER SUMMARY:

2012: 11th-229 (-368), 2/6, Average Qualifying Spot: 13.6, Left First: 42.8%

2011: 16th-299 (-2241), 2/7, Average Qualifying Spot: 13.8, 2 DNQ's, Left First: 33.3%

2010: 16th-481 (-2140), 6/10, 1 Win, 1 Final, Average Qualifying Spot: 10.4, Left First: 42.8%

2009: 17th-295 (-2252), 0/8, Average Qualifying Spot: 12, 4 DNQ's, Left First: 25%

2008: 21st-200 (-2361), 3/3, Average Qualifying Spot: 12, 7 DNQ's, 1 By 3 Thousandths, Left First: 33.3%

2007: 24th-70 (-3108), 7 DNQ's

2006: 23rd-91 (-1545), 0/1, Average Qualifying Spot: 13, 6 DNQ's, Left First: 0%

2005: 23rd-102 (-1414), 0/2, Average Qualifying Spot: 15.5, 4 DNQ's, Left First: 66.6%

2004: 18th-240 (-1643), 0/7, Average Qualifying Spot: 13.1, 2 DNQ's, Left First: 50%

2003: 20th-284 (-1484), 2/7, Average Qualifying Spot: 11.1, 2 DNQ's, Left First: 25%

2002: 18th-485 (-1291), 3/11, Average Qualifying Spot: 12.1, 8 DNQ's, Left First: 7.1%

2001: 22nd-133 (-1867), 0/2, Average Qualifying Spot: 13.5, 7 DNQ's, Left First: 0%

Phil Burkart Date Of Birth: May 15, 1968 From: Yorkville, NY

Pro Debut: 1998 Starts: 89 Consecutive Qualified Starts: 20

Win Percentage In Final Round: 44.4% Average Career Qualifying Spot: 10.3

AT THE TREE:

Career Holeshot Win/Loss Record: 7/3 Career Left Firsts/Left On: 89/61 = 59.3%

STATS:

Career Best E.T./Speed: 1000ft: 4.208/298.87 1320ft.: 4.734/330.07

Career Wins: 4

Career Finals: 9

Last Win: 2006 Reading

Last Final: 2007 Pomona-2

Most Successful Event: Denver: 7/2, 1 Win, 2 Finals

Elimination Round Win/Loss Record: 73/90 = 44.7%

Career Provisional # 1 Qualifiers: 2

Top Ten Point Finishes: 2

Career Best Points Finish: Countdown: 20th-291 (-2887)

Pre-Countdown (2006 And Before): 8th-1034 (-602)

YEARLY CAREER SUMMARY:

2010: 28th-31 (-2590), 0/1, Average Qualifying Spot: 16, Left First: 0%

2007: 20th-291 (-2887), 8/4, 2 Finals, Average Qualifying Spot: 8, Left First: 90.9%

2006: 8th-1034 (-602), 17/20, 1 Win, 1 Final, Average Qualifying Spot: 10.4, 2 DNQ's, Left First: 77.7%

2005: 12th-912 (-604), 12/20, 2 Finals, Average Qualifying Spot: 11, 3 DNQ's, Left First: 53.3%

2004: 10th-1159 (-724), 21/21, 2 Wins, 2 Finals, Average Qualifying Spot: 9.26, Left First: 48.7%

2003: 17th-413 (-1355), 7/8, 1 Final, Average Qualifying Spot: 8.75, 3 DNQ's, Left First: 54.5%

2002: 26th-74 (-1702), 0/1, Average Qualifying Spot: 5, 4 DNQ's, Left First: 0%

2001: 25th-60 (-1940), 6 DNQ's, 1 By 8 Thousandths

2000: 23rd-199 (-1793), 1/5, Average Qualifying Spot: 11.8, 2 DNQ's, 1 By 2 Thousandths, Left First: 50%

1999: 6/5, 1 Win, 1 Final, Average Qualifying Spot: 11.5, 1 DNQ, Left First: 54.5%

1998: 1/5, Average Qualifying Spot: 13.8, Left First: 33%

Jon Capps Date Of Birth: N/A From: Las Vegas, NV
Sponsor: Biesenbach Inc. Crew Chief: Chuck Worsham
Owner: Chuck Worsham Body: '10 Dodge Charger Engine: BAE 500
Pro Debut: 2007 Starts: 5 Consecutive Qualified Starts: 0
Average Career Qualifying Spot: 12.2

AT THE TREE:

Career Left Firsts/Left On: 4/3 = 57.1%

STATS:

Career Best E.T./Speed: 1000ft: 4.152/299.20 1320ft.: 4.826/318.47
Career Finals: 0 IHRA: FC: 1 Most Successful Event: Dallas: 2/1
Elimination Round Win/Loss Record: 3/5 = 37.5%
Career # 1 Qualifiers: 0 IHRA: FC: 1

Career Best Points Finish: Countdown: 18th-191 (-2349)

YEARLY CAREER SUMMARY:

2012: 28th-10 (-587), 1 DNQ

2011: 18th-191 (-2349), 2/4, Average Qualifying Spot: 11.2, 2 DNQ's, Left First: 60%

2007: 23rd-71 (-3107), 1/1, Average Qualifying Spot: 16, 2 DNQ's, Left First: 50%

2005: Finished 79th In The Top Alcohol Dragster National Points

2004: Finished 7th In The Division 7 Top Alcohol Funny Car Points, 43rd Nationally

2002: Finished 15th In The Division 7 Top Alcohol Funny Car Points, 59th Nationally

2001: Finished 123rd In The Top Alcohol Dragster National Points

Ron Capps Date Of Birth: June 28, 1966 From: Carlsbad, CA

Sponsor: Napa Auto Parts Crew Chief: Rahn Tobler Assistant Crew Chief: John Collins

Owner: Don Schumacher

Body: '12 Dodge Charger Engine: Dodge 496

Pro Debut: FC: 1997 TF: 1995 Starts: 354 FC: 337 TF: 17

Consecutive Qualified Starts: FC: 2

Win Percentage In Final Round: 47.1% TF: 50% FC: 47%

Average Career Qualifying Spot: FC: 7.46

AT THE TREE:

Career Holeshot Win/Loss Record: FC: 22/21 Career Left Firsts/Left On: FC: 405/291 = 58.1%

Career Final Rounds Won/Lost On A Holeshot: FC: 3/4

STATS:

Career Best E.T./Speed: 1000ft.: 4.023/315.64 1320ft.: TF: 4.794/302.62 FC: 4.694/331.61

Career Wins: 33 TF: 1 FC: 32

Career Finals: 70 TF: 2 FC: 68

Last Win: 2011 Las Vegas-2

Last Final: 2012 Houston

Most Successful Event: FC: Madison: 26/8, 3 Wins, 4 Finals, 2 DNQ's

Elimination Round Win/Loss Record: 436/322 = 57.5%

TF: 11/16 = 40.7% FC: 425/306 = 58.1%

Career # 1 Qualifiers: FC: 11

Career Provisional # 1 Qualifiers: FC: 12

Top Five Finishes: FC: 8

Top Ten Point Finishes: FC: 14, 7 Consecutive

Career Best Points Finish: Countdown: 3rd-2433 (-114)

Pre-Countdown (2006 And Before): TF: 15th-7677 (-766) FC: 2nd-1508 (-8)

Best/Worst Points Finish If Countdown Never Was: 2nd/8th

YEARLY CAREER SUMMARY:

2012: 3rd-379 (-218), 9/5, 1 Final, Average Qualifying Spot: 5.6, 1 DNQ, Left First: 53.8%

2011: 6th-2397 (-143), 30/19, 2 Wins, 5 Finals, Average Qualifying Spot: 7.19, Qualified # 1 Once, 1 DNQ, Left First: 73.3%

2010: 7th-2284 (-337), 23/22, 1 Win, 3 Finals, Including 2 Consecutive, Average Qualifying Spot: 5.6, Left First: 34.8%

2009: 3rd-2433 (-114), 39/19, 5 Wins, Including 2 Consecutive, 7 Finals, Average Qualifying Spot: 6.95, Qualified # 1 Three Times, Left First: 52.6%, Appeared In 3 Consecutive Finals Between End Of 2008 And Start Of 2009

2008: 8th-2302 (-259), 20/24, 2 Finals, Average Qualifying Spot: 9.37, Left First: 47.6%

2007: 4th-3067 (-111), 32/19, 3 Wins, 7 Finals, Including 3 Consecutive, Average Qualifying Spot: 7, 1 DNQ, Left First: 51%, Lost 5 Rounds On A Holeshot

2006: 3rd-1503 (-133), 37/18, 5 Wins, 8 Finals, Including 4 Consecutive, Average Qualifying Spot: 8.08, Left First: 63.4%, Won 4 Rounds On A Holeshot, Including 2 Finals

2005: 2nd-1508 (-8), 37/20, 3 Wins, 7 Finals, Including 2 Consecutive, Average Qualifying Spot: 7.95, Qualified # 1 Once, Left First: 60.7%, Lost Championship By Smallest Points Difference In Class History

2004: 12th-819 (-1064), 6/21, Average Qualifying Spot: 10.4, 2 DNQ's, Left First: 70.3%

2003: 8th-1105 (-663), 20/21, 1 Win, 2 Finals, Average Qualifying Spot: 9.27, 1 DNQ, Left First: 60%

2002: 6th-1148 (-628), 23/20, 1 Win, 3 Finals, Average Qualifying Spot: 7.28, 2 DNQ's, Left First: 57.1%, Won $100,000 Shootout

2001: 4th-1451 (-549), 33/20, 3 Wins, 5 Finals, Including 2 Consecutive, Average Qualifying Spot: 6.34, 1 DNQ, Left First: 66.6%, Won 4 Rounds On A Holeshot

2000: 2nd-1551 (-441), 41/22, 1 Win, 7 Finals, Including 2 Consecutive Three Times, 3 Consecutive Once, Average Qualifying Spot: 6.86, Qualified # 1 Twice, Left First: 56.6%

1999: 9th-891 (-1180), 11/19, 1 Final, Average Qualifying Spot: 7.73, Qualified # 1 Once, 3 DNQ's, Left First: 51.7%, Won $100,000 Shootout, Joining Al Hofmann As The Only Driver To Win 2 Consecutive

1998: 2nd-1528 (-135), 40/18, 5 Wins, 8 Finals, Including 2 Consecutive Twice, Average Qualifying Spot: 4.52, Qualified # 1 Once, Left First: 62.9%, Won 100,000 Shootout

1997: 5th-1174 (-691), 24/19, 2 Wins, 3 Finals, Average Qualifying Spot: 7.71, Qualified # 1 Twice, 2 DNQ's, Left First: 66.6%, Auto Club Road To The Future Award Winner

1996: 21st, 2/4, 2 DNQ's, Only FC Following Seasons

1995: 14th, 9/12, 1 Win, 2 Finals, 1 DNQ

Dale Creasy Jr. Date Of Birth: July 31, 1959 From: Beecher, IL

Sponsor: Tek Pak Inc. Crew Chief: N/A

Owner: Dale Creasy Jr. Body: '09 Chevrolet Impala SS Engine: BAE 500

Pro Debut: 1997 Starts: 81 Consecutive Qualified Starts: 0

Win Percentage In Final Round: 0% IHRA: FC: 76.9% Average Career Qualifying Spot: 13.6

AT THE TREE:

Career Left Firsts/Left On: 40/40 = 50%

STATS:

Championships: 0 IHRA: FC: 2

Career Best E.T./Speed: 1000ft: 4.180/297.16 1320ft.: 4.836/312.42

Career Wins: 0 IHRA: FC: 10

Career Finals: 0 IHRA: FC: 13

Most Successful Event: Reading: 3/4, 5 DNQ's

Elimination Round Win/Loss Record: 14/81 = 14.7%

Career # 1 Qualifiers: 0 IHRA: FC: 7

Top Five Finishes: 0 IHRA: FC: 2

Top Ten Point Finishes: 0 IHRA: FC: 3

Career Best Points Finish: Countdown: 17th-206 (-2334)

Pre-Countdown (2006 And Before): 16th-655 (-1121)

YEARLY CAREER SUMMARY:

2012: 26th-20 (-577), 2 DNQ's

2011: 17th-206 (-2334), 2/5, Average Qualifying Spot: 14.2, 1 DNQ, Left First: 28.5%

2010: 19th-208 (-2413), 1/6, Average Qualifying Spot: 13.6, Left First: 66.6%

2009: 31st-20 (-2527), 2 DNQ's

2007: 28th-20 (-3158), 2 DNQ's, Won IHRA Funny Car Championship

2006: 35th-10 (-1626), 1 DNQ, Won IHRA Funny Car Championship

2005: 21st-173 (-1343), 2/3, Average Qualifying Spot: 15.6, 4 DNQ's, Left First: 100%

2004: 26th-40 (-1843), 4 DNQ's

2003: 16th-546 (-1222), 1/14, Average Qualifying Spot: 14.3, 9 DNQ's, Left First: 61.5%

2002: 16th-655 (-1121), 3/17, Average Qualifying Spot: 12.7, 6 DNQ's, Left First: 27.7%

2001: 21st-211 (-1789), 0/1, Average Qualifying Spot: 16, 18 DNQ's, Left First: 0%

2000: 21st-252 (-1740), 0/2, Average Qualifying Spot: 15.5, 19 DNQ's, Left First: 100%

1999: 5/17, Average Qualifying Spot: 12.7, 5 DNQ's, Left First: 55.5%

1998: 0/14, Average Qualifying Spot: 14, 6 DNQ's, Left First: 50%

1997: 0/2, Average Qualifying Spot: 13, 6 DNQ's, 1 By 2 Thousandths, Left First: 100%

James Day Date Of Birth: 1978 From: Mission Viejo, CA
Pro Debut: 2007 Starts: 1 Consecutive Qualified Starts: 0
Win Percentage In Final Round: 0% IHRA: PFC: 100%
Average Career Qualifying Spot: 13

AT THE TREE:

Career Left Firsts/Left On: 0/1 = 0%

STATS:

Career Best E.T./Speed: 1000ft.: FC: 4.846/173.29 1320ft.: FC: 5.198/273.77
Career Wins: 0 IHRA: PFC: 2
Career Finals: 0 IHRA: PFC: 2
Most Successful Event: Denver: 0/1, 1 DNQ
Elimination Round Win/Loss Record: 0/1 = 0%
Top Ten Point Finishes: 0 IHRA: PFC: 1
Career Best Points Finish: Countdown: 22th-51 (-2570)
Pre-Countdown (2006 And Before): 29th-20 (-3158)

YEARLY CAREER SUMMARY:

2012: 28th-15 (-582), 2 DNQ's
2011: 30th-20 (-2520), 2 DNQ's
2010: 22nd-51 (-2570), 0/1, Average Qualifying Spot: 13, 2 DNQ's, Left First: 0%

2008: 28th-10 (-2551), 1 DNQ

2007: 29th-20 (-3158), 2 DNQ's

2006: Finished 110th In The Top Alcohol Dragster National Points

2005: Finished 16th In The Division 4 Top Alcohol Dragster Points, 92nd Nationally

2002: Finished109th In The Top Alcohol Dragster NationalPoints

Alexis DeJoria Date Of Birth: September 24, 1977 From: Venice, CA

Sponsor: Patron Tequila Crew Chief: Del Worsham

Owner: Connie Kalitta Body: '12 Toyota Camry Engine: TFX 500

Pro Debut: 2011 Starts: 8 Consecutive Qualified Starts: 4

Win Percentage In Final Round: 33.3% TAFC: 33.3% Average Career Qualifying Spot: 11.1

AT THE TREE:

Career Holeshot Win/Loss Record: 0/1 Career Left Firsts/Left On: 1/7 = 14.2%

STATS:

Career Best E.T./Speed: 1000ft.: 4.115/310.27

Career Wins: 1 TAFC: 1

Career Finals: 3 TAFC: 3

Most Successful Event: Gainesville: 1/1

Elimination Round Win/Loss Record: 1/8 = 11.1%

Career Best Points Finish: Countdown: 5th-2123 (-2416)

YEARLY CAREER SUMMARY:

2012: 14th-190 (-407), 1/5, Average Qualifying Spot: 11.2, 1 DNQ, Left First: 16.6%

2011: 25th-107 (-2433), 0/3, Average Qualifying Spot: 11, 1 DNQ, Left First: 0%

2010: Finished 4th In The Division 2 Top Alcohol Funny Car Points, 18th Nationally

2009: Finished 4th In The Division 2 Top Alcohol Funny Car Points, 11th Nationally

2008: Finished 4th In The Division 7 Top Alcohol Funny Car Points, 28th Nationally

2007: Finished 14th In The Division 7 Top Alcohol Funny Car Points, 53rd Nationally

2006: Finished 14th In The Division 7 Super Comp Points, 64th Nationally

Gary Densham Date Of Birth: October 20, 1946 From: Belleflower, CA

Sponsor: Densham Motorsports Crew Chief: Greg Amaral Owner: Gary Densham

Body: '09 Dodge Charger Engine: BAE 500

Pro Debut: 1979 Starts: 372 Consecutive Qualified Starts: 2

Win Percentage In Final Round: 40% IHRA: FC: 66.6%

Average Career Qualifying Spot: 1997-2011: 8.62

AT THE TREE: 1997-2011:

Career Holeshot Win/Loss Record: 9/10 Career Left Firsts/Left On: 158/243 = 39.4%

Career Final Rounds Won/Lost On A Holeshot: 0/1

STATS:

U.S. Nationals Wins/Finals: 1/1

Career Best E.T./Speed: 1000ft.: 4.100/304.53 1320ft.: 4.706/329.75

Career Wins: 8 IHRA: FC: 2

Career Finals: 20 IHRA: FC: 3

Last Win: 2004 Indianapolis

Last Final: 2008 Sonoma

Most Successful Event: 1994-2011, 96 Unknown:

Brainerd: 17/11, 1 Win, 4 Finals, Including 2 Consecutive

Elimination Round Win/Loss Record: 214/364 = 37%

Career # 1 Qualifiers: 9 IHRA: FC: 2

Career Provisional # 1 Qualifiers: 1997-2011: 10

Top Five Finishes: 3

Top Ten Point Finishes: 8 IHRA: FC: 1

Career Best Points Finish: Countdown: 10th-2217 (-344)

Pre-Countdown (2006 And Before): 4th-485 (-1291)

Best/Worst Points Finish If Countdown Never Was: 10th

YEARLY CAREER SUMMARY:

2012: 15th-167 (-430), 3/3, Average Qualifying Spot: 11.3, 1 DNQ, Left First: 20%

2011: 19th-188 (-2352), 1/5, Average Qualifying Spot: 12.2, 1 DNQ, Left First: 16.6%

2010: 18th-234 (-2387), 0/7, Average Qualifying Spot: 9.57, Left First: 14.2%

2009: 16th-343 (-2204), 4/9, Average Qualifying Spot: 12.2, 1 DNQ, Left First: 7.6%

2008: 10th-2217 (-344), 20/22, 2 Finals, Average Qualifying Spot: 11.6, 2 DNQ's, Left First: 45%

2007: 17th-728 (-2450), 4/19, Average Qualifying Spot: 11.3, 4 DNQ's, Left First: 35%

2006: 12th-794 (-842), 5/21, Average Qualifying Spot: 11, Qualified # 1 Once, 2 DNQ's, Left First: 23%

2005: 15th-662 (-854), 3/18, Average Qualifying Spot: 13.8, 5 DNQ's, 1 By 7 Thousandths, Left First: 52.6%

2004: 4th-1405 (-478), 30/21, 2 Wins, 3 Finals, Average Qualifying Spot: 4.65, Qualified # 1 Twice, Left First: 41.6%, Doubled Up U.S. Nationals Weekend Winning Shootout And Event Netting $150,000

2003: 5th-1343 (-425), 28/20, 2 Wins, 3 Finals, Including 2 Consecutive, Average Qualifying Spot: 4.59, Qualified # 1 Three Times, 1 DNQ, Left First: 34.1%

2002: 4th-1412 (-364), 31/21, 2 Wins, 4 Finals, Average Qualifying Spot: 5.6, Qualified # 1 Twice, Left First: 42.8%

2001: 8th-1147 (-853), 21/19, 2 Wins, 2 Finals, Average Qualifying Spot: 8.28, Qualified # 1 Once, 3 DNQ's, Left First: 40.5%

2000: 14th-635 (-1357), 3/16, Average Qualifying Spot: 12.4, 7 DNQ's, 1 By 7 Thousandths, Left First: 47%

1999: 14th, 7/18, 1 Final, Average Qualifying Spot: 10.9, 4 DNQ's, Left First: 65.2%

1998: 12th, 5/20, Average Qualifying Spot: 10, 2 DNQ's, Left First: 54.5%

1997: 10th-924 (-941), 11/21, Average Qualifying Spot: 8.52, 1 DNQ, Left First: 29.6%

1996: 10th, 8/18, 1 Final, 1 DNQ

1995: 9th, 12/15, 3 Finals, 4 DNQ's
1994: 12th, 8/16, 1 Final, 2 DNQ's
1993: 14th, 2/12, 2 DNQ's
1992: 13th, 5/12, 4 DNQ's
1991: 12th, 2/14, 5 DNQ's
1990: 23rd, 0/5, 4 DNQ's
1989: 22nd, 1/3, 3 DNQ's
1988: 23rd, 0/2, 4 DNQ's
1987: 31st, 0/1, 2 DNQ's
1986: 34th, 0/2
1985: 22nd, 0/2, 1 DNQ
1984: 47th, 1 DNQ
1983: 29th, 0/1, 1 DNQ
1982: 33rd, 0/1
1981: 2 DNQ's
1979: 1 DNQ

Jeff Diehl Date Of Birth: July 27, 1964 From: Salinas, CA

Sponsor: J.G. Parks And Son Crew Chief: Jeff Diehl Owner: Jeff Diehl

Body: '09 Chevrolet Monte Carlo Engine: BAE 500

Pro Debut: 2006 Starts: 14 Consecutive Qualified Starts: 0

Win Percentage In Final Round: 0% IHRA: 50% FC: 100%

Average Career Qualifying Spot: 15

AT THE TREE:

Career Holeshot Win/Loss Record: 0/1 Career Left Firsts/Left On: 2/10 = 16.6%

STATS:

Career Best E.T./Speed: 1000ft.: 4.192/298.67 1320ft.: 5.632/218.02

Career Wins: 0 IHRA: 1 FC: 1

Career Finals: 0 IHRA: 2 FC: 1 PFC: 1

Most Successful Event: Denver/Sonoma: 0/2

Elimination Round Win/Loss Record: 0/14 = 0%

Top Ten Point Finishes: 0 IHRA: FC: 3

Career Best Points Finish: Countdown: 17th-400 (-2221)

Pre-Countdown (2006 And Before): 27th-20 (-1616)

YEARLY CAREER SUMMARY:

2012: 22nd-20 (-577), 2 DNQ's

2011: 21st-154 (-2386), 0/4, Average Qualifying Spot: 15.2, 4 DNQ's, Left First: 33.3%

2010: 17th-400 (-2221), 0/10, Average Qualifying Spot: 15, 9 DNQ's, Left First: 12.5%

2009: 30th-30 (-2517), 3 DNQ's

2006: 27th-20 (-1616), 2 DNQ's

Grant Downing Date Of Birth: N/A From: Fullerton, CA
Formally: New Zealand

Sponsor: Worsham Racing Crew Chief: Chuck Worsham Owner: Chuck Worsham

Body: '10 Dodge Charger Engine: BAE 500

Pro Debut: 2003 Starts: 6 Consecutive Qualified Starts: 1

Average Career Qualifying Spot: 15.5

AT THE TREE:

Career Left Firsts/Left On: 1/5 = 16.6%

STATS:

Championships: 1 SCS: 1

Career Best E.T./Speed: 1000ft.: 4.211/291.89 1320ft.: FC: 4.900/315.78

Career Finals: 0 IHRA: FC: 1

Most Successful Event: Phoenix/Denver/Dallas: 0/1

Elimination Round Win/Loss Record: 0/6 = 0%

Career Best Points Finish: Countdown: 18th-175 (-2372)

Pre-Countdown (2006 And Before): 27th-30 (-1853)

YEARLY CAREER SUMMARY:

2012: 25th-31 (-566), 0/1, Average Qualifying Spot: 16, Left First: 100%

2011: 31st-20 (-2520), 2 DNQ's

2010: 30th-30 (-2591), 3 DNQ's, 1 By 8.62 MPH

2009: 18th-175 (-2372), 0/5, Average Qualifying Spot: 15.4, 2 DNQ's, Left First: 0%

2007: 30th-20 (-3158), 2 DNQ's

2006: 28th-20 (-1616), 2 DNQ's

2005: 29th-20 (-1496), 2 DNQ's

2004: 27th-30 (-1853), 3 DNQ's
2003: 28th-20 (-1748), 2 DNQ's
2002: Sport Compact Series Pro Champion

Jim Epler Date Of Birth: September 13, 1957 From: Phoenix, AZ
Pro Debut: 1991 Starts: 71 Consecutive Qualified Starts: 0
Win Percentage In Final Round: 33%
Average Career Qualifying Spot: 7.19

AT THE TREE: 1997-2012:

Career Holeshot Win/Loss Record: 5/0 Career Left Firsts/Left On: 42/73 = 36.5%

STATS:

U.S. Nationals Wins/Finals: 1/2, Including 2 Consecutive Finals
Career Best E.T./Speed: 1320ft.: 4.818/315.22
Career Wins: 4
Career Finals: 12
Last Win: 2000 Indianapolis
Last Final: 2001 Sonoma
Most Successful Event: 1997-2011:
Indianapolis: 8/2, 1 Win, 2 Finals, Including 2 Consecutive, 2 DNQ's
Elimination Round Win/Loss Record: 1997-2011: 61/69 = 46.9%
Career # 1 Qualifiers: 3
Career Provisional # 1 Qualifiers: 1997-2011: 4
Top Five Point Finishes: 1
Top Ten Point Finishes: 5
Career Best Points Finish: 5th-1242 (-750)

YEARLY CAREER SUMMARY:

2001:14th-776 (-1224), 10/17, 1 Final, Average Qualifying Spot: 12.5, 5 DNQ's, Left First: 36%

2000: 5th-1242 (-750), 25/20, 2 Wins, 3 Finals, Including 2 Consecutive, Average Qualifying Spot: 5.86, 1 Qualified # 1 Twice, DNQ, Left First: 50%

1999: 6th-960 (-1111), 18/17, 2 Finals, Average Qualifying Spot: 8.82, Qualified # 1 Once, 4 DNQ's, Left First: 40.6%

1998: 8/12, 1 Final, Average Qualifying Spot: 10.1, 5 DNQ's, Left First: 37.5%

1997: 0/3, Average Qualifying Spot: 11.6, 1 DNQ, Left First: 0%

1995: 10th-714 (-976),

1994: 7th-7922 (-8854), 1 Final,

1993: 7th-7252 (-10822), 1 Win, 2 Finals, First Driver To Break The 300 MPH Barrier, 300.40, At Topeka-2, Mike Kloeber Was The Crew Chief

1992: 1 Win, 2 Finals

Bonus Fact: Sold Computer Software Business To Race Full Time In 1994

Chuck Etchells Date Of Birth: N/A From: Putnam, CT

Pro Debut: 1979 Starts: 1997-2011: 60 Consecutive Qualified Starts: 0

Win Percentage In Final Round: 50% IHRA: FC: 80%

Average Career Qualifying Spot: 1997-2011: 7.41

AT THE TREE: 1997-2011:

Career Holeshot Win/Loss Record: 2/4 Career Left Firsts/Left On: 44/66 = 40%

STATS:

Championships: 0 IHRA: FC: 1

Career Best E.T./Speed: 1320ft.: 4.813/315.56

Career Wins: 13 IHRA: FC: 4

Career Finals: 26 IHRA: FC: 5

Most Successful Event: 1997-2011: Richmond: 8/0, 2 Wins, 2 Finals, Including 2 Consecutive

Elimination Round Win/Loss Record: 1997-2011: 69/56 = 55.2%

Career # 1 Qualifiers: 15 IHRA: FC: 7

Career Provisional # 1 Qualifiers: 1997-2011: 4

Top Five Finishes: 7 IHRA: FC: 1

Top Ten Point Finishes: 7 IHRA: FC: 1

Career Best Points Finish: 2nd-12320 (-5754)

YEARLY CAREER SUMMARY:

2001: 17th-611 (-1389), 5/14, Average Qualifying Spot: 12.7, 7 DNQ's, 1 By 19.88 MPH, Left First: 47%

1999: 0/1, Average Qualifying Spot: 16, Left First: 0%

1998: 4th-1430 (-233), 36/19, 3 Wins, 4 Finals, Average Qualifying Spot: 5.59, 1 DNQ, Left First: 47%

1997: 4th-1298 (-567), 28/22, 1 Win, 4 Finals, Average Qualifying Spot: 5.08, Qualified # 1 Four Times, Left First: 28.5%

1996: 5th-1001 (-1022), 1 Win, 4 Finals

1995: 4th-1202 (-488), 2 Wins, 3 Finals, Qualified # 1 Three Times,

1994: 4th-10852 (-5924), 2 Finals, Including 2 Consecutive, Qualified # 1 Twice,

1993: 2nd-12320 (-5754), 2 Wins, 5 Finals, Including 2 Consecutive, Qualified # 1 Five Times, Including 2 Consecutive, First Driver To Break The 4 Second Barrier, 4.987, At Topeka-2, Tim Richards Was The Crew Chief

1992: 5th-10256 (-4990), 3 Wins, 3 Finals, Qualified # 1 Once,

1990: 1 Win, 1 Final, Won IHRA Funny Car Championship

Ashley Force-Hood Date Of Birth: November 29, 1982 From: Anaheim Hills, CA

Pro Debut: 2007 Starts: 88 Consecutive Qualified Starts: 69

Win Percentage In Final Round: 42.8% FC: 33.3% TAD: 55.5%

Average Career Qualifying Spot: 5.02

AT THE TREE:

Career Holeshot Win/Loss Record: 3/13 Career Left Firsts/Left On: 58/125 = 31.6%

Career Final Rounds Won/Lost On A Holeshot: 0/1

STATS:

U.S. Nationals Wins/Finals: 3/0 FC: 2/0, Both Consecutive TAD: 1/0

Career Best E.T./Speed: 1000ft.: 4.032/316.38 1320ft.: 4.730/329.10

Career Wins: 9 FC: 4 TAD: 5

Career Finals: 21 FC: 12 TAD: 9

Most Successful Event: Atlanta: 12/3, 1 Win, 3 Finals, Including 3 Consecutive

Elimination Round Win/Loss Record: 105/84 = 55.5%

Career # 1 Qualifiers: 20 FC: 15 TAD: 5

Career Provisional # 1 Qualifiers: 24 FC: 19 TAD: 6

Career Best Points Finish: Countdown: 2nd-2481 (-66)

Best/Worst Points Finish If Countdown Never Was: 2nd/10th

YEARLY CAREER SUMMARY:

2010: 3rd-2449 (-172), 25/22, 1 Win, 2 Finals, Average Qualifying Spot: 4.52, Qualified # 1 Six Times, Including 2 Consecutive Twice, Left First: 39.1%

2009: 2nd-2481 (-66), 39/22, 2 Wins, 6 Finals, Including 3 Consecutive, Average Qualifying Spot: 4.2, Qualified # 1 Six Times, Including 2 Consecutive, Left First: 33.3%

2008: 6th-2385 (-176), 25/22, 1 Win, 3 Finals, Including 3 Consecutive, Average Qualifying Spot: 5.08, Qualified # 1 Three Times, Including 2 Consecutive, 1 DNQ, Left First: 40%, Lost 6 Rounds On A Holeshot

2007: 10th-960 (-2218), 16/18, 1 Final, Average Qualifying Spot: 6.66, 3 DNQ's, 1 By 6 Thousandths, Left First: 6.2%

2006: Finished 2nd In The Division 2 Top Alcohol Dragster Points, 5th Nationally

2005: Finished 3rd In The Division 4 Top Alcohol Dragster Points, 7th Nationally

2004: Division 4 Top Alcohol Dragster Champion, Finished 4th Nationally, Won With Her Dad, John, In Pomona, The First Father-Daughter To Win Together

2003: Finished 14th In The Division 3 Super Comp Points, 41st Nationally

2002: Finished 34th In The Division 7 Super Comp Points, 221st Nationally

Courtney Force Date Of Birth: June 20, 1988 From: Yorba Linda, CA
Sponsor: Traxxas Crew Chief: Ron Douglas/Danny Hood
Owner: John Force Body: '10 Ford Mustang Engine: Ford 500
Pro Debut: 2012 Starts: 6 Consecutive Qualified Starts: 6
Win Percentage In Final Round: 50% TAD: 50% Average Career Qualifying Spot: 9.66

AT THE TREE:

Career Left Firsts/Left On: 3/6 = 33.3%

STATS:

Career Best E.T./Speed: 1000ft.: 4.099/313.88
Career Wins: 1 TAD: 1
Career Finals: 2 TAD: 2
Most Successful Event: Phoenix: 2/1
Elimination Round Win/Loss Record: 4/6 = 40%
Career # 1 Qualifiers: 1 TAD: 1
Career Provisional # 1 Qualifiers: 2 TAD: 2

YEARLY CAREER SUMMARY:

2012: 9th-268 (-329), 4/6, Average Qualifying Spot: 9.66, Left First: 33.3%

2009: Finished 9th In The Division 7 Top Alcohol Dragster Points, 24th Nationally

2008: Finished 16th In The Division 7 Top Alcohol Dragster Points, 48th Nationally

2007: Finished 69th In The Division 7 Super Comp Points, 187th Nationally

2006: Finished 75th In The Division 7 Super Comp Points, 170th Nationally

2005: Finished 162nd In The Division 7 Super Comp Points, 803rd Nationally

John Force Date Of Birth: May 4, 1949 From: Yorba Linda, CA

Sponsor: Castrol GTX High Mileage Crew Chief: Dean Antonelli/ Danny DeGennaro

Owner: John Force Body: '12 Ford Mustang Engine: Ford 500

Pro Debut: 1978 Starts: 579 Consecutive Qualified Starts: 80

Win Percentage In Final Round: 62.5%

Average Career Qualifying Spot: 1997-2012: 1541/342 = 4.5

AT THE TREE: 1997-2012:

Career Holeshot Win/Loss Record: 28/20 Career Left Firsts/Left On: 446/385 = 53.6%

Career Final Rounds Won/Lost On A Holeshot: 7/4

STATS:

Championships: 15, Holds Record For The Most Championships Won In NHRA History As Well As Winning 10 Consecutive Championships

U.S. Nationals Wins/Finals: 4/7

Career Best E.T./Speed: 1000ft.: 4.011/319.22 1320ft.: 4.664/333.58

Career Wins: 135, Most In NHRA History

Career Finals: 216, Most In NHRA History IHRA: FC: 1

Last Win: 2012 Pomona-1

Last Final: 2012 Pomona-1

Most Successful Event: Elimination Record 1997-2011:

Brainerd: 34/10, 11 Wins, Including 4 Consecutive, 13 Finals,

Elimination Round Win/Loss Record: 1105/444 = 71.3%

Career # 1 Qualifiers: 139, Most In NHRA History

Career Provisional # 1 Qualifiers: 1997-2011: 69

Top Five Finishes: 25, 2 Consecutive

Top Ten Point Finishes: 29, 27 Consecutive IHRA: FC: 1

Career Best Points Finish: Countdown: 1st-2621

Pre-Countdown (2006 And Before): 1st-2071

Best/Worst Points Finish If Countdown Never Was: 1st/10th

YEARLY CAREER SUMMARY:

2012: 7th-323 (-274), 6/5, 1 Win, 1 Final, Average Qualifying Spot: 8, Left First: 80%

2011: 9th-2232 (-308), 14/21, 1 Win, 1 Final, Average Qualifying Spot: 5.9, Qualified # 1 Five Times, Including 4 Consecutive, Left First: 56.2%

2010: 1st-2621, 44/17, 6 Wins, Including 2 Consecutive, 11 Finals, Including 2 Consecutive Twice, Average Qualifying Spot: 5.65, Qualified # 1 Three Times, Left First: 71.6%

2009: 9th-2268 (-279), 23/24, Average Qualifying Spot: 5.95, Left First: 66.6%, First Season in 23 years, 1986, Without A National Event Win, First In 25 Years, 1984, Without A Final Round Appearance

2008: 7th-2303 (-258), 23/19, 1 Win, 2 Finals, Average Qualifying Spot: 5.7, 4 DNQ's, Left First: 51.2%

2007: 7th-2191 (-987), 25/14, 3 Wins, 5 Finals, Including 4 Consecutive, Average Qualifying Spot: 7.29, 2 DNQ's, Left First: 38.8%, Had Season Ending Accident In Dallas, First Season In 20 Years, 1987, To Record A DNQ Breaking A Consecutive Qualifying Streak Of 397 Events

2006: 1st-1636, 41/20, 3 Wins, 8 Finals, Including 2 Consecutive Twice, Average Qualifying Spot: 4.17, Qualified # 1 Six Times, Including 2 Consecutive, Left First: 47.3%, Won $100,000 Shootout, Won 4 Rounds On A Holeshot, Including 2 Finals

2005: 3rd-1484 (-32), 35/18, 5 Wins, Including 3 Consecutive, 7 Finals, Average Qualifying Spot: 5.26, Qualified # 1 Once, Left First: 38%

2004: 1st-1883, 53/18, 5 Wins, 12 Finals, Including 3 Consecutive, Average Qualifying Spot: 4.3, Qualified # 1 Seven Times, Including 3 Consecutive, Left First: 45.3%, Lost Five Rounds On A Holeshot, Shared Pomona-2 Win With His Daughter, Ashley, As They Both Dominated FC And TAD, Second Time In His Career He Set The National Speed Record At A Faster Speed Then The Top-Fuel National Speed Record, Only Funny Car Driver To Do It, Broke The 4.6 Second Barrier For The Class At Chicago-2, 4.697 Austin Coil And Bernie Fedderly Were The Crew Chiefs

2003: 3rd-1504 (-264), 33/20, 3 Wins, Including 2 Consecutive, 5 Finals, Including 4 Consecutive, Average Qualifying Spot: 3.73, Qualified # 1 Five Times, Left First: 72.9%, Broke A Streak Of Winning 10 Consecutive Championships As A Driver, But Won 11th Consecutive As An Owner

2002: 1st-1776, 48/15, 8 Wins, Including 3 Consecutive, 10 Finals, Average Qualifying Spot: 4.3, Qualified # 1 Six Times, Including 2 Consecutive Twice, Left First: 61.6%, Won 6 Rounds On A Holeshot, Including 1 Final, Broke The 100 National Event Wins Barrier

2001: 1st-2000, 55/18, 6 Wins, Including 2 Consecutive Twice, 13 Finals, Including 4 Consecutive Twice, Average Qualifying Spot:

2.83, Qualified # 1 Six Times, Including 2 Consecutive, Left First: 53.6%

2000: 1st-1992, 58/12, 11 Wins, Including 3 Consecutive, 13 Finals, Including 5 Consecutive, Average Qualifying Spot: 2.78, Qualified # 1 Eleven Times, 2 Consecutive Three Times, Left First: 43.9%, Won $100,000 Shootout

1999: 1st-2071, 61/11, 11 Wins, Including 3 Consecutive Twice, 13 Finals, Including 4 Consecutive, Average Qualifying Spot: 2.27, Qualified # 1 Nine Times, Including 2 Consecutive Three Times, Left First: 40.8%

1998: 1st-1663, 44/20, 3 Wins, 9 Finals, Including 4 Consecutive, Average Qualifying Spot: 3.78, Qualified # 1 Four Times, Left First: 57.3%, Set The National Speed Record At A Faster Speed Then The Top-Fuel National Speed Record

1997: 1st-1865, 57/16, 7 Wins, Including 3 Consecutive, 11 Finals, Including 4 Consecutive, Average Qualifying Spot: 3.56, Qualified # 1 Six Times, Including 3 Consecutive, Left First: 57.1%

1996: 1st-2023, 65/6, 13 Wins, Including 3 Consecutive Three Times, 16 Finals, Qualified # 1 Thirteen Times, Including 5 Consecutive, First Drag Racer Ever To Win The Driver of the Year Award, Won $100,000 Shootout

1995: 1st-1690, 50/13, 6 Wins, Including 2 Consecutive, 11 Finals, Qualified # 1 Nine Times, Including 2 Consecutive Three Times, 2 Consecutive Between Seasons

1994: 1st-16776, 50/8, 10 Wins, Including 5 Consecutive, 11 Finals, Qualified # 1 Twelve Times, Including 6 Consecutive

1993: 1st-18074, 56/7, 11 Wins, Including 5 Consecutive, 13 Finals, Qualified # 1 Seven Times, Including 2 Consecutive, Won $100,000 Shootout

1992: 2nd-14008 (-1238), 39/14, 4 Wins, Including 2 Consecutive, 8 Finals, Qualified # 1 Eight Times, Including 4 Consecutive

1991: 1st-15538, 48/13, 5 Wins, Including 3 Consecutive, 10 Finals, Qualified # 1 Twice

1990: 1st-15564, 45/12, 7 Wins, Including 3 Consecutive, 7 Finals, Qualified # 1 Ten Times, Including 4 Consecutive, Won $100,000 Shootout

1989: 6th, 21/18, 1 Win, 2 Finals, Qualified # 1 Once

1988: 3rd-11336 (-1026), 28/13, 3 Wins, 4 Finals, Qualified # 1 Five Times, Including 2 Consecutive

1987: 4th-8992 (-3696), 21/12, 1 Win, 5 Finals, Qualified # 1 Twice, 1 DNQ, Won $100,000 Shootout

1986: 4th-8200 (-4586), 16/14, 3 Finals, Qualified # 1 Once

1985: 5th-7240 (-5412), 15/12, 1 Final,

1984: 13th, 5/8, 2 DNQ's

1983: 4th-6810 (-3125), 12/10, 2 Finals, 1 DNQ

1982: 20th, 3/2, 1 DNQ

1981: 16th, 2/3, 2 DNQ's

1980: 26th, 1/4, 1 DNQ

1979: 8th-4193 (-2830), 8/6, 2 Finals, 2 DNQ's

1978: 23rd, 0/1

Bob Gilbertson Date Of Birth: April 7, 1955 From: Gastonia, NC
Pro Debut: 1999 Starts: 139 Consecutive Qualified Starts: 0
Win Percentage In Final Round: 20% IHRA: FC: 50% Average Career Qualifying Spot: 12.8

AT THE TREE:

Career Holeshot Win/Loss Record: 6/0 Career Left Firsts/Left On: 114/65 = 63.6%

STATS:

Career Best E.T./Speed: 1000ft.: 4.161/296.83 1320ft.: 4.764/325.45

Career Wins: 1 IHRA: FC: 3
Career Finals: 5 IHRA: FC: 6
Last Win: 2000 Houston-1
Last Final: 2006 Houston
Most Successful Event: Houston-1: 8/9, 1 Win, 2 Finals
Elimination Round Win/Loss Record: 56/138 = 28.8%
Career # 1 Qualifiers: 0 IHRA: FC: 10
Career Provisional # 1 Qualifiers: 1
Top Five Finishes: 0 IHRA: 4 FC: 3 AFC: 1
Top Ten Point Finishes: 0 IHRA: 4 FC: 3 AFC: 1
Career Best Points Finish: Countdown: 21st-268 (-2910)
Pre-Countdown (2006 And Before): 11th-908 (-1092)

YEARLY CAREER SUMMARY:

2011: 34th-10 (-2530), 1 DNQ

2010: 29th-31 (-2590), 0/1, Average Qualifying Spot: 13, Left First: 0%

2009: 28th-31 (-2516), 0/1, Average Qualifying Spot: 16, Left First: 100%

2008: 24th-62 (-2499), 0/1, Average Qualifying Spot: 11, 3 DNQ's, Left First: 100%

2007: 21st-268 (-2910), 2/5, Average Qualifying Spot: 12.4, 7 DNQ's, Left First: 57.1%

2006: 16th-703 (-933), 9/15, 1 Final, Average Qualifying Spot: 13.1, 5 DNQ's, Left First: 39.1%

2005: 14th-719 (-797), 6/17, 1 Final, Average Qualifying Spot: 12.2, 6 DNQ's, 1 By 5 Thousandths, Left First: 57.1%

2004: 14th-640 (-1243), 5/16, Average Qualifying Spot: 13.5, 5 DNQ's, Left First: 52.3%

2003: 15th-649 (-1119), 3/17, Average Qualifying Spot: 14, 6 DNQ's, Left First: 53.3%

2002: 15th-722 (-1054), 5/18, Average Qualifying Spot: 12.1, 5 DNQ's, Left First: 71.4%

2001: 11th-908 (-1092), 11/21, 2 Finals, Average Qualifying Spot: 12.4, 3 DNQ's, 1 By 2 Thousandths, Left First: 80.6%

2000: 12th-899 (-1093), 13/18, 1 Win, 1 Final, Average Qualifying Spot: 12.9, 3 DNQ's, Left First: 75%, Won 4 Rounds On A Holeshot

1999: 0/1, Average Qualifying Spot: 13.7, 8 DNQ's, 1 By 7 Thousandths, Left First: 77.7%

Johnny Gray Date Of Birth: March 20, 1953 From: Carlsbad, NM

Sponsor: Service Central Crew Chief: Rob Wendland Assistant Crew Chief: Rip Reynolds

Owner: Don Schumacher Body: '12 Dodge Charger Engine: Dodge 496

Pro Debut: FC: 1999 PS: 1993 Starts: 147 FC: 89 PS: 58

Consecutive Qualified Starts: FC: 17 PS: 0

Win Percentage In Final Round: 26.6% FC: 11.1% TAD: 100% TAFC: 100%

Average Career Qualifying Spot: 9.68 FC: 9.47 PS: 10

AT THE TREE:

Career Holeshot Win/Loss Record: 10/5 FC: 5/0 PS: 5/5

Career Left Firsts/Left On: 114/121 = 48.5% FC: 78/74 = 51.3% PS: 36/47 = 43.3%

STATS:

U.S. Nationals Wins/Finals: FC: 0/1

Career Best E.T./Speed: 1000ft.: 4.010/318.62 1320ft.: FC: 4.813/324.67 PS: 6.566/210.47

Career Wins: 4 FC: 1 TAD: 1 TAFC: 2

Career Finals: 15 FC: 9 PS: 3 TAD: 1 TAFC: 2

Last Win: 2011 Brainerd

Last Final: 2012 Gainesville

Most Successful Event: Gainesville: 9/8, 1 Final

FC: Gainesville: 7/5, 1 Final Won At: Brainerd: 4/0, 1 Win, 1 Final PS: Denver, 4/3

Elimination Round Win/Loss Record: 107/146 = 42.2% FC: 70/89 = 44% PS: 37/58 = 38.9%

Career # 1 Qualifiers: 4 FC: 2 TAFC: 2

Career Provisional # 1 Qualifiers: 9 FC: 4 TAFC: 5

Top Five Finishes: 2 TAFC: 2

Top Ten Point Finishes: 6 FC: 1 PS: 2 TAD: 1 TAFC: 2

Career Best Points Finish: Countdown: FC: 11th-1223 (-3432) PS: 9th-2300 (-382)

Pre-Countdown (2006 And Before): FC:10th-941 (-835) PS: 35th

Best/Worst Points Finish If Countdown Never Was: FC: 7th PS: 9th/9th

YEARLY CAREER SUMMARY:

2012: 6th-333 (-264), 6/6, 1 Final, Average Qualifying Spot: 43/6 = 7.16, Qualified # 1 Once, Left First: 25%

2011: 11th-1236 (-1304), 26/18, 1 Win, 5 Finals, Including 3 Consecutive, Average Qualifying Spot: 7.1, Qualified # 1 Once, 3 DNQ's, Left First: 28.5%

2010: 10th-2200 (-391), 14/20, 1 Final, Average Qualifying Spot: 8.9, 3 DNQ's, Left First: 39.2%, Back To FC Following Seasons

2009: 9th-2300 (-382), 14/24, 2 Finals, Average Qualifying Spot: 9.08, Left First: 47%

2008: 15th-722 (-1801), 9/14, Average Qualifying Spot: 13.1, 10 DNQ's, 1 By 8 Thousandths, 1 By 3 Thousandths, Left First: 42.8%

2006: 33rd-10, 1 DNQ, Back To PS Following Seasons

2004: 20th-190 (-1693), 0/6, Average Qualifying Spot: 11.6, Left First: 60%

2003: 13th-792 (-976), 14/16, 3 Finals, Average Qualifying Spot: 9, 1 DNQ's, Left First: 80%

2002: 10th-941 (-835), 12/21, Average Qualifying Spot: 9.85, 2 DNQ's, Left First: 77.4%

2001: 13th-824 (-1176), 11/17, Average Qualifying Spot: 11.1, 6 DNQ's, 1 By 3 Thousandths, 1 By 8 Thousandths, Left First: 37%

2000: 25th-165 (-1827), 1/4, Average Qualifying Spot: 13.7, 3 DNQ's, Left First: 40%

1999: 41st, 1 DNQ

1998: Division 7 Top Alcohol Funny Car Champion; Top 5 Nationally

1997: Division 5 Top Alcohol Funny Car Champion; Top 5 Nationally

1996: Finished 6th In Top Alcohol Dragster National Points

1994: 35th, 7 DNQ's, Moved To FC

1993: 43rd, 3 DNQ's

Bonus Facts: Has Run In 7 Different Classes In His Career, Made The First Gasoline Powered 200 MPH Run In Comp Eliminator, Tuned His Funny Car In 2000

Terry Haddock Date Of Birth: December 15, 1970 From: Temple, TX

Sponsor: Acme Refining Crew Chief: Terry Haddock Owner: Terry Haddock

Body: '09 Impala Engine: BAE 500

Pro Debut: FC: 1998 TF: 2008 Starts: 42 FC: 16 TF: 26

Consecutive Qualified Starts: TF: 0 FC: 1

Win Percentage In Final Round: 0% IHRA: FC: 66.6%

Average Career Qualifying Spot: 13.6 TF: 13.1 FC: 14.5

AT THE TREE:

Career Holeshot Win/Loss Record: 0/2 TF: 0/2 FC: 0/1

Career Left Firsts/Left On: 7/36 = 16.2% TF: 7/17 = 29.1% FC: 0/19 = 0%

STATS:

Championships: 0 IHRA: FC: 1

Career Best E.T./Speed: 1000ft.: TF: 3.899/306.05 FC: 4.276/296.24 1320ft.: FC: 4.840/313.88

Career Wins: IHRA: FC: 2

Career Finals: IHRA: FC: 3

Most Successful Event: Madison: 2/3 TF: Madison: 1/1 FC: Madison: 1/2

Elimination Round Win/Loss Record: 4/42 = 8.6% TF: 2/26 = 7.1% FC: 2/16 = 11.1%

Career # 1 Qualifiers: 0 IHRA: FC: 1

Top Five Finishes: 0 IHRA: FC: 3

Top Ten Point Finishes: 0 IHRA: 4 TF: 1 FC: 3

Career Best Points Finish: Countdown: TF: 12th-595 (-1976) FC: 24th-111 (-2429)

Pre-Countdown (2006 And Before): FC: 19th-224 (-1659)

YEARLY CAREER SUMMARY:

2012: 20th-41 (-556), 0/1, Average Qualifying Spot: 16, 1 DNQ, Left First: 0%

2011: 24th-111 (-2429), 0/1, Average Qualifying Spot: 14, 10 DNQ's, Left First: 0%

2010: TF: 15th-331 (-2353), 1/8, Average Qualifying Spot: 13.3, 6 DNQ's, Left First: 37.5% FC: 26th-40 (-2581), 4 DNQ's, FC Only In Following Seasons

2009: TF: 12th-595 (-1976), 1/18, Average Qualifying Spot: 13, 1 DNQ, Left First: 25% FC: 26th-41 (-2506), 0/1, Average Qualifying Spot: 16, 1 DNQ, Left First: 0%

2008: TF: 35th-10 (-2693), 1 DNQ FC: 27th-50 (-2511), 5 DNQ's

2007: 26th-60 (-3118), 6 DNQ's

2006: 21st-100 (-1536), 10 DNQ's

2005: 20th-202 (-1314), 1/2, Average Qualifying Spot: 16, 12 DNQ's, Left First: 0%

2004: 19th-224 (-1659), 0/4, Average Qualifying Spot: 14.2, 10 DNQ's, Left First: 0%

2003: 21st-244 (-1524), 1/4, Average Qualifying Spot: 15.2, 10 DNQ's, Left First: 0%

2002: 22nd-122 (-1654), 0/1, Average Qualifying Spot: 9, 9 DNQ's, Left First: 0%

2001: 23rd-110 (-1890), 11 DNQ's

2000: 26th-132 (-1860), 0/1, Average Qualifying Spot: 12, 10 DNQ's, Left First: 0%

1999: 27th, 0/1, Average Qualifying Spot: 15, 4 DNQ's, Left First: 0%

1998: 37th, 2 DNQ's

Matt Hagan Date Of Birth: November 18, 1982 From: Christiansburg, VA

Sponsor: Aaron's Crew Chief: Tommy Delago Assistant Crew Chief: Glen Huszar

Owner: Don Schumacher Body: '12 Dodge Charger Engine: Dodge 496

Pro Debut: FC: 2008 PM: 2006 Starts: 75 Consecutive Qualified Starts: 1

Win Percentage In Final Round: 45.4% IHRA: 75% FC: 100%

Average Career Qualifying Spot: 6.41

AT THE TREE:

Career Holeshot Win/Loss Record: 2/6 Career Left Firsts/Left On: 81/83 = 49.3%

Career Final Rounds Won/Lost On A Holeshot: 0/1

STATS:

Championships: 1

Career Best E.T./Speed: 1000ft.: 3.995/322.27

Career Wins: 5 IHRA: FC: 3

Career Finals: 11 IHRA: FC: 3 PM: 1

Last Win: 2011 Pomona-2

Last Final: 2011 Pomona-2

Most Successful Event: Concord-2: 8/2, 1 Win, 2 Finals

Elimination Round Win/Loss Record: 87/70 = 55.4%

Career # 1 Qualifiers: 10 IHRA: FC: 2

Career Provisional # 1 Qualifiers: 10

Top Five Finishes: 2, 2 Consecutive IHRA FC: 1

Top Ten Point Finishes: 2, 2 Consecutive IHRA: 2 FC: 1 PM: 1

Career Best Points Finish: Countdown: 1st-2540

Best/Worst Points Finish If Countdown Never Was: 2nd/3rd

YEARLY CAREER SUMMARY:

2012: 13th-202 (-395), 1/5, Average Qualifying Spot: 9, 1 DNQ, 1 By 6.22 MPH, Left First: 83.3%

2011: 1st-2540, 33/20, 2 Wins, 4 Finals, Average Qualifying Spot: 5.09, Qualified # 1 Four Times, Left First: 48%, Ran The Fastest Speed Ever To 1000 Feet At Reading, 322.27, (Missed Backing By 0.35 MPH) Tommy Delago Was The Crew Chief

2010: 2nd-2579 (-42), 37/20, 3 Wins, 5 Finals, Average Qualifying Spot: 5.39, Qualified # 1 Four Times, Left First: 61.4%

2009: 11th-1139 (-1408), 16/24, 2 Finals, Average Qualifying Spot: 7.66, Qualified # 1 Twice, Left First: 41%, Lost 4 Rounds On A Holeshot

2008: 25th-61 (-2500), 0/1, Average Qualifying Spot: 16, 3 DNQ's, Left First: 0%

Frank Hawley Date Of Birth: N/A, 1954 From: Gainesville, FL

Pro Debut: TF: 1988 FC: 1982 Starts: 1997-2011: 5 Consecutive Qualified Starts: FC: 4

Win Percentage In Final Round: 47.3% TF: 33.3% FC: 53.8%

Average Career Qualifying Spot: 1997-2011: 5.8

AT THE TREE: 1997-2011:

Career Holeshot Win/Loss Record: 0/1 Career Left Firsts/Left On: 0/8 = 0%

STATS:

Championships: 2 U.S. Nationals Wins/Finals: TF: 0/1

Career Best E.T./Speed: 1000ft.: 4.072/307.16 1320ft.: 4.849/321.04

Career Wins: 9 TF: 2 FC: 7

Career Finals: 19 TF: 6 FC: 13

Last Win: TF: 1990 Dallas FC: 1983 Denver

Last Final: TF: 1990 Indianapolis FC: 2008 Reading

Most Successful Event: 1997-2011: Reading: 3/1, 1 Final

Elimination Round Win/Loss Record: 1997-2011: 3/5 = 37.5%

Career # 1 Qualifiers: 7 TF: 3 FC: 4

Career Provisional # 1 Qualifiers: 1997-2011: 1

Top Five Finishes: 4 TF: 1 FC: 3

Top Ten Point Finishes: 5 TF: 2 FC: 3

Career Best Points Finish: Countdown: 20th-235 (-2326)

Pre-Countdown (2006 And Before): 1st-7446

YEARLY CAREER SUMMARY:

2008: 20th-235 (-2326), 3/5, 1 Final, Average Qualifying Spot: 5.8, Qualified # 1 Once, 1 DNQ, Left First: 0%

1991: 4th-9882 (-4506), Qualified # 1 Three Times, Including 2 Consecutive, FC Only Following Season

1990: 9th-8664 (-7394), 2 Wins, 4 Finals, Qualified # 1 Three Times

1989: 1 Final

1988: 1 Final

1984: 4th-6668 (-2220), 2 Finals, TF Only Following Seasons

1983: 1st-9935, 4 Wins, 5 Finals, Qualified # 1 Once

1982: 1st-7446, 3 Wins, 5 Finals, Qualified # 1 Twice

Jim Head Date Of Birth: September 5, 1948 From: Columbus, OH

Sponsor: Head Inc. Crew Chief: Jim Head Owner: Jim Head

Body: '08 Toyota Solara Engine: TFX 500

Pro Debut: FC: 1984 TF: 1980 Starts: 389 TF: 223 FC: 166

Consecutive Qualified Starts: TF: 17 FC: 1

Win Percentage In Final Round: 33.3% TF: 37.5% FC: 30% IHRA: 20% TF: 25%

Average Career Qualifying Spot: 1997-2011: 10.6 TF: 9.86 FC: 11.3

AT THE TREE: 1997-2011:

Career Holeshot Win/Loss Record: 7/9 TF: 5/2 FC: 2/7

Career Left Firsts/Left On: 160/148 = 51.9% TF: 90/52 = 63.3% FC: 70/96 = 42.1%

Career Final Rounds Won/Lost On A Holeshot: TF: 0/1

STATS:

U.S. Nationals Wins/Finals: 2/0 TF: 1/0 FC: 1/0, 1 Of Only 4 Drivers To Win In Both Classes

Career Best E.T./Speed: 1000ft.: FC: 4.077/311.20 1320ft.: TF: 4.532/331.20 FC: 4.759/326.87

Career Wins: 6 TF: 3 FC: 3 IHRA: TF: 2

Career Finals: 18 TF: 8 FC: 10 IHRA: 10 TF: 8 FC: 2

Last Win: TF: 1997 Memphis FC: 1985 Brainerd

Last Final: TF: 2003 Reading FC: 2009 Pomona-1

Most Successful Event: Elimination Record 1997-2011: Indianapolis: 80-83, 85-96: Unknown:

10/11, 2 Wins, 2 Finals TF: Memphis: 7/1, 1 Win, 2 Finals

FC: Bristol: 6/6,1 Win, 1 Final, 2 DNQ's

Elimination Round Win/Loss Record: 216/383 = 36%

TF: 117/220 = 34.7% FC: 99/163 = 37.7%

Career # 1 Qualifiers: 2 TF: 1 FC: 1

Career Provisional # 1 Qualifiers: 1997-2011: 5 TF: 4 FC: 1

Top Five Finishes: 0 IHRA: 3 TF: 2 FC: 1

Top Ten Point Finishes: 7 TF: 2 FC: 5 IHRA: 6 TF: 5 FC: 1

Career Best Points Finish: Countdown: FC: 8th-2621

Pre-Countdown (2006 And Before): TF: 8th-1083 (-698) FC: 6th-5990 (-2898)

Best/Worst Points Finish If Countdown Never Was: 9th

YEARLY CAREER SUMMARY:

2012: 18th-154 (-443), 1/2, Average Qualifying Spot: 7.66, 3 DNQ's, Left First: 50%

2011: 14th-640 (-1900), 5/15, Average Qualifying Spot: 10.2, 2 DNQ's, Left First: 15%

2010: 14th-724 (-1897), 9/17, Average Qualifying Spot: 11.8, Left First: 48%

2009: 15th-662 (-1885), 5/17, 1 Final, Average Qualifying Spot: 11.1, Left First: 37.5%

2008: 17th-606 (-1955), 7/13, Average Qualifying Spot: 10, Qualified # 1 Once, 4 DNQ's, 1 By 9 Thousandths, Left First: 50%

2007: 8th-2163 (-1015), 16/19, 1 Final, Average Qualifying Spot: 11.1, 4 DNQ's, 1 By 1 Thousandth, Left First: 39.3%

2006: 17th-673 (-963), 7/16, Average Qualifying Spot: 11.1, 2 DNQ's, Left First: 40.9%

2005: 18th-336 (-1180), 2/6, Average Qualifying Spot: 14.3, 11 DNQ's, Left First: 62.5%

2004: 17th-402 (-1481), 0/10, Average Qualifying Spot: 14.4, 9 DNQ's, 1 By A Thousandth, Left First: 70%, Return To FC

2003: 12th-802 (-1192), 14/16, 1 Final, Average Qualifying Spot: 9.37, Left First: 57.1%

2002: 17th-314 (-1637), 2/8, Average Qualifying Spot: 10.8, 2 DNQ's, Left First: 40%

1999: 12th, 12/22, 1 Final, Average Qualifying Spot: 11.7, Left First: 80.6%, Won Blaine Johnson Award

1998: 8th-1083 (-698), 21/21, 2 Finals, Average Qualifying Spot: 8.42, 2 DNQ's, Left First: 58.5%

1997: 9th-955 (-882), 17/17, 2 Wins, 2 Finals, Average Qualifying Spot: 8.21, 4 DNQ's, Left First: 65.6%

1996: 11th, 11/16, 1 Win, 1 Final, 1 DNQ

1995: 13th, 5/18, 1 DNQ

1994: 13th, 3/16, 2 DNQ's

1993: 12th, 8/16, Qualified # 1 Once, 2 DNQ's

1992: 13th, 5/10, 1 Final, 5 DNQ's

1991: 11th, 2/17, 1 DNQ

1990: 12th, 3/16, 2 DNQ's

1989: 12th, 7/13, 5 DNQ's

1988: TF: 22nd, 1/4, 1 DNQ FC: 14th, 9/9, 1 Final, 1 DNQ, TF Only In Following Seasons

1987: 9th-5442 (-7246), 8/10, 1 Final, 4 DNQ's

1986: 8th-5932 (-6854), 9/12, 2 Finals, 1 DNQ
1985: 9th-6014 (-6638), 11/9, 2 Wins, 2 Finals, 1 DNQ
1984: 6th-5990 (-2898), 10/8, 1 Win, 2 Finals
1983: 17th, 1/3, 3 DNQ's, FC Only In Following Seasons
1982: 15th, 1/4, 1 DNQ
1981: 15th, 1/2, 3 DNQ's
1980: 30th, 3/1

Leif Helander Date Of Birth: 1944 From: Sweden
Pro Debut: 2009 Starts: 1 Consecutive Qualified Starts: 0
Average Career Qualifying Spot: 16

AT THE TREE:

Career Left Firsts/Left On: 0/1 = 0%

STATS:

Career Best E.T./Speed: 1000ft.: 4.813/208.42
Most Successful Event: Dallas: 0/1 Elimination Round Win/Loss Record: 0/1 = 0%
Career Best Points Finish: Countdown: 27th-41 (-2506)

YEARLY CAREER SUMMARY:

2009: 27th-41, 0/1, Average Qualifying Spot: 16, 1 DNQ, Left First: 0%

Al Hofmann Date Of Birth: November 28, 1947 From: Eustis, FL

Died 2008—Heart Attack

Pro Debut: 1991 Starts: 1997-2011: 94 Consecutive Qualified Starts: 5

Win Percentage In Final Round: 46.8% Average Career Qualifying Spot: 1997-2011: 10.7

AT THE TREE: 1997-2011:

Career Holeshot Win/Loss Record: 4/2 Career Left Firsts/Left On: 54/79 = 40.6%

STATS:

U.S. Nationals Wins/Finals: 0/1

Career Best E.T./Speed: 1320ft.: 4.855/317.46

Career Wins: 15

Career Finals: 32

Last Win: 1998 Memphis

Last Final: 2001 Bristol

Most Successful Event: 1997-2011: Memphis: 8/4, 1 Win, 1 Final

Elimination Round Win/Loss Record: 55/91 = 37.6%

Career # 1 Qualifiers: 8

Career Provisional # 1 Qualifiers: 1997-2011: 2

Top Five Finishes: 5

Top Ten Point Finishes: 7

Career Best Points Finish: 2nd-1508 (-182)

YEARLY CAREER SUMMARY:

2002: 23rd-115 (-1661), 1/3, Average Qualifying Spot: 11, Left First: 25%

2001: 16th-699 (-1301), 7/15, 1 Final, Average Qualifying Spot: 13.8, 9 DNQ's, 1 By 6 Thousandths, 1 By 1 Thousandth, Left First: 23.8%

2000: 13th-832 (-1160), 7/21, Average Qualifying Spot: 11.1, 2 DNQ's, Left First: 50%

1999: 6/20, Average Qualifying Spot: 11.8, 2 DNQ's, Left First: 62.5%

1998: 9th-1044 (-619), 20/18, 1 Win, 3 Finals, Average Qualifying Spot: 7.63, Qualified # 1 Twice, Including 2 Consecutive, 4 DNQ's, Left First: 22.5%

1997: 14/14, 2 Wins, 3 Finals, Average Qualifying Spot: 9.68, 2 DNQ's, Left First: 48.1%

1996: 4th-1122 (-901), 1 Win, Including 2 Consecutive Between Seasons, 2 Finals, Qualified # 1 Once

1995: 2nd-1508 (-182), 5 Wins, Including 2 Consecutive, 7 Finals, Including 4 Consecutive, Qualified # 1 Twice

1994: 3rd-11496 (-5280), 1 Win, 5 Finals, Qualified # 1 Once

1993: 4th-11496 (-6578), 4 Finals, Qualified # 1 Once

1992: 3rd-12510 (-2736), 3 Wins, Including 2 Consecutive, 5 Finals, Qualified # 1 Once

1991: 7th-9956 (-5582), 2 Wins, Including 2 Consecutive, 2 Finals

Robert Hight Date Of Birth: August 20, 1969 From: Anaheim Hills, CA
Sponsor: Auto Club Of Southern California Crew Chief: Jimmy Prock
Assistant Crew Chief: Eric Lane Owner: John Force

Body: '12 Ford Mustang Engine: Ford 500

Pro Debut: 2005 Starts: 161 Consecutive Qualified Starts: 29

Win Percentage In Final Round: 65.8% Average Career Qualifying Spot: 4.7

AT THE TREE:

Career Holeshot Win/Loss Record: 6/4 Career Left Firsts/Left On: 171/181 = 48.5%

Career Final Rounds Won/Lost On A Holeshot: 2/1

STATS:

Championships: 1 U.S. Nationals Wins/Finals: 2/4, Including 4 Consecutive Finals

Career Best E.T./Speed: 1000ft.: 4.005/320.81 1320ft.: 4.636/333.08

Career Wins: 27

Career Finals: 41

Last Win: 2012 Las Vegas-1

Last Final: 2012 Las Vegas-1

Most Successful Event: Pomona-1: 17/5, 3 Wins, 4 Finals

Elimination Round Win/Loss Record: 237/134 = 63.8%

Career # 1 Qualifiers: 42

Career Provisional # 1 Qualifiers: 44

Top Five Point Finishes: 6

Top Ten Point Finishes: 7 Consecutive

Career Best Points Finish: Countdown: 1st-2547

Pre-Countdown (2006 And Before): 2nd-1524 (-112)

Best/Worst Points Finish If Countdown Never Was: 1st/5th

YEARLY CAREER SUMMARY:

2012: 1st-597, 17/2, 4 Wins, Including 4 Consecutive, 4 Finals, Average Qualifying Spot: 3.33, Qualified # 1 Three Times, Including 2 Consecutive, Left First: 61.1%

2011: 4th-2447 (-93), 28/17, 5 Wins, 6 Finals, Average Qualifying Spot: 5.95, Qualified # 1 Once, Left First: 63.8%

2010: 8th-2277 (-344), 29/18, 4 Wins, Including 3 Consecutive, 5 Finals, Including 4 Consecutive, Average Qualifying Spot: 4.27, Qualified # 1 Six Times, Including 3 Consecutive, 1 DNQ, Left First: 41.4%

2009: 1st-2547, 30/19, 3 Wins, Including 2 Consecutive, 4 Finals, Including 3 Consecutive, Average Qualifying Spot: 6.09, Qualified # 1 Four Times, Including 2 Consecutive, 2 DNQ's, Left First: 51%, Qualified For The Countdown In 10th Place At The Very Last Pre-Countdown Race

2008: 4th-2442 (-119), 36/20, 3 Wins, 6 Finals, Including 2 Consecutive, Average Qualifying Spot: 5.86, Qualified # 1 Five Times, 1 DNQ, Left First: 52.8%, 3 Consecutive Finals Between 2008 And 2007 Seasons

2007: 2nd-3159 (-19), 34/17, 3 Wins, Including 2 Consecutive, 6 Finals, Including 2 Consecutive Twice, Average Qualifying Spot: 4.15, Qualified # 1 Eight Times, Including 2 Consecutive Twice, 2 DNQ's, Left First: 54.3%, Ran The Quickest E.T. Ever At 4.636 (Missed Backing Nationally By Just Over A Tenth Of A Second, 4.783), 4.636 Run Was Also The Quickest Run To 1000ft. At A 3.955, Still A Mark Left To Be Matched In The 1000ft. Era, Lost Championship By Smallest Points Difference In Class History Under The Countdown Points Format, Jimmy Prock Was The Crew Chief

2006: 2nd-1524 (-112), 35/20, 3 Wins, 6 Finals, Including 3 Consecutive, Average Qualifying Spot: 3.08, Qualified # 1 Nine Times, Including 2 Consecutive Twice, Left First: 45%

2005: 5th-1379 (-137), 28/21, 2 Wins, 4 Finals, Including 2 Consecutive, Average Qualifying Spot: 3.86, Qualified # 1 Six Times, Including 2 Consecutive Twice, Left First: 26.5%, Won Auto Club Road To The Future Award

Tommy Johnson Jr. Date Of Birth: April 6, 1968 From: Avon, IN

Pro Debut: FC: 1999 TF: 1989 Starts: 1997-2011: 189 FC: 183 TF: 6

Consecutive Qualified Starts: 1997-2011: TF: 6 FC: 0

Win Percentage In Final Round: 1997-2011: 37% TF: 40% FC: 41.1% TAD: 33.3%

IHRA: 50% TF: 50% AFC: 50%

Average Career Qualifying Spot: 1997-2011: 8.08 TF: 11 FC: 7.98

AT THE TREE: 1997-2011:

Career Holeshot Win/Loss Record: FC: 15/12

Career Left Firsts/Left On: 198/125 = 61.3% TF: 4/3 = 57.1% FC: 194/122 = 61.3%

Career Final Rounds Won/Lost On A Holeshot: FC: 0/3

STATS:

U.S. Nationals Wins/Finals: 0/1

Career Best E.T./Speed: 1000ft.: FC: 4.070/305.49 1320ft.: TF: 4.663/315.71 FC: 4.672/331.45

Career Wins: 10 TF: 2 FC: 7 TAD: 1 IHRA: 5 TF: 4 AFC: 1

Career Finals: 27 TF: 5 FC: 17 TAD: 3 Sportsman: 2 IHRA: 10 TF: 8 AFC: 2

Last Win: TF: 1994 Memphis FC: 2007 Englishtown

Last Final: TF: 1995 Brainerd FC: 2007 Englishtown

Most Successful Event: 1997-2011: TF: Topeka-1: 1/1 FC: Englishtown: 12/7, 1 Win, 1 Final

Elimination Round Win/Loss Record: 1997-2011: 158/182 = 46.4%

TF: 1/6 = 14.2% 157/176 = 47.1%

Career # 1 Qualifiers: 9 TF: 1 FC: 8

Career Provisional # 1 Qualifiers: 1997-2011: 11 TF: 1 FC: 10

Top Five Finishes: 0 IHRA: TF: 1

Top Ten Point Finishes: FC: 6 IHRA: TF: 3 AFC: 1

Career Best Points Finish: Countdown: 13th-916 (-2262)

Pre-Countdown (2006 And Before): TF: 8th-859 (-716) FC: 6th-1322 (-314)

YEARLY CAREER SUMMARY:

2008: 18th-578 (-1983), 4/12, Average Qualifying Spot: 10.4, 12 DNQ's, Left First: 62.5%

2007: 13th-916 (-2262), 12/18, 1 Win, 1 Final, Average Qualifying Spot: 7.94, Qualified # 1 Twice, 4 DNQ's, 1 By 7 Thousandths, Left First: 53.5%

2006: 6th-1322 (-314), 27/21, 2 Wins, 3 Finals, Average Qualifying Spot: 6.69, Qualified # 1 Twice, Left First: 65.9%, Won 4 Rounds On A Holeshot

2005: 6th-1294 (-222), 26/22, 1 Win, 2 Finals, Average Qualifying Spot: 7, Left First: 76%

2004: 11th-888 (-995), 9/21, Average Qualifying Spot: 9.19, 2 DNQ's, Left First: 53.5%

2003: 9th-1051 (-717), 15/23, 1 Final, Average Qualifying Spot: 7.82, Left First: 40%

2002: 7th-1129 (-647), My Points Do Not Match NHRA—Unknown Reason, 23/20, 4 Finals, Including 2 Consecutive, Average

Qualifying Spot: 11, 3 DNQ's, Left First: 60.4%, Won 5 Rounds On A Holeshot

2001: 10th-1127 (-873), 18/21, 1 Win, 2 Finals, Average Qualifying Spot: 6.18, Qualified # 1 Once, 2 DNQ's, Left First: 71%

2000: 18th-305 (-1697), 2/7, Average Qualifying Spot: 12.4, Qualified # 1 Once, 3 DNQ's, Left First: 77.7%

1999: 10th-881 (-1190), 21/11, 2 Wins, 4 Finals, Including 4 Consecutive, Average Qualifying Spot: 4.15, Qualified # 1 Twice, Left First: 55.1%, Ran 13 Of 22 Events And Still Finished In The Top Ten

1997: 1/6, Average Qualifying Spot: 11, Left First: 57.1%

1995: 8th-859 (-716), 1 Final

1994: 9th-8414 (-5186), 1 Win, 1 Final, Qualified # 1 Once

1993: 10th-8196 (-4602), 1 Win, 2 Finals

1991: 1 Final

Scott Kalitta Date Of Birth: February 18, 1962 From: Ypsilanti, MI

Died In 2008—Racing Accident Pro Debut: FC: 1986 TF: 1982

Starts: 1997-2012: 121 FC: 39 TF: 82 Consecutive Qualified Starts: TF: FC: 2

Win Percentage In Final Round: 50% TF: 50% FC: 50%

Average Career Qualifying Spot: 1997-2012: 7.5 TF: 6.26 FC: 10.1

AT THE TREE 1997-2012:

Career Holeshot Win/Loss Record: 5/3 TF: 4/3 FC: 1/0

Career Left Firsts/Left On: 101/115 = 46.7% TF: 88/76 = 53.6% FC: 13/39 = 25%

Career Final Rounds Won/Lost On A Holeshot: TF: 0/1

STATS:

Championships: 2 TF: 2

Career Best E.T./Speed: 1320ft.: TF: 4.455/333.95 FC: 4.726/325.69

Career Wins: 18 TF: 17 FC: 1

Career Finals: 36 TF: 34 FC: 2 IHRA: FC: 2

Last Win: TF: 2005 Chicago FC: 1989 Houston

Last Final: TF: 2005 Chicago FC: 2008 Chicago

Most Successful Event: 1997-2012: Dallas: 10/6, 2 Finals, 1 DNQ

TF: Dallas: 10/5, 2 Finals FC: Chicago: 3/2, 1 Final, 1 DNQ

Elimination Round Win/Loss Record: 1997-2012: 112/117 = 48.9%

TF: 97/78 = 55.4% FC: 15/39 = 27.7%

Career # 1 Qualifiers: TF: 20

Career Provisional # 1 Qualifiers: 1997-2012: 6 TF: 4 FC: 2

Top Five Finishes: TF: 6 IHRA: TF: 1 FC: 2

Top Ten Point Finishes: 10 TF: 8 FC: 2 IHRA: TF: 1 FC: 3

Career Best Points Finish: Countdown: 18th-668 (-2250)

Pre-Countdown (2006 And Before): TF: 1st-1575 FC: 9th-7764

YEARLY CAREER SUMMARY:

2008: 19th-311 (-2250), 4/6, 1 Final, Average Qualifying Spot: 11.3, 5 DNQ's, Left First: 11.1%

2007: 18th-668 (-2510), 4/16, Average Qualifying Spot: 8.93, 7 DNQ's, 1 By 15.46 MPH, Left First: 36.8%

2006: 15th-748 (-888), 7/17, Average Qualifying Spot: 10.7, 6 DNQ's, Left First: 20.8%

2005: 8th-1142 (-839), 19/21, 2 Wins, 2 Finals, Average Qualifying Spot: 7.82, Left First: 40.5%

2004: 4th-1440 (-554), 32/22, 1 Win, 2 Finals, Average Qualifying Spot: 5.13, Qualified # 1 Twice, Left First: 51.9%

2003: 17th-459 (-1535), 11/7, 2 Finals, Average Qualifying Spot: 5.71, Left First: 43.7%

2000: 35th-32 (-1858), 0/1, Average Qualifying Spot: 9, Left First: 0%

1999: 6/7, Average Qualifying Spot: 4.85, Qualified # 1 Once, 2 DNQ's, Left First: 33.3%

1997: 4th-1301 (-536), 29/20, 1 Win, 2 Finals, Average Qualifying Spot: 6.33, Qualified # 1 Once, 2 DNQ's, Left First: 76%

1996: 2nd-1197 (-218), 1 Win, 2 Finals, 5 Finals, Qualified # 1 Twice, Including 2 Consecutive

1995: 1st-1575, 6 Wins, Including 3 Consecutive Twice, 7 Finals, Qualified # 1 Three Times

1994: 1st-13600, 5 Wins, Including 4 Consecutive, 9 Finals, Including 6 Consecutive Then 2 Consecutive, Qualified # 1 Three Times

1993: 2nd-11542 (-1256), 1 Win, 3 Finals, Including 2 Consecutive, Qualified # 1 Seven Times, Including 3 Consecutive

1990: 9th-6538 (-9026), Following Seasons TF

1989: 9th-7764 (-8374), 1 Win, 1 Final

1988: Qualified # 1 Once

1983: 10th-4141 (-6789), Following Seasons FC

Andy Kelley Date Of Birth: 1973 From: Piedmont, SC

Pro Debut: 2006 Starts: 1 Consecutive Qualified Starts: 0

Win Percentage In Final Round: 0% IHRA: FC: 50%

Average Career Qualifying Spot: 16

AT THE TREE:

Career Left Firsts/Left On: 1/0 = 100%

STATS:

Career Best E.T./Speed: 1000ft.: 4.292/282.54 1320ft.: 5.191/255.63
Career Wins: 0 IHRA: FC: 2
Career Finals: 0 IHRA: FC: 4
Most Successful Event: Bristol: 0/1
Elimination Round Win/Loss Record: 0/1 = 0%
Top Five Point Finishes: 0 IHRA: FC: 2
Top Ten Point Finishes: 0 IHRA: FC: 3
Career Best Points Finish: Countdown: 24th-51 (-2496)
Pre-Countdown (2006 And Before): 37th-10 (-1626)

YEARLY CAREER SUMMARY:

2009: 24th-51 (-2496), 0/1, Average Qualifying Spot: 16, 2 DNQ's, Left First:

2006: 37th-10 (-1626), 1 DNQ

2001: Finished 10th In The Division 2 Top Alcohol Funny Car Points, 77th Nationally

John Lawson Date Of Birth: June 6, 1957 From: Joliet, IL
Pro Debut: 2000 Starts: 17 Consecutive Qualified Starts: 0
Win Percentage In Final Round: 60% TAFC: 60% Average Career Qualifying Spot: 13.2

AT THE TREE:

Career Holeshot Win/Loss Record: 0/1 Career Left Firsts/Left On: 6/12 = 33.3%

STATS:

Career Best E.T./Speed: 1000ft.: 4.299/282.90 1320ft.: 4.854/316.08

Career Wins: 3 TAFC: 3

Career Finals: 5 TAFC: 5 IHRA: PFC: 1

Most Successful Event: Chicago-1: 3/4, 5 DNQ's

Elimination Round Win/Loss Record: 7/17 = 29.1%

Career # 1 Qualifiers: 1 TAFC: 1

Career Provisional # 1 Qualifiers: 3 TAFC: 2

Top Ten Point Finishes: 0 IHRA: PFC: 1

Career Best Points Finish: Countdown: 31st-20 (-3158)

Pre-Countdown (2006 And Before): 19th-354 (-1422)

YEARLY CAREER SUMMARY:

2009: 32nd-10 (-2537), 1 DNQ

2007: 31st-20 (-3158), 2 DNQ's

2006: 29th-20 (-1616), 2 DNQ's

2005: 26th-40 (-1476), 4 DNQ's

2004: 29th-20 (-1863), 2 DNQ's

2003: 24th-102 (-1616), 2/2, Average Qualifying Spot: 15.5, Left First: 25%

2002: 19th-354 (-1422), 3/8, Average Qualifying Spot: 12.2, 3 DNQ's, Left First: 30%

2001: 20th-305 (-1695), 1/3, Average Qualifying Spot: 12.3, 17 DNQ's, Left First:

2000: 24th-174 (-1818), 1/4, Average Qualifying Spot: 14.7, 5 DNQ's, Left First: 50%

1999: Finished 2nd In The Division 3 Top Alcohol Funny Car Points

Cory Lee Date Of Birth: November 13, 1959 From: Sierra Del Oro, CA

Pro Debut: 1996? Starts: 44 Consecutive Qualified Starts: 1

Average Career Qualifying Spot: 11.5

AT THE TREE: 1997-2011:

Career Holeshot Win/Loss Record: 2/0 Career Left Firsts/Left On: 23/36 = 38.9%

STATS:

Career Best E.T./Speed: 1000ft: 6.021/119.05 1320ft.: 4.822/321.27

Career Finals: 2 IHRA: FC: 1 Last Final: 2003 Pomona-2

Most Successful Event: 1997-2011: Gainesville: 5/2, 1 Final

Elimination Round Win/Loss Record: 1997-2011: 29/44 = 39.7%

Career Provisional # 1 Qualifiers: 0 IHRA: FC: 1

Top Ten Point Finishes: 0 IHRA: FC: 1

Career Best Points Finish: Countdown: 29th-31 (-2516)

Pre-Countdown (2006 And Before): 12th-N/A (-N/A)

YEARLY CAREER SUMMARY:

2011: 35th-10 (-2530), 1 DNQ

2009: 29th-31 (-2516), 0/1, Average Qualifying Spot: 14, Left First: 0%

2005: 33rd-10 (-1506), 1 DNQ

2004: 21st-154 (-1729), 3/2, Average Qualifying Spot: 11, 3 DNQ's, Left First: 0%

2003: 19th-287 (-1481), 5/5, 1 Final, Average Qualifying Spot: 13.2, 3 DNQ's, Left First: 25%

2002: 21st-125 (-1651), 1/3, Average Qualifying Spot: 12.6, 1 DNQ, Left First: 25%

2000: 22nd-228 (-1764), 0/5, Average Qualifying Spot: 12, 7 DNQ's, Left First: 60%

1999: 12th, 13/17, 1 Final, Average Qualifying Spot: 11.3, 5 DNQ's, 1 By 9 Thousandths, Left First: 44.4%

1998: 6/8, Average Qualifying Spot: 9.62, 1 DNQ, Left First: 50%

1997: 1/3, Average Qualifying Spot: 12.3, 3 DNQ's, Left First: 0%

Paul Lee Date Of Birth: September 16, 1957 From: Anaheim Hills, CA

Pro Debut: 2005 Starts: 37 Consecutive Qualified Starts: 0

Win Percentage In Final Round: 75% TAFC: 75% IHRA: FC: 14.2%

Average Career Qualifying Spot: 12.7

AT THE TREE:

Career Left Firsts/Left On: 18/24 = 42.8%

STATS:

Career Best E.T./Speed: 1000ft.: 4.089/309.49 1320ft.: 4.863/318.17

Career Wins: 3 TAFC: 3 IHRA: FC: 1

Career Finals: 4 TAFC: 4 IHRA: FC: 7

Most Successful Event: Tied With 5 Tracks He Got A Round Win: 1/0

Elimination Round Win/Loss Record: 9/37 = 19.5%

Career # 1 Qualifiers: 0 IHRA: FC: 1

Top Five Point Finishes: 0 IHRA: FC: 1

Top Ten Point Finishes: 1 TAFC: 1 IHRA: FC: 3

Career Best Points Finish: Countdown: 13th-767 (-1854)

Pre-Countdown (2006 And Before): 26th-40 (-1476)

YEARLY CAREER SUMMARY:

2011: 13th-650 (-1890), 3/18, Average Qualifying Spot: 12.8, 4 DNQ's, Left First: 50%

2010: 13th-767 (-1854), 6/19, Average Qualifying Spot: 12.6, 4 DNQ's, Left First: 36.3%

2006: 25th-60 (-1576), 6 DNQ's, Including 1 By 6 Thousandths

2005: 26th-40 (-1476), 4 DNQ's

2004: Finished 4th In The Division 3 Top Alcohol Funny Car Points, 10th Nationally

2003: Finished 4th In The Division 2 Top Alcohol Funny Car Points, 17th Nationally

2002: Finished 4th In The Division 1 Top Alcohol Funny Car Points, 22nd Nationally

2001: Finished 4th In The Division 1 Top Alcohol Funny Car Points, 41st Nationally

Todd Lesenko Date Of Birth: February 22, 1963 From: Alberta, Canada

Sponsor: Tap It Brewing Crew Chief: Jim Dunn

Owner: Jim Dunn Body: '12 Chevrolet Impala Engine: BAE 500

Pro Debut: 2011 Starts: 5 Consecutive Qualified Starts: 0

Win Percentage In Final Round: 0% IHRA: PFC: 50% Average Career Qualifying Spot: 13.8

AT THE TREE:

Career Left Firsts/Left On: 3/3 = 50%

STATS:

Career Best E.T./Speed: 1000ft.: 4.168/298.60

Career Wins: 0 IHRA: PFC: 1

Career Finals: 0 IHRA: PFC: 2

Most Successful Event: Pomona-1: 1/1

Elimination Round Win/Loss Record: 2/5 = 28.5%

Career Best Points Finish: Countdown: 26th-73 (-2467)

YEARLY CAREER SUMMARY:

2012: 16th-163 (-434), 2/3, Average Qualifying Spot: 14, 3 DNQ's, Left First: 25%

2011: 26th-73 (-2467), 0/2, Average Qualifying Spot: 13.5, 1 DNQ, Left First: 100%

Eric Medlen Date Of Birth: August 13, 1973 From: Indianapolis, IN

Died In 2007—Testing Accident Pro Debut: 2004 Starts: 72 Consecutive Qualified Starts: 72

Win Percentage In Final Round: 66.6% Average Career Qualifying Spot: 4.98

AT THE TREE:

Career Holeshot Win/Loss Record: 5/9 Career Left Firsts/Left On: 64/93 = 40.7%

Career Final Rounds Won/Lost On A Holeshot: 1/0

STATS:

Career Best E.T./Speed: 1320ft.: 4.681/328.54

Career Wins: 6

Career Finals: 9

Last Win: 2006 Virginia

Last Final: 2006 Virginia

Most Successful Event: Brainerd: 9/1, 2 Wins, 2 Finals, Including 2 Consecutive

Elimination Round Win/Loss Record: 95/66 = 59%

Career # 1 Qualifiers: 7

Career Provisional # 1 Qualifiers: 9

Top Five Point Finishes: 3

Top Ten Point Finishes: 3

Career Best Points Finish: Countdown: 22nd-159 (-3019)

Pre-Countdown (2006 And Before): 4th-1411 (-105)

YEARLY CAREER SUMMARY:

2007: 22nd-159 (-3019), 3/3, Average Qualifying Spot: 7.66, Left First: 83.3%

2006: 4th-1407 (-229), 32/21, 2 Wins, 2 Finals, Average Qualifying Spot: 4.08, Qualified # 1 Three Times, Left First: 49%

2005: 4th-1411 (-105), 31/20, 3 Wins, Including 2 Consecutive, 5 Finals, Average Qualifying Spot: 5.26, Qualified # 1 Twice, Left First: 34%

2004: 5th-1375 (-508), 29/22, 1 Win, 2 Finals, Average Qualifying Spot: 5.26, Qualified # 1 Twice, Left First: 34%, Lost 4 Rounds On A Holeshot

2002: Finished 18th In The Division 7 Top Alcohol Dragster Points, 127th Nationally

Mike Neff Date Of Birth: September 16, 1966 From: Indianapolis, IN

Sponsor: Castrol GTX Crew Chief: Mike Neff/Bernie Fedderly

Assistant Crew Chief: Jon Schaffer Owner: John Force

Body: '12 Ford Mustang Engine: Ford 500

Pro Debut: 2007 Starts: 76 Consecutive Qualified Starts: 56

Win Percentage In Final Round: 38.8% Average Career Qualifying Spot: 6.1

AT THE TREE:

Career Holeshot Win/Loss Record: 3/9 Career Left Firsts/Left On: 62/93 = 40%

Career Final Rounds Won/Lost On A Holeshot: 0/1

STATS:

U.S. Nationals Wins/Finals: 1/1

Career Best E.T./Speed: 1000ft.: 4.036/316.97 1320ft.: 4.783/326.40

Career Wins: 7

Career Finals: 18

Last Win: 2012 Houston

Last Final: 2012 Houston

Most Successful Event: Englishtown: 8/2, 1 Win, 2 Finals

Elimination Round Win/Loss Record: 95/69 = 57.9%

Career # 1 Qualifiers: 5

Career Provisional # 1 Qualifiers: 6

Top Five Point Finishes: 2

Top Ten Point Finishes: 4

Career Best Points Finish: Countdown: 5th-2123 (-2416)

Best/Worst Points Finish If Countdown Never Was: 1st/10th

YEARLY CAREER SUMMARY:

2012: 2nd-489 (-108), 13/5, 1 Win, 3 Finals, Average Qualifying Spot: 4.83, Left First: 47%

2011: 5th-2440 (-100), 40/17, 5 Wins, Including 2 Consecutive, 9 Finals, Including 4 Consecutive, Average Qualifying Spot: 4.86, Qualified # 1 Once, Left First: 30.1%, Lost 4 Rounds On A Holeshot

2009: 10th-2235 (-312), 22/23, 1 Win, 3 Finals, Average Qualifying Spot: 6.41, Qualified # 1 Twice, Left First: 50%

2008: 9th-2284 (-277), 20/22, 3 Finals, Including 2 Consecutive, Average Qualifying Spot: 7.13, Qualified # 1 Twice, 2 DNQ's, Left First: 41.4%

2007: 25th-65 (-3113), 0/2, Average Qualifying Spot: 8.5, Left First: 0%

Mark Oswald Date Of Birth: N/A From: Houma, LA

Pro Debut: FC: 1983 TF: 1981 Starts: 1997-2011: 21 Consecutive Qualified Starts: 19

Win Percentage In Final Round: 50% TF: 66.6% FC: 47.3%

IHRA: 54.2% TF: 44.4% FC: 57.6% Average Career Qualifying Spot: 1997-2011: 10

AT THE TREE: 1997-2011:

Career Holeshot Win/Loss Record: 1/0 Career Left Firsts/Left On: 5/24 = 17.2%

STATS:

Championships: 1 FC: 1 IHRA: FC: 3
Career Best E.T./Speed: 1320ft.: TF: 5.618/257.14 FC: 4.757/328.46
Career Wins: 20 TF: 2 FC: 18 IHRA: 19 TF: 4 FC: 15
Career Finals: 41 TF: 3 FC: 38 IHRA: 35 TF: 9 FC: 26
Last Win: TF: 1982 Englishtown FC: 1994 Englishtown
Last Final: TF: 1982 Englishtown FC: 1997 Gainesville
Most Successful Event: 1997-2011: Gainesville: 3/1, 1 Final
Elimination Round Win/Loss Record: 1997-2011: 10/20 = 33.3%
Career # 1 Qualifiers: 18 TF: 1 FC: 17
Top Five Finishes: FC: 8 IHRA: 9 TF: 3 FC: 6
Top Ten Point Finishes: FC: 10 IHRA: 9 TF: 3 FC: 6
Career Best Points Finish: Countdown: 26th-57 (-2504)
Pre-Countdown (2006 And Before): TF: N/A FC: 1st-8888

YEARLY CAREER SUMMARY:

2008: 26th-57 (-2504), 1/1, Average Qualifying Spot: 2, Left First: 0%

1997: 10/20, 1 Final, Average Qualifying Spot: 10.5, 2 DNQ's, Left First: 18.5%

1996: 6th-934, 1 Final

1995: 1 Final, Qualified # 1 Once

1994: 1 Win, 1 Final

1992: 7th-7986 (-7260), 1 Final, Qualified # 1 Once

1991: 5th-11172 (-4366), 2 Wins, 5 Finals

1990: 4th-12956 (-2608), 3 Wins, 5 Finals

1989: 4th-12390 (-3748), 1 Win, 6 Finals, Qualified # 1 Three Times, Including 2 Consecutive

1988: 2nd-11710 (-652), 2 Wins, 4 Finals

1987: 2nd-9846 (-2842), 2 Wins, 3 Finals, Qualified # 1 Four Times, Including 2 Consecutive, Won IHRA Funny Car Championship

1986: 2nd-10510 (-2276), 3 Wins, 3 Finals, Qualified # 1 Three Times, Including 3 Consecutive, Won IHRA Funny Car Championship

1984: 1st-8888, 2 Wins, 3 Finals, Qualified # 1 Twice, Won IHRA Funny Car Championship

1983: 2nd-8148 (-1787), 2 Wins, 4 Finals, Including 2 Consecutive, Qualified # 1 Three Times, Won IHRA Funny Car Championship

1982: 2 Wins, 2 Finals, Qualified # 1 Once, Following Seasons FC Only

1981: 1 Final

Bonus Facts: Current Co-Crew Chief For Antron Brown

Cruz Pedregon Date Of Birth: September 19, 1963 From: Brownsburg, IN

Sponsor: Snap-On Tools Crew Chief: Lee Beard Owner: Cruz Pedregon

Body: '10 Toyota Camry Engine: TFX 500

Pro Debut: FC: 1992 TF: 1991 Starts: 373 TF: 10 FC: 363

Consecutive Qualified Starts: FC: 4

Win Percentage In Final Round: 44.7% FC: 44.7 TAD: 100% TAFC: 50%

Average Career Qualifying Spot: 1997-2012: FC: 7.52

AT THE TREE: 1997-2012:

Career Holeshot Win/Loss Record: 14/14 Career Left Firsts/Left On: 266/213 = 55.5%

Career Final Rounds Won/Lost On A Holeshot: 1/2

STATS:

Championships: 2 FC: 2 U.S. Nationals Wins/Finals: FC: 3/4, Including 2 Consecutive Wins

Career Best E.T./Speed: 1000ft.: FC: 4.015/316.75 1320ft.: TF: 4.968/289.01 FC: 4.680/330.80

Career Wins: 34 FC: 30 TAD: 3 TAFC: 1

Career Finals: 72 FC: 67 TAD: 3 TAFC: 2

Last Win: FC: 2011 Dallas

Last Final: FC: 2012 Concord

Most Successful Event: Elimination Record 1997-2011: 91, 93, 95 Unknown:

FC: Dallas: 25/9, 3 Wins, 6 Finals, 4 DNQ's

Elimination Round Win/Loss Record: 452/343 = 56.8% TF: 3/10 = 23% FC: 449/333 = 57.4%

Career # 1 Qualifiers: FC: 48 IHRA: FC: 1

Career Provisional # 1 Qualifiers: 1997-2011: FC: 25

Top Five Finishes: FC: 8

Top Ten Point Finishes: FC: 12

Career Best Points Finish: Countdown: FC: 1st-2561

Pre-Countdown (2006 And Before): TF: 15th FC: 1st-15246

Best/Worst Points Finish If Countdown Never Was: 2nd/10th

YEARLY CAREER SUMMARY:

2012: 5th-342 (-255), 6/5, 1 Final, Average Qualifying Spot: 3.8, Qualified # 1 Twice, 1 DNQ, Left First: 81.8%

2011: 3rd-2465 (-75), 29/21, 1 Win, 3 Finals, Average Qualifying Spot: 4.36, Qualified # 1 Six Times, Left First: 34.7%

2010: 11th-1118 (-1503), 17/20, 2 Wins, 2 Finals, Average Qualifying Spot: 8.13, Qualified # 1 Once, 1 DNQ, Left First: 55.5%

2009: 12th-1103 (-1444), 15/24, Average Qualifying Spot: 8.2, Qualified # 1 Twice, Left First: 54.2%

2008: 1st-2561, 37/20, 3 Wins, Including 3 Consecutive, 5 Finals, Average Qualifying Spot: 6.39, Qualified # 1 Three Times, 1 DNQ, Left First: 73%, Won $100,000 Shootout

2007: 12th-925 (-2253), 18/16, 3 Finals, Average Qualifying Spot: 11.3, Qualified # 1 Once, 7 DNQ's, Left First: 56.2%

2006: 10th-956 (-680), 15/20, 1 Win, 3 Finals, Average Qualifying Spot: 10, 2 DNQ's, Left First: 68.5%

2005: 10th-1074 (-442), 20/20, 1 Final, Average Qualifying Spot: 8.4, Qualified # 1 Twice, 3 DNQ's, Left First: 52.6%

2004: 9th-1188 (-695), 22/23, 4 Finals, Including 2 Consecutive, Average Qualifying Spot: 7.78, Qualified # 1 Once, Left First: 64.2%

2003: 11th-995 (-773), 15/21, 2 Finals, Average Qualifying Spot: 10.8, 2 DNQ's, Left First: 71.4%

2002: 13th-754 (-1022), 7/17, Average Qualifying Spot: 9.52, 6 DNQ's, Left First: 60.8%

2000: 19th-289 (-1703), 6/3, 1 Win, 1 Final, Average Qualifying Spot: 10,7, 4 DNQ's, Left First: 77.7%

1999: 16th, 15/11, 2 Finals, Average Qualifying Spot: 6.27, 3 DNQ's, Left First: 31.8%

1998: 3rd-1445 (-218), 33/17, 5 Wins, Including 2 Consecutive, 6 Finals, Average Qualifying Spot: 2.31, Qualified # 1 Thirteen Times, Including 4 Consecutive Twice, 2 Consecutive Twice, 1 DNQ, Left First: 33.3%

1997: 7th-1166 (-699), 24/20, 4 Finals, Average Qualifying Spot: 5.35, Qualified # 1 Twice, Including 2 Consecutive, 3 DNQ's, Including 1 By 5 Thousandths, Left First: 52.5%

1996: 3rd-1286 (-737), 31/18, 1 Win, 4 Finals, Qualified # 1 Once

1995: 3rd-1351 (-339), 34/14, 5 Wins, 7 Finals, Qualified # 1 Four Times

1994: 2nd-12512 (-4264), 33/15, 3 Wins, Including 2 Consecutive, 7 Finals, Qualified # 1 Twice

1993: 3rd-11850 (-6224), 29/16, 2 Wins, 4 Finals, Qualified # 1 Four Times, Including 2 Consecutive Twice

1992: 1st-15246, 43/12, 6 Wins, Including 5 Consecutive, 8 Finals, Qualified # 1 Four Times, Including 2 Consecutive

1991: 15th, 3/10, 2 DNQ's, Only Year In TF

Frank Pedregon Date Of Birth: October 23, 1962 From: Phillips Ranch, CA

Pro Debut: 1998 Starts: 115 Consecutive Qualified Starts: 0

Win Percentage In Final Round: 50% Average Career Qualifying Spot: 10

AT THE TREE:

Career Holeshot Win/Loss Record: 3/4 Career Left Firsts/Left On: 103/94 = 52.2%

STATS:

U.S. Nationals Wins/Finals: 1/2

Career Best E.T./Speed: 1320ft.: 4.732/326.08

Career Wins: 4

Career Finals: 8 FC: 7 TAD: 1

Last Win: 2001 Atlanta

Last Final: 2005 Dallas

Most Successful Event: Indianapolis: 9/5, 1 Win, 2 Finals, 2 DNQ's

Elimination Round Win/Loss Record: 92/126 = 42.2%

Career Provisional # 1 Qualifiers: TAD: 1

Top Five Point Finishes: 1

Top Ten Point Finishes: 2

Career Best Points Finish: 4th-1028 (-1043)

YEARLY CAREER SUMMARY:

2006: 20th-163 (-1473), 0/2, Average Qualifying Spot: 11, 10 DNQ's, Left First: 50%

2005: 17th-547 (-969), 7/11, 2 Finals, Average Qualifying Spot: 9.81, 5 DNQ's, Left First: 33.3%

2004: 24th-61 (-1822), 0/1, Average Qualifying Spot: 16, 3 DNQ's, Left First: 100%

2003: 12th-923 (-845), 14/19, Average Qualifying Spot: 10.3, 3 DNQ's, Left First: 41.2%

2002: 14th-733 (-1043), 8/17, Average Qualifying Spot: 11.4, 3 DNQ's, Left First: 58.3%

2001: 7th-1149 (-851), 20/22, 1 Win, 1 Final, Average Qualifying Spot: 8.45, 2 DNQ's, Left First: 72.5%, Won $100,000 Shootout

2000: 11th-949 (-1043), 12/22, Average Qualifying Spot: 8.95, 1 DNQ, Left First: 39.3%

1999: 4th-1028 (-1043), 17/20, 1 Win, 2 Finals, Average Qualifying Spot: 9.47, 1 DNQ, Left First: 54.5%

1998: 12/13, 2 Wins, 2 Finals, Average Qualifying Spot: 12.1, 4 DNQ's, Left First: 50%

Tony Pedregon Date Of Birth: March 8, 1965 From: Brownsburg, IN

Sponsor: K-Love Crew Chief: Mike Guger Owner: Tony Pedregon

Body: '09 Chevrolet Impala Engine: TFX 500

Pro Debut: FC: 1995 TF: 1992 Starts: 380 TF: 6 FC: 374

Consecutive Qualified Starts: TF: 0 FC: 2 Win Percentage In Final Round: 56.5%

Average Career Qualifying Spot: 1997-2012: 6.96

AT THE TREE: 1997-2011:

Career Holeshot Win/Loss Record: 43/12 Career Left Firsts/Left On: 481/232 = 67.4%

Career Final Rounds Won/Lost On A Holeshot: 7/1

STATS:

Championships: FC: 2 U.S. Nationals Wins/Finals: FC: 0/1

Career Best E.T./Speed: 1000ft.: FC: 4.041/311.49 1320ft.: TF: 4.867/291.54 FC: 4.659/331.28

Career Wins: FC: 43

Career Finals: FC: 76

Last Win: FC: 2009 Brainerd

Last Final: FC: 2010 Las Vegas-1

Most Successful Event: FC: 30/13, 3 Wins, 4 Finals

Elimination Round Win/Loss Record: 503/337 = 59.8% TF: 2/6 = 20% FC: 501/331 = 60.2%

Career # 1 Qualifiers: FC: 37

Career Provisional # 1 Qualifiers: 1997-2011: FC: 31

Top Five Finishes: FC: 10

Top Ten Point Finishes: FC: 15

Career Best Points Finish: Countdown: FC: 1st-3178

Pre-Countdown (2006 And Before): TF: 20th FC: 1st-1768

Best/Worst Points Finish If Countdown Never Was: 1st/12th

YEARLY CAREER SUMMARY:

2012: 17th-162 (-435), 0/5, Average Qualifying Spot: 12.2, 1 DNQ, Left First: 60%

2011: 12th-783 (-1757), 8/20, Average Qualifying Spot: 12.4, 2 DNQ's, Left First: 69.2%, First Season In 16 Years That He Finished Outside The Top Ten, 1995

2010: 9th-2251 (-370), 14/23, 1 Final, Average Qualifying Spot: 12.3, Left First: 75%, Won 4 Rounds On A Holeshot

2009: 6th-2403 (-144), 41/21, 3 Wins, Including 2 Consecutive, 8 Finals, Including 3 Consecutive, Average Qualifying Spot: 6.08, Qualified # 1 Three Times, Left First: 71.9%, Won 5 Rounds On A Holeshot

2008: 5th-2440 (-121), 35/20, 4 Wins, 5 Finals, Average Qualifying Spot: 8.08, Qualified # 1 Three Times, Left First: 87.7%, Won

5 Rounds On A Holeshot, Won The Last Quarter Mile National Event

2007: 1st-3178, 30/18, 4 Wins, 5 Finals, Average Qualifying Spot: 7.18, 1 DNQ, Left First: 84.4%, Holds National E.T. Record With A 4.659 At Phoenix, The Last National E.T. Record Set At 1320 Feet, Dickie Venables And Kurt Elliot Were The Crew Chiefs

2006: 5th-1370 (-266), 32/19, 3 Wins, Including 2 Consecutive, 5 Finals, Average Qualifying Spot: 7, 1 DNQ, Left First: 63.8%

2005: 7th-1239 (-277), 23/21, 2 Wins, 3 Finals, Including 2 Consecutive, Average Qualifying Spot: 7.08, Qualified # 1 Three Times, Including 2 Consecutive, Left First: 69%

2004: 8th-1192 (-691), 20/23, 1 Final, Average Qualifying Spot: 6.21, Qualified # 1 Three Times, Including 2 Consecutive, Left First: 39%,

2003: 1st-1768, 47/15, 8 Wins, Including 2 Consecutive, 8 Finals, Average Qualifying Spot: 3.6, Qualified # 1 Eight Times, Including 2 Consecutive Three Times, Left First: 63.7%

2002: 2nd-1698 (-78), 44/17, 6 Wins, Including 3 Consecutive, 8 Finals, Average Qualifying Spot: 4.26, Qualified # 1 Seven Times, Including 3 Consecutive, Left First: 63.7%, Won 4 Rounds On A Holeshot

2001: 5th-1406 (-594), 30/20, 3 Wins, Including 2 Consecutive, 5 Finals, Average Qualifying Spot: 5.3, Qualified # 1 Once, 1 DNQ, Left First: 52%

2000: 4th-1444 (-548), 35/20, 2 Wins, 6 Finals, Average Qualifying Spot: 6.5, 1 DNQ, Left First: 70.2%, Won 4 Rounds On A Holeshot

1999: 2nd-1604 (-467), 42/19, 3 Wins, 7 Finals, Including 3 Consecutive, Average Qualifying Spot: 5.31, Qualified # 1 Four Times, Left First: 66.6%

1998: 6th-1256 (-407), 27/21, 2 Wins, 2 Finals, Average Qualifying Spot: 7.56, Left First: 63%

1997: 2nd-1411 (-454), 32/20, 2 Wins, 5 Finals, Average Qualifying Spot: 4.81, Qualified # 1 Three Times, 1 DNQ, Left First: 74%

1996: 2nd-1387 (-636), 36/18, 1 Win, 7 Finals, Including 2 Consecutive Twice, Won Auto Club Road To The Future Award

1995: 15th, 5/11, 1 DNQ

1994: 34th, 4 DNQ's

1993: 20th, 2/5, 1 DNQ

1992: 36th, 0/1

Cristen Powell Date Of Birth: March 22, 1979 From: Portland, OR

Pro Debut: FC: 1999 TF: 1997 Starts: 41 TF: 28 FC: 13

Consecutive Qualified Starts: TF: 2 FC: 0 Win Percentage In Final Round: TF: 100%

Average Career Qualifying Spot: 9.21 TF: 9.14 FC: 9.38

AT THE TREE:

Career Holeshot Win/Loss Record: 1/2 TF: 1/0 FC: 0/2

Career Left Firsts/Left On: 15/38 = 28.3% TF: 12/24 = 33.3% FC: 3/14 = 17.6%

STATS:

Career Best E.T./Speed: 1320ft.: TF: 4.590/308.85 FC: 4.921/307.90

Career Wins: 1 TF: 1

Career Finals: 1 TF: 1

Last Win: TF: 1997 Englishtown

Last Final: TF: 1997 Englishtown

Most Successful Event: Englishtown: 5/1, 1 Win, 1 Final TF: Englishtown: 4/0, 1 Win, 1 Final

FC: Englishtown: 1/1 Ex-Track Since 2000: Dallas-1: 1/1

Elimination Round Win/Loss Record: 19/40 = 32.2% TF: 15/27 = 35.7% FC: 4/13 = 23.5%

Career # 1 Qualifiers: 2 TF: 1 TAD: 1

Career Provisional # 1 Qualifiers: 1997-2011: TF: 1

Career Best Points Finish: TF: N/A FC: 17th-438 (-1554)

YEARLY CAREER SUMMARY:

2000: 17th-418 (-1574), 2/10, Average Qualifying Spot: 10.4, 8 DNQ's, Left First: 25%

1999: 2/3, Average Qualifying Spot: 6, 1 DNQ, Left First: 0%

1998: 6/14, Average Qualifying Spot: 8, Qualified # 1 Once, 3 DNQ's, Left First: 40%

1997: 9/13, 1 Win, 1 Final, Average Qualifying Spot: 10.2, 1 DNQ, Left First: 28.5%, Youngest Female Top-Fuel Winner In NHRA History, 18

Leah Pruett Date Of Birth: 1990 From: Cherry Valley, CA

Pro Debut: 2009 Starts: 1 Consecutive Qualified Starts: 1

Win Percentage In Final Round: 66.6% PM: 66.6% Average Career Qualifying Spot: 16

AT THE TREE:

Career Left Firsts/Left On: 1/0 = 100%

STATS:

Career Best E.T./Speed: 1000ft.: 4.644/212.43

Career Wins: 2 PM: 2

Career Finals: 3 PM: 3

Most Successful Event: Reading: 0/1

Elimination Round Win/Loss Record: 0/1 = 0%

Career # 1 Qualifiers:

Career Provisional # 1 Qualifiers: 1 PM: 1

Career Best Points Finish: Countdown: 29th-31 (-2509)

YEARLY CAREER SUMMARY:

2011: Somehow Not A Part Of NHRA Points, Author's Input, 29th-31 (-2509), 0/1, Average Qualifying Spot: 16, Left First: 100%

2009: 33rd-10 (-2537), 1 DNQ

Dale Pulde Date Of Birth: N/A From: Sylmar, CA

Pro Debut: 1971 Starts: 1997-2011: 4 Consecutive Qualified Starts: 0

Win Percentage In Final Round: 40% IHRA: 55.5% FC: 57.1%

Average Career Qualifying Spot: 10.7

AT THE TREE: 1997-2011:

Career Left Firsts/Left On: 5/3 = 62.5%

STATS:

Championships: 0 IHRA: FC: 3

Career Best E.T./Speed: 1320ft.: 4.893/306.01

Career Wins: 6 IHRA: FC: 20

Career Finals: 15 IHRA: 36 FC: 35 PFC: 1

Last Win: 1996 Dallas

Last Final: 1998 Pomona-2

Most Successful Event: 1997-2011: Pomona-2: 3/2, 1 Final, 2 DNQ's

Elimination Round Win/Loss Record: 1997-2011: 4/4 = 50%

Career # 1 Qualifiers: 5

Top Five Point Finishes: 1 IHRA: FC: 10

Top Ten Point Finishes: 9 IHRA: FC: 10

Career Best Points Finish: 3rd-7612 (-5040)

YEARLY CAREER SUMMARY:

2005: 24th-60 (-1456), 6 DNQ's

2004: 29th-20 (-1863), 2 DNQ's

1999: 1/1, Average Qualifying Spot: 7, Left First: 0%

1998: 3/1, 1 Final, Average Qualifying Spot: 13, Left First: 75%

1997: 0/2, Average Qualifying Spot: 11.5, Left First: 100%

1996: 1 Win, 1 Final

1992: Qualified # 1 Once

1990: 1 Win, 1 Final

1988: 9th-5978 (-6384), 1 Win, 1 Final

1985: 3rd-7612 (-5040), 2 Finals, Qualified # 1 Twice, Won IHRA Funny Car Championship

1984: 7th-5788 (-3100), Qualified # 1 Once

1983: 9th-5558 (-4377), 1 Final

1982: 9th-3131 (-4315), Won IHRA Funny Car Championship

1981: 8th-3805 (-3681), 1 Final, Qualified # 1 Once

1980: 8th-4152 (-4296), 2 Wins, 2 Finals

1979: 1 Final

1978: 10th-5457 (-8256), 1 Win, 2 Finals

1977: 6th-5588 (-8620), Won IHRA Funny Car Championship

1972: 1 Final

1971: 1 Final

Peter Russo Date Of Birth: N/A From: Australia

Sponsor: Russo Racing Crew Chief: N/A Owner: Peter And Helen Russo

Body: N/A Chevrolet Monte Carlo Engine: N/A

Pro Debut: 1999 Starts: 0 Consecutive Qualified Starts: 0

STATS:

Championships: 0 ANDRA: FC: 4

Career Best E.T./Speed: 1000ft.: 7.025/99.79 1320ft.: 5.035/286.13

Most Successful Event: Seattle/Dallas-2: 1 DNQ

Career Best Points Finish: Countdown: 32nd-20 (-2520)

Pre-Countdown (2006 And Before): 29th-20 (-1863)

YEARLY CAREER SUMMARY:

2011: 32nd-20 (-2520), 2 DNQ's

2007: 33rd-20 (-3158), 2 DNQ's

2006: 31st-20 (-1616), 2 DNQ's

2004: 29th-20 (-1863), 2 DNQ's

2002: 31st-30 (-1746), 3 DNQ's

2000: 32nd-30 (-1962), 3 DNQ's

1999: 1 DNQ

Bonus Fact: First Australian Funny Car Driver Over 280 MPH!

Bruce Sarver Date Of Birth: January 11, 1962 From: Bakersfield, CA
Died In 2005—Suicide
Pro Debut: 1996 Starts: 1997-2011: 108 FC: 59 TF: 49
Consecutive Qualified Starts: TF: 19 FC: 22 Win Percentage In Final Round: 20% FC: 25%
Average Career Qualifying Spot: 1997-2011: 8.13 TF: 9.3 FC: 7.16

AT THE TREE: 1997-2011:

Career Holeshot Win/Loss Record: 5/5 TF: 3/2 FC: 2/3
Career Left Firsts/Left On: 63/111 = 36.2% TF: 28/36 = 43.7% FC: 35/75 = 31.8%
Career Final Rounds Won/Lost On A Holeshot: TF: 0/1

STATS:

Career Best E.T./Speed: 1320ft.: TF: 4.575/317.46 FC: 4.768/320.39
Career Wins: FC: 2
Career Finals: 10 TF: 2 FC: 8
Last Win: FC: 2001 Pomona-1
Last Final: TF: 1998 Sonoma FC: 2002 Dallas
Most Successful Event: 1997-2011: Pomona-1: 8/2, 1 Win, 1 Final
TF: Englishtown/Sonoma: 3/2, 1 Final FC: Pomona-1: 6/2, 1 Win, 1 Final
Elimination Round Win/Loss Record: 1997-2011: 87/106 = 45%
TF: 26/49 = 34.6% FC: 61/57 = 51.6%

Career # 1 Qualifiers: FC: 6

Career Provisional # 1 Qualifiers: FC: 5

Top Ten Point Finishes: 3 TF: 1 FC: 2

Career Best Points Finish: TF: 10th-957 (-824) FC: 6th-1283 (-717)

YEARLY CAREER SUMMARY:

2003: 25th-32 (-1736), 0/1, Average Qualifying Spot: 9, Left First: 0%

2002: 11th-914 (-862), 18/16, 4 Finals, Average Qualifying Spot: 6.12, Qualified # 1 Three Times, Left First: 33.3%

2001: 6th-1283 (-717), 25/22, 1 Win, 2 Finals, Including 3 Consecutive Between Seasons, Average Qualifying Spot: 7.47, Qualified # 1 Twice, 1 DNQ, Left First: 36.5%

2000: 9th-1035 (-957), 18/18, 1 Win, 2 Finals, Average Qualifying Spot: 7.57, Qualified # 1 Once, 4 DNQ's, Left First: 25.7%

1999: 2/7, Average Qualifying Spot: 12.8, Left First: 28.5%

1998: 10th-957 (-824), 13/21, 1 Final, Average Qualifying Spot: 9.09, 1 DNQ, Left First: 43.3%

1997: 11/21, 1 Final, Average Qualifying Spot: 8.33, Left First: 48.1%

Gary Scelzi Date Of Birth: August 11, 1960 From: Fresno, CA RETIRED

Pro Debut: FC: 2002 TF: 1997 Starts: 251 FC: 137 TF: 114

Consecutive Qualified Starts: TF: 65 FC: 6

Win Percentage In Final Round: 61.4% TF: 64.1% FC: 60% TAD: 54.5%

Average Career Qualifying Spot: 5.55 TF: 3.59 FC: 7.18

AT THE TREE:

Career Holeshot Win/Loss Record: 12/26 TF: 2/9 FC: 10/17

Career Left Firsts/Left On: 295/265 = 52.6% TF: 160/131 = 54.9% FC: 135/134 = 50.1%

Career Final Rounds Won/Lost On A Holeshot: FC: 1/2

STATS:

Championships: 4 TF: 3 FC: 1 U.S. Nationals Wins/Finals: TF: 1/1

Career Best E.T./Speed: 1000ft: FC: 4.081/303.64 1320ft.: TF: 4.480/329.58 FC: 4.690/333.49

Career Wins: 43 TF: 25 FC: 12 TAD: 6

Career Finals: 70 TF: 39 FC: 20 TAD: 11

Last Win: TF: 2001 Reading FC: 2007 Richmond

Last Final: TF: 2001 Reading FC: 2007 Richmond

Most Successful Event: Reading: 22/6, 4 Wins, 5 Finals, 1 DNQ

TF: Madison/Reading: 15/2, 3 Wins, 4 Finals FC: Chicago-1: 12/4, 2 Wins, 2 Finals

Elimination Round Win/Loss Record: 380/214 = 63.9%

TF: 223/89 = 71.4% FC: 157/125 = 55.6%

Career # 1 Qualifiers: 46 TF: 35 FC: 11

Career Provisional # 1 Qualifiers: 42 TF: 33 FC: 9

Top Five Finishes: 8 TF: 5 Consecutive FC: 3

Top Ten Point Finishes: 10 TF: 5 Consecutive FC: 5

Career Best Points Finish: Countdown: 3rd-3092 (-86)

Pre-Countdown (2006 And Before): TF: 1st-1890 FC: 1st-1516

Best/Worst Points Finish If Countdown Never Was: 4th

YEARLY CAREER SUMMARY:

2008: 14th-817 (-1744), 7/20, Average Qualifying Spot: 11.6, 4 DNQ's, 1 For Illegal Ballast Left First: 53.8%

2007: 3rd-3092 (-86), 27/18, 4 Wins, 4 Finals, Average Qualifying Spot: 7.77, Qualified # 1 Twice, 1 DNQ, Left First: 51.2%

2006: 7th-1204 (-432), 23/21, 1 Win, 3 Finals, Average Qualifying Spot: 7.54, 1 DNQ, Left First: 51.1%, Lost 5 Rounds On A Holeshot

2005: 1st-1516, 35/20, 3 Wins, 5 Finals, Average Qualifying Spot: 3.73, Qualified # 1 Six Times, Left First: 50.9%, Lost 4 Rounds On A Holeshot

2004: 3rd-1565 (-318), 39/20, 3 Wins, 6 Finals, Average Qualifying Spot: 5.91, Qualified # 1 Once, Left First: 57.8, Won 4 Rounds On A Holeshot, The First Driver To Break The 330 MPH Barrier, Possibly The Last Great Speed Barrier, At Chicago-1 Running 330.15, Mike Neff Was The Crew Chief

2003: 6th-1159 (-609), 20/21, 1 Win, 1 Final, Average Qualifying Spot: 6.59, Qualified # 1 Twice, 1 DNQ, Left First: 38.4%

2002: 20th-301 (-1475), 6/5, 1 Final, Average Qualifying Spot: 9.6, 2 DNQ's, Left First: 30%

2001: 5th-1581 (-521), 37/22, 2 Wins, 5 Finals, Average Qualifying Spot: 3.95, Qualified # 1 Five Times, Including 4 Consecutive, Left First: 55.3%, Won Postponed 2000 $100,000 Shootout

2000: 1st-1890, 54/14, 9 Wins, Including 3 Consecutive, 11 Finals, Including 4 Consecutive, Average Qualifying Spot: 3.13, Qualified # 1 Nine Times, Including 3 Consecutive, Left First: 68.7%

1999: 2nd-1380 (-108), 30/18, 3 Wins, 4 Finals, Average Qualifying Spot: 4.04, Qualified # 1 Six Times, 1 DNQ, Left First: 48.8%, Lost 4 Rounds On A Holeshot, Won $100,000 Shootout

1998: 1st-1781, 49/17, 6 Wins, Including 3 Consecutive, 8 Finals, Including 3 Consecutive Twice, Average Qualifying Spot: 4,

Qualified # 1 Eight Times, Including 3 Consecutive Then 2 Consecutive Twice, Left First: 43.1%

1997: 1st-1837, 52/18, 5 Wins, Including 2 Consecutive, 10 Finals, Including 3 Consecutive Then 2 Consecutive Three Times, Average Qualifying Spot: 2.86, Qualified # 1 Seven Times, Including 3 Consecutive, Left First: 55.2%, Became The First Professional Drive To Win First 2 Races and 10 Elimination Rounds Of His Career, Won $100,000 Shootout

Justin Schriefer Date Of Birth: N/A From: Grant Park, IL
Sponsor: Creasy Family Racing Crew Chief: Dale Creasy
Assistant Crew Chief: Justin Schriefer
Owner: Dale Creasy Body: '04 Chevrolet Camaro Engine: TFX 500
Pro Debut: 2009 Starts: 5 Consecutive Qualified Starts: 0
Average Career Qualifying Spot: 12.6

AT THE TREE:

Career Left Firsts/Left On: 1/0 = 100%

STATS:

Career Best E.T./Speed: 1000ft.: 4.337/279.79
Most Successful Event: Chicago: 0/2, 1 DNQ
Elimination Round Win/Loss Record: 0/5 = 0%
Career Best Points Finish: Countdown: 19th-122 (-2425)

YEARLY CAREER SUMMARY:

2011: 28th-41 (-2499), 0/1, Average Qualifying Spot: 16, 1 DNQ, Left First: 0%

2010: 20th-112 (-2509), 0/2, Average Qualifying Spot: 16, 5 DNQ's, Left First: 100%

2009: 19th-122 (-2425), 0/2, Average Qualifying Spot: 15, 6 DNQ's, Left First: 0%

Todd Simpson Date Of Birth: N/A From: Pounder, TX

Sponsor: Simpson Racing Crew Chief: Bryan Simpson Owner: Dick Simpson

Body: '01 Chevrolet Camaro Engine: Chvy 496

Pro Debut: TF: 2009 FC: 2006 Starts: 8 TF: 4 FC: 4

Consecutive Qualified Starts: TF: 1 FC: 0

Win Percentage In Final Round: 71.4% TAFC: 71.4%

Average Career Qualifying Spot: 15.1 TF: 14.7 FC: 15.5

AT THE TREE:

Career Left Firsts/Left On: 2/4 = 33.3% TF: 2/1 = 66.6% FC: 0/3 = 0%

STATS:

Career Best E.T./Speed: 1000ft.: TF: 4.247/269.13 FC: 4.335/273.83 1320ft.: FC: 5.222/293.28

Career Wins: 5 TAFC: 5

Career Finals: 7 TAFC: 7 IHRA: FC: 1

Most Successful Event: Dallas: 0/2, 2 DNQ's TF: All Qualified Starts FC: Dallas: 0/2, 1 DNQ

Elimination Round Win/Loss Record: 0/8 = 0% TF: 0/4 = 0% FC: 0/4 = 0%

Career # 1 Qualifiers: 1 TAFC: 1

Career Provisional # 1 Qualifiers: 3 TAFC: 3

Top Ten Point Finishes: 1 TAFC: 1 IHRA: FC: 2

Career Best Points Finish: Countdown: TF: 31st-103 (-2468) FC: 24th-41 (-2580)

Pre-Countdown (2006 And Before): 32nd-20 (-1616)

YEARLY CAREER SUMMARY:

2012: 29th-10 (-587), 1 DNQ

2011: 27th-72 (-2468), 0/2, Average Qualifying Spot: 15.5, 1 DNQ, Left First: 0%

2010: 24th-41 (-2580), 0/1, Average Qualifying Spot: 15, 1 DNQ, Left First: 0%

2009: 31st-103 (-2468), 0/4, Average Qualifying Spot: 14.7, Left First: 66.6%, FC Only Following Season

2007: 27th-31 (-3147), 0/1, Average Qualifying Spot: 16, Left First: 0%, TF Only Following Season

2006: 32nd-20 (-1616), 2 DNQ's

2002: Finished 4th In The Division 4 Top Alcohol Funny Car Points, 25th Nationally

2001: Finished 2nd In The Division 4 Top Alcohol Funny Car Points, 15th Nationally

2000: Finished 3rd In The Division 4 Top Alcohol Funny Car Points, 10th Nationally

1999: Finished 2nd In The Division 4 Top Alcohol Funny Car Points

Dean Skuza Date Of Birth: December 27, 1966 From: Brecksville, OH RETIRED

Pro Debut: 1994 Starts: 1997-2011: 147 Consecutive Qualified Starts: 0

Win Percentage In Final Round: 16.6% Average Career Qualifying Spot: 1997-2011: 7.95

AT THE TREE: 1997-2011:

Career Holeshot Win/Loss Record: 5/6 Career Left Firsts/Left On: 148/114 = 56.4%

STATS:

Career Best E.T./Speed: 1320ft.: 4.794/317.19

Career Wins: 2

Career Finals: 12

Last Win: 1998 Reading

Last Final: 2003 Dallas

Most Successful Event: 1997-2011: Reading: 10/6, 1 Win, 1 Final

Elimination Round Win/Loss Record: 1997-2011: 115/145 = 44.2%

Career # 1 Qualifiers: 3

Career Provisional # 1 Qualifiers: 1997-2011: 2

Top Five Point Finishes: 1

Top Ten Point Finishes: 9, 7 Consecutive

Career Best Points Finish: 5th-977 (-1094)

YEARLY CAREER SUMMARY:

2003: 10th-1039 (-729), 19/19, 3 Finals, Average Qualifying Spot: 8.52, 4 DNQ's, Left First: 45.7%

2002: 9th-1001 (-775), 15/21, Average Qualifying Spot: 8.95, 2 DNQ's, Left First: 54.8%

2001: 9th-1128 (-872), 17/23, 1 Final, Average Qualifying Spot: 7.17, Qualified # 1 Twice, 1 DNQ, Left First: 60%

2000: 10th-995 (-997), 14/21, 1 Final, Average Qualifying Spot: 7.47, Qualified # 1 Once, 2 DNQ's, Left First: 57.5%

1999: 5th-977 (-1094), 13/20, Average Qualifying Spot: 6.6, 2 DNQ's, Left First: 68.7%

1998: 8th-1117 (-546), 20/20, 1 Win, 4 Finals, Average Qualifying Spot: 9.3, 2 DNQ's, Left First: 56.7%

1997: 8th-1083 (-898), 17/21, 1 Wins, 2 Finals, Average Qualifying Spot: 8.18, 1 DNQ, Left First: 76.3%

1995: 6th-937 (-753), 1 Final

1994: 8th-7832 (-8944),

John Smith Date Of Birth: January 30, 1967 From: Anderson, SC

Sponsor: John Smith Racing Crew Chief: John Smith Owner: John Smith

Body: N/A Chevrolet Monte Carlo Engine: N/A

Pro Debut: FC: 2009 TF: 1998 Starts: 98 TF: 92 FC: 6

Consecutive Qualified Starts: TF: 5 FC: 3

Average Career Qualifying Spot: 12.3 TF: 12.1 FC: 15.1

AT THE TREE:

Career Holeshot Win/Loss Record: TF: 1/1

Career Left Firsts/Left On: 81/42 = 65.8% TF: 76/39 = 66% FC: 5/3 = 62.5%

STATS:

Career Best E.T./Speed: 1000ft.: FC: 4.143/299.80 1320ft.: TF: 4.540/325.77

Career Finals: 0 IHRA: TF: 2 Last Final: TF: 2003 Gainesville

Most Successful Event: Chicago: 6/4, 1 DNQ TF: Chicago-1: 6/4, 1 DNQ FC: Concord-1: 1/1

Ex-Track Since 2009: Richmond: 1/1

Elimination Round Win/Loss Record: 33/98 = 25.1% TF: 31/92 = 25.2% FC: 2/6 = 25%

Top Ten Point Finishes: 2 IHRA: TF: 1

Career Best Points Finish: Countdown: FC: 21st-72 (-2416)

Pre-Countdown (2006 And Before): TF: 8th-938 (-1056)

YEARLY CAREER SUMMARY:

2011: 23rd-124 (-2416), 1/3, Average Qualifying Spot: 14.3, 1 DNQ, Left First: 75%

2010: 21st-72 (-2549), 0/2, Average Qualifying Spot: 16, 1 DNQ, Left First: 0%

2009: 25th-51 (-2496), 1/1, Average Qualifying Spot: 16, Left First: 100%

2005: 12th-721 (-1260), 6/19, Average Qualifying Spot: 13.3, 4 DNQ's, Left First: 79.1%, FC Only Following Seasons

2004: 11th-700 (-1294), 3/19, Average Qualifying Spot: 12.5, 4 DNQ's, Left First: 65%

2003: 8th-938 (-1056), 12/21, 1 Final, Average Qualifying Spot: 9.8, 2 DNQ's, Left First: 53.1%

2002: 10th-846 (-1105), 8/21, Average Qualifying Spot: 12, 2 DNQ's, Left First: 69.2%

2001: 13th-395 (-1707), 2/11, Average Qualifying Spot: 13.6, 2 DNQ's, Left First: 75%

1998: 0/1, Average Qualifying Spot: 14, 2 DNQ's, Left First: 0%

Mike Smith Date Of Birth: N/A From: Boynton Beach, FL

Sponsor: Ultimate Warrior Motorsports Crew Chief: Mike Smith Owner: Paul Weiss

Body: '08 Dodge Stratus Engine: TFX 496

Pro Debut: FC: 2009 TF: 1996? Starts: 1997-2011: 21 TF: 19 FC: 2

Consecutive Qualified Starts: TF: 3 FC: 0

Win Percentage In Final Round: 0% IHRA: TF: 50%

Average Career Qualifying Spot: 1997-2011: 13.8 TF: 13.8 FC: 13.5

AT THE TREE: 1997-2011:

Career Left Firsts/Left On: 8/13 = 38% TF: 8/11 = 42.1% FC: 0/2 = 0%

STATS:

Career Best E.T./Speed: 1000ft.: FC: 4.192/297.75 1320ft.: TF: 4.647/321.09 FC: 5.412/191.97

Career Wins: 0 IHRA: TF: 1

Career Finals: 0 IHRA: 2 TF: 1 FC: 1

Most Successful Event: 1997-2011: Houston: 1/2 TF: Houston-1: 1/1 FC: Atlanta: 0/1

Elimination Round Win/Loss Record: 1997-2011: 3/21 = 12.5%

TF: 3/19 = 13.6% FC: 0/2 = 0%

Top Ten Point Finishes: 0 IHRA: TF: 2

Career Best Points Finish: Countdown: FC: 23rd-62 (-2485)

Pre-Countdown (2006 And Before): TF: 25th-145 (-1849)

YEARLY CAREER SUMMARY:

2011: 33rd-20 (-2520), 2 DNQ's

2009: 23rd-62 (-2485), 0/2, Average Qualifying Spot: 13.5, Left First: 0%

2008: 29th-10 (-2551), 1 DNQ

2003: 25th-145 (-1849), 0/4, Average Qualifying Spot: 13.2, 2 DNQ's, Left First: 66.6%, FC Only Following Seasons

2002: 28th-113 (-1838), 0/3, Average Qualifying Spot: 14.3, 2 DNQ's, Left First: 50%

2000: 26th-134 (-1756), 2/3, Average Qualifying Spot: 12.6, 1 DNQ, Left First: 40%

1999: 0/4, Average Qualifying Spot: 14.7, 2 DNQ's, Left First: 25%

1998: 0/2, Average Qualifying Spot: 12, 1 DNQ, Left First: 0%

1997: 1/3, Average Qualifying Spot: 15.3, 7 DNQ's, Left First: 66.6%

Bob Tasca III Date Of Birth: October 14, 1975 From: Cranston, RI

Sponsor: Ford Motorcraft Crew Chief: Dickie Venables/Chris Cunningham/Marc Denner

Owner: Bob Tasca III Body: '12 Ford Mustang Engine: Ford 500

Pro Debut: 2008 Starts: 97 Consecutive Qualified Starts: 77

Win Percentage In Final Round: 31.2% FC: 37.5% TAFC: 25%

Average Career Qualifying Spot: 789/97 = 8.13

AT THE TREE:

Career Holeshot Win/Loss Record: 5/6 Career Left Firsts/Left On: 98/75 = 56.6%

Career Final Rounds Won/Lost On A Holeshot: 1/0

STATS:

U.S. Nationals Wins/Finals: 0/2 FC: 0/1 TAFC: 0/1

Career Best E.T./Speed: 1000ft.: 4.056/314.46 1320ft.: 4.798/321.42

Career Wins: 5 FC: 3 TAFC: 2

Career Finals: 16 FC: 8 TAFC: 8

Last Win: 2010 Englishtown

Last Final: 2012 Las Vegas-1

Most Successful Event: Gainesville: 8/4, 1 Win, 2 Finals

Elimination Round Win/Loss Record: 87/94 = 48%

Career # 1 Qualifiers: 3 FC: 2 TAFC: 1

Career Provisional # 1 Qualifiers: 5 FC: 4 TAFC: 1

Top Five Point Finishes: 2 FC: 1 TAFC: 1

Top Ten Point Finishes: 3 FC: 1 TAFC: 1

Career Best Points Finish: Countdown: 5th-2123 (-2416)

Best/Worst Points Finish If Countdown Never Was: 5th/8th

YEARLY CAREER SUMMARY:

2012: 8th-319 (-278), 5/6, 1 Final, Average Qualifying Spot: 5.33, Left First: 45.4%

2011: 7th-2327 (-213), 19/22, 2 Finals, Average Qualifying Spot: 8.36, Qualified # 1 Once, Left First: 69.2%

2010: 5th-2395 (-226), 29/22, 1 Win, 2 Finals, Average Qualifying Spot: 7.5, Left First: 47%

2009: 8th-2326 (-221), 26/22, 2 Wins, 3 Finals, Average Qualifying Spot: 7.25, Qualified # 1 Once, Left First: 55.5%

2008: 12th-893 (-1668), 8/22, Average Qualifying Spot: 10.6, 2 DNQ's, Left First: 62.9%

2007: Finished 2nd In The Division1 Top Alcohol Funny Car Points, 4th Nationally

2006: Finished 6th In The Division 1 Top Alcohol Funny Car Points, 17th Nationally

Brian Thiel Date Of Birth: January 11, 1975 From: Pleasant Grove, CA
Sponsor: N&S Tractor Crew Chief: Johnny West
Owner: Brian Thiel Body: N/A Dodge Charger Engine: N/A
Pro Debut: 2008 Starts: 7 Consecutive Qualified Starts: 2
Average Career Qualifying Spot: 14.4

AT THE TREE:

Career Left Firsts/Left On: 4/2 = 66.6%

STATS:

Career Best E.T./Speed: 1000ft.: 4.182/298.47
Most Successful Event: Seattle: 0/2
Elimination Round Win/Loss Record: 0/7 = 0%
Career Best Points Finish: Countdown: 20th-169 (-2371)

YEARLY CAREER SUMMARY:

2011: 20th-169 (-2371), 0/4, Average Qualifying Spot: 15.7, 6 DNQ's, Left First: 100%

2010: 23rd-51 (-2570), 0/1, Average Qualifying Spot: 15, 2 DNQ's, Left First: 0%

2009: 20th-84 (-2463), 0/2, Average Qualifying Spot: 11.5, 2 DNQ's, Left First: 50%

2008: Finished 11th In The Division 7 Top Alcohol Dragster Points, 76th Nationally

Jerry Toliver Date Of Birth: September 23, 1950 From: Compton, CA

Pro Debut: 1998 Starts: 137 Consecutive Qualified Starts: 1

Win Percentage In Final Round: 50% Average Career Qualifying Spot: 9.11

AT THE TREE:

Career Holeshot Win/Loss Record: 1/6 Career Left Firsts/Left On: 81/112 = 41.9%

Career Final Rounds Won/Lost On A Holeshot: 1/1

STATS:

Career Best E.T./Speed: 1000ft: 4.066/307.37 1320ft.: 4.738/328.22

Career Wins: 5

Career Finals: 10

Last Win: 2006 Reading

Last Final: 2007 Pomona-2

Most Successful Event: Pomona-1: 8/5, 2 Wins, 2 Finals, 1 DNQ

Elimination Round Win/Loss Record: 75/132 = 36.2%

Career # 1 Qualifiers: 2

Career Provisional # 1 Qualifiers: 5

Top Five Point Finishes: 1

Top Ten Point Finishes: 2

Career Best Points Finish: Countdown: 14th-774 (-1773)

Pre-Countdown (2006 And Before): 3rd-1513 (-479)

YEARLY CAREER SUMMARY:

2009: 14th-774 (-1773), 4/21, Average Qualifying Spot: 12.6, 3 DNQ's, Left First: 28%

2008: 15th-734 (-1827), 2/20, Average Qualifying Spot: 9.9, 4 DNQ's, Left First: 31.8%

2007: 19th-472 (-2706), 2/11, Average Qualifying Spot: 11.3, 8 DNQ's, Left First: 38.4%

2004: 13th-783 (-1100), 12/15, 1 Win, 2 Finals, Average Qualifying Start: 12.8, 7 DNQ's, Left First: 50%

2002: 25th-75 (-1701), 0/2, Average Qualifying Spot: 8.5, 1 DNQ, Left First: 0%

2001: 15th-703 (-1297), 2/19, Average Qualifying Spot: 11.2, Qualified # 1 Once, 4 DNQ's, Left First: 31.5%

2000: 3rd-1513 (-479), 37/19, 3 Wins, 7 Finals, Including 3 Consecutive, Average Qualifying Spot: 5.86, Qualified # 1 Once, 1 DNQ, Left First: 53.8%

1999: 8th-923 (-1148), 13/18, 1 Win, 1 Final, 3 DNQ's, Left First: 37%

1998: 3/7, Average Qualifying Spot: 13.7, 5 DNQ's, Left First: 71.4%

Melanie Troxel Date Of Birth: August 31, 1972 From: Denver, CO

Pro Debut: FC: 2008 TF: 2000 Starts: 131 FC: 48 TF: 83

Consecutive Qualified Starts: 16 TF: 57 FC: 16

Win Percentage In Final Round: 34.6% TF: 26.6% FC: 100% PM: 33.3% TAD: 50%

Average Career Qualifying Spot: 8.29 TF: 7.91 FC: 8.95

AT THE TREE:

Career Holeshot Win/Loss Record: 8/6 TF: 6/6 FC: 2/0

Career Left Firsts/Left On: 100/131 = 43.2% TF: 68/91 = 42.7% FC: 32/40 = 44.4%

STATS:

Career Best E.T./Speed: 1000ft.: FC: 4.042/313.73 1320ft.: TF: 4.458/332.51 FC: 4.752/327.90

Career Wins: 9 TF: 4 FC: 1 PM: 2 TAD: 2

Career Finals: 26 TF: 15 FC: 1 PM: 6 TAD: 4

Last Win: TF: 2007 Memphis FC: 2008 Bristol

Last Final: TF: 2007 Richmond FC: 2008 Bristol

Most Successful Event: Indianapolis: 10/6 Won At: Pomona-1: 6/3, 1 Win, 1 Final

TF: Phoenix: 7/4, 2 Finals FC: Bristol: 5/2, 1 Win, 1 Final

Elimination Round Win/Loss Record: 114/126 = 47.5% TF: 87/79 = 52.4% FC: 27/47 = 36.4%

Career # 1 Qualifiers: 12 TF: 3 FC: 1 TAD: 4 PM: 4

Career Provisional # 1 Qualifiers: 14 TF: 3 FC: 2 TAD: 5 PM: 4

Top Five Finishes: TF: 1

Top Ten Point Finishes: TF: 2

Career Best Points Finish: Countdown: TF: 9th-1173 (-2013) FC: 11th-932 (-1629)

Pre-Countdown (2006 And Before): TF: 4th-1471 (-210)

Best/Worst Points Finish If Countdown Never Was: 7th

YEARLY CAREER SUMMARY:

2011: 15th-455 (-2085), 8/16, Average Qualifying Spot: 8.75, 5 DNQ's, Left First: 47.8%

2010: 15th-571 (-2050), 7/13, Average Qualifying Spot: 11.9, 2 DNQ's, Left First: 36.8%

2008: 11th-932 (-1629), 12/18, 1 Win, 1 Final, Average Qualifying Spot: 7.1, Qualified # 1 Once, 5 DNQ's, 1 For Illegal Ballast, Left First: 46.6%

2007: 9th-1173 (-2013), 20/21, 2 Wins, 4 Finals, Average Qualifying Spot: 7.43, Qualified # 1 Once, Left First: 46.1%, Following Seasons FC Only

2006: 4th-1471 (-210), 36/21, 2 Wins, 9 Finals, Average Qualifying Spot: 7, Qualified # 1 Twice, Left First: 29%, Lost 4 Rounds On A Holeshot, Holds TF Record For The Most Consecutive Finals To Begin A Season, 5, First Quarter Driver Of The Year, Sportswoman Of The Year By Billie Jean King's Women's Sports Foundation

2005: 14th-529 (-1452), 8/11, 1 Final, Average Qualifying Spot: 7.36, Left First: 47%

2003: 18th-384 (-1610), 6/8, Average Qualifying Spot: 12.3, 1 DNQ, Left First: 57%

2002: 13th-407 (-1544), 7/8, Average Qualifying Spot: 10, 2 DNQ's, Left First: 60%

2000: 13th-517 (-1373), 10/10, 1 Final, Average Qualifying Spot: 6.5, Left First: 47.3%, Won Auto Club Road To The Future Award

1999: Division 6 Top Alcohol Dragster Champion

Daniel Wilkerson Date Of Birth: 1988 From: Springfield, IL

Sponsor: Summit Racing Equipment Crew Chief: Tim Wilkerson Owner: Tim Wilkerson

Body: '11 Ford Mustang Engine: TFX 500

Pro Debut: 2009 Starts: 6 Consecutive Qualified Starts: 6

Average Career Qualifying Spot: 9

AT THE TREE:

Career Left Firsts/Left On: 1/6 = 14.2%

STATS:

Career Best E.T./Speed: 1000ft.: 4.090/307.37

Career Finals: 0 IHRA: FC: 1

Most Successful Event: Norwalk/Indianapolis: 1/1

Elimination Round Win/Loss Record: 2/6 = 25%

Career # 1 Qualifiers: 0 IHRA: FC: 1

Career Best Points Finish: Countdown: 22nd-140 (-2400)

YEARLY CAREER SUMMARY:

2011: 22nd-140 (-2400), 2/3, Average Qualifying Spot: 9.33, Left First: 0%

2010: 27th-33 (-2588), 0/1, Average Qualifying Spot: 10, Left First: 0%

2009: 22nd-66 (-2481), 0/2, Average Qualifying Spot: 8, Left First: 50%

2008: Finished 4th In The Division 3 Top Alcohol Funny Car Points, 29th Nationally

2007: Division 3 Top Alcohol Funny Car Champion, 15th Nationally

2006: Finished 12th In The Division 3 Top Alcohol Funny Car Points, 81st Nationally

Tim Wilkerson Date Of Birth: December 29, 1960 From: Springfield, IL

Sponsor: Levi, Ray, & Shoup Crew Chief: Tim Wilkerson Owner: Tim Wilkerson

Body: '12 Ford Mustang Engine: TFX 500

Pro Debut: 1996 Starts: 296 Consecutive Qualified Starts: 4

Win Percentage In Final Round: 54.5% FC: 58.6% TAFC: 25%

Average Career Qualifying Spot: 1997-2012: 8.11

AT THE TREE: 1997-2011:

Career Holeshot Win/Loss Record: 10/15 Career Left Firsts/Left On: 203/292 = 41%

STATS:

U.S. Nationals Wins/Finals: 1/2

Career Best E.T./Speed: 1000ft.: 4.027/310.13 1320ft.: FC: 4.723/330.47

Career Wins: 18 FC: 17 TAFC: 1

Career Finals: 33 FC: 29 TAFC: 4

Last Win: 2011 Seattle

Last Final: 2011 Seattle

Most Successful Event: 1997-2011:

Sonoma: 16/7, 2 Wins, 3 Finals, 2 DNQ's

Elimination Round Win/Loss Record: 259/279 = 48.1%

Career # 1 Qualifiers: 16

Career Provisional # 1 Qualifiers: 1997-2011: 16

Top Five Finishes: 2

Top Ten Point Finishes: 7

Career Best Points Finish: Countdown: 2nd-2468 (-93)

Pre-Countdown (2006 And Before): 7th-1218 (-665)

Best/Worst Points Finish If Countdown Never Was: 1st/11th

YEARLY CAREER SUMMARY:

2012: 12th-214 (-383), 2/5, Average Qualifying Spot: 9.8, 1 DNQ, Left First: 33.3%

2011: 10th-2212 (-328), 14/21, 1 Win, 2 Finals, Including 2 Consecutive, Average Qualifying Spot: 7.45, Qualified # 1 Once, Left First: 32.3%

2010: 10th-2242 (-379), 25/18, 3 Wins, Including 2 Consecutive, 4 Finals, Including 3 Consecutive, Average Qualifying Spot: 8.23, Qualified # 1 Once, 2 DNQ's, Left First: 60.9%

2009: 4th-2430 (-117), 31/21, 2 Wins, Including 2 Consecutive, 3 Finals, Average Qualifying Spot: 7.86, 1 DNQ, Left First: 47%

2008: 2nd-2468 (-93), 42/18, 6 Wins, Including 2 Consecutive, 7 Finals, Average Qualifying Spot: 7.33, Qualified # 1 Four Times, Including 2 Consecutive Twice, Left First: 34.4%, Won The First 1000ft. National Event

2007: 15th-884 (-2294), 14/16, Average Qualifying Spot: 8.93, Qualified # 1 Twice, 7 DNQ's, Left First: 39.2%

2006: 18th-610 (-1026), 2/16, Average Qualifying Spot: 13.6, 7 DNQ's, Left First: 33.3%

2005: 11th-952 (-564), 11/22, 1 Final, Average Qualifying Spot: 9.5, 1 DNQ, Left First: 34.3%

2004: 7th-1218 (-665), 23/20, 2 Wins, 3 Finals, Average Qualifying Spot: 6.4, Qualified # 1 Twice, 1 DNQ, Left First: 31.7%

2003: 7th-1117 (-651), 19/20, 2 Wins, Including 2 Consecutive, 3 Finals, Including 3 Consecutive, Average Qualifying Spot: 8.86, Qualified # 1 Twice, 1 DNQ, Left First: 47.3%

2002: 12th-826 (-950), 14/16, 1 Final, Average Qualifying Spot: 6.12, Left First: 34.4%

2001: 18th-569 (-1431), 7/12, Average Qualifying Spot: 8.25, 3 DNQ's, Left First: 52.6%

2000: 15th-501 (-1491), 5/11, Average Qualifying Spot: 7.81, 5 DNQ's, Left First: 46.6%

1999: 15th, 12/12, 1 Win, 2 Finals, Including 2 Consecutive, Average Qualifying Spot: 6.46, Qualified # 1 Twice, 6 DNQ's, Left First: 36.3%

1998: 7th-1143 (-520), 20/22, 2 Finals, Average Qualifying Spot: 5.31, Qualified # 1 Twice, 1 DNQ, Left First: 35.1%

1997: 14th, 11/18, 1 Final, Average Qualifying Spot: 9.94, 1 DNQ, Left First: 53.8%

1996: 14th, 7/11

1995: Division 3 Top Alcohol Funny Car Champion

1994: Division 3 Top Alcohol Funny Car Champion

Jack Wyatt Date Of Birth: N/A From: Seymour, IA

Sponsor: Steve Plueger Crew Chief: Steve Plueger

Owner: Steve Plueger Body: '07 Dodge Stratus Engine: TFX 500

Pro Debut: 1998? Starts: 15 Consecutive Qualified Starts: 0

Win Percentage In Final Round: 0 IHRA: FC: 57.1% Average Career Qualifying Spot: 15

AT THE TREE:

Career Left Firsts/Left On: 7/7 = 50%

STATS:

Career Best E.T./Speed: 1000ft: 4.272/280.49 1320ft.: 4.847/312.42

Career Wins: 0 IHRA: FC: 4

Career Finals: 0 IHRA: FC: 7

Most Successful Event: Bristol: 2/1, 2 DNQ's

Elimination Round Win/Loss Record: 4/15 = 21%

Career Provisional # 1 Qualifiers: 1

Top Five Finishes: 0 IHRA: FC: 2

Top Ten Point Finishes: 0 IHRA: FC: 3

Career Best Points Finish: Countdown: 21st-82 (-2465)

Pre-Countdown (2006 And Before): 18th-336 (-1432)

YEARLY CAREER SUMMARY:

2012: 26th-10 (-587), 1 DNQ

2010: 25th-41 (-2580), 0/1, Average Qualifying Spot: 16, 1 DNQ, Left First: 0%

2009: 21st-82 (-2465), 1/2, Average Qualifying Spot: 15, Left First: 100%

2006: 24th-80 (-1556), 8 DNQ's

2005: 19th-323 (-1193), 2/3, Average Qualifying Spot: 15.6, 19 DNQ's, Left First: 40%

2004: 25th-60 (-1823), 6 DNQ's

2003: 18th-336 (-1432), 0/5, Average Qualifying Spot: 14.2, 18 DNQ's, Left First: 0%

2002: 27th-60 (-1716), 6 DNQ's

2001: 30th-20 (-1980), 2 DNQ's

2000: 38th-10 (-1982), 1 DNQ

1999: 8 DNQ's, 1 By 8 Thousandths

1998: 1/4, Average Qualifying Spot: 15.5, 4 DNQ's, Left First: 100%

A POINTS HISTORY ANALYSIS:1997-2011:

- The Countdown Was A New Points System Invented In 2007 And Almost Guaranteed That Season Ending Point Races Would Never Be A Runaway Again. At The Beginning Of 6 Races Left On The Schedule, If You Were In The Top Ten (Top 8 For 2007) You Were Going To Be Qualified For The Program. There Would Be A New Set Of Points Adjusted By Setting The Qualifiers 120 Points Apart And Resetting The Qualified Driver's Point Total To The Position They Qualified.

- The Points Leader Would Be # 1 With 2110 And Have A 30 Point Lead Over # 2 With 10 Points Between Each Driver Down To Tenth.

- In 2007 It Was The Top 8 Drivers Separated By 10 Points Each (2070-2000) Until The Final 2 Races Of The Season. The New Top 4 Drivers Would Be Separated By 10 Points Each (3030-3000) And They Would Compete For The Championship.

- 2007-2011 Features An In-depth Look At Countdown To 1 Finishes In Comparison To If There Was Never A Countdown System. Qualifying Bonus Points Awarded After Every Qualifying Session To The # 1, 2, And 3 Qualifiers Are Also Taken Out Of The Non-Countdown System Comparison.)

- The NHRA Did Not Award Points For National Records When The Switch To 1000ft. Was Made In 2008 And Did Not Begin Awarding Points Until The 2009 Start Of The Countdown. I Have Decided That I Will Award Points For National Records Beginning With The Inception Of 1000ft. In Denver 2008 And Ending At Indy 2009. My System Ends And NHRA Continues It. Due To This, Countdown Results Will Be Different Than What NHRA Recorded.

- This Look Is Given To Show What The Points Would Have Been Under Normal Points For An Entire Season And To Show Who Benefited Or Got Affected The Most By The Program. I Am Not A Fan Of The Countdown. I Am A Fan Of Teams Being Able/Having To Dominate In Hopes Of Winning The Championship. The Countdown Was Invented To Provide Tight Season Ending Point Finishes, Yet Regular Points Provided At Times Even Better Point Races.

- It's not possible for this comparison to take into account what the frame of mind would have been for teams under a regular points system. Actual final points and championship winners could have been different than what is shown under a different psychological environment for teams and their crew chiefs vs. if the countdown actually helped or hurt tuning decisions.

2011:

Top-Fuel Countdown Results:

1. Del Worsham 2627
2. Spencer Massey 2569 -58
3. Antron Brown 2542 -85
4. Larry Dixon 2540 -87
5. Tony Schumacher 2467 -160
6. Brandon Bernstein 2381 -246

7. David Grubnic 2273 -354
8. Doug Kalitta 2239 -388
9. Shawn Langdon 2208 -419
10. Morgan Lucas 2138 -489
11. Bob Vandergriff Jr. 952 -1675

Top-Fuel Regular Points:

1. Del Worsham 1867
2. Antron Brown 1744 -123
3. Spencer Massey 1656 -211
4. Larry Dixon 1581 -286
5. Tony Schumacher 1522 -345
6. Brandon Bernstein 1131 -736
7. Doug Kalitta 1031 -836
8. Bob Vandergriff Jr. 943 -924
9. Shawn Langdon 909 -958
10. David Grubnic 885 -982
11. Morgan Lucas 824 -1043

Best Result: I Must Point Out That Larry Dixon Qualified # 4 For The Countdown And Tony Schumacher Qualified # 5, After Points

Adjustment They Actually Switch Qualifying Spots, It Had No Effect On The Countdown, Morgan Lucas Finishes In The Top 10

Worst Result: Bob Vandergriff Jr. Is Denied A Top 10 Finish

Summary: Outside Of The Different Championship Winners, The Class Stayed Almost The Same

Funny Car Countdown Results:

1. Matt Hagan 2540
2. Jack Beckman 2468 -72
3. Cruz Pedregon 2465 -75
4. Robert Hight 2447 -93
5. Mike Neff 2440 -100
6. Ron Capps 2397 -143
7. Bob Tasca III 2327 -213
8. Jeff Arend 2303 -237
9. John Force 2232 -308
10. Tim Wilkerson 2212 -328
11. Johnny Gray 1219 -1321

Funny Car Regular Points:

1. Mike Neff 1564
2. Jack Beckman 1441 -123
3. Matt Hagan 1438 -126
4. Robert Hight 1400 -164
5. Cruz Pedregon 1354 -210
6. Ron Capps 1318 -246
7. Johnny Gray 1219 -345
8. Bob Tasca III 1108 -446
9. Jeff Arend 1100 -464
10. John Force 1039 -525
11. Tim Wilkerson 986 -578

Best Result: I Must Point Out That Cruz Pedregon Qualified # 4 For The Countdown, Ron Capps # 5, Matt Hagan # 6, Bob Tasca III # 8, And Jeff Arend # 9, After Points Adjustment Ron Capps # 4, Matt Hagan # 5, Cruz Pedregon # 6, Jeff Arend # 8, Bob Tasca # 9, Only Cruz Pedregon And Robert Hight Were Effected As They Would Of Switched Spots In The Final Countdown Points, Matt Hagan Wins Championship, Cruz Pedregon Finishes 3rd, Tim Wilkerson Finishes 10th

Worst Result: Mike Neff Loses Championship By 100 Points When He Would Of Won It By 123, Johnny Gray Is Denied A Top 10 Finish

Overall Summary: Johnny Gray Is The Biggest Example Of How The Countdown Can Hurt A Team That Finds Success At The Wrong Time. In The History Of The Countdown, He Earned 517 Points In The Countdown, If He Only Qualified In The Countdown # 7, He Would Have Been The Funny Car Champion, Even Under Regular Points It Is Quite An Accomplishment To Go From 11th To 7th.

Author's Opinion: The Sport Needs To Ditch The Countdown Because No Team Should Be Denied A Spot In The Top 10 When They Perform Better Than The Locked In 10th Place And Possibly Beyond. It Does Not Sit Well With Me That Johnny Gray Had The Best Final 6 Races In The Class And The Best He Could Finish Was 11th.

2010:

Top-Fuel Countdown Results:

1. Larry Dixon 2684
2. Tony Schumacher 2582 -102
3. Cory McClenathan 2551 -133
4. Antron Brown 2460 -224
5. Shawn Langdon 2431 -253
6. Doug Kalitta 2371 -313
7. Brandon Bernstein 2366 -318
8. Steve Torrence 2289 -395
9. David Grubnic 2288 -396
10. Morgan Lucas 2252 -432

Best Result: None

Worst Result: None

Top-Fuel Regular Points:

1. Larry Dixon 2081
2. Tony Schumacher 1776 -305
3. Cory McClenathan 1743 -338
4. Antron Brown 1529 -552
5. Doug Kalitta 1516 -565
6. Brandon Bernstein 1401 -680
7. Shawn Langdon 1195 -886
8. Morgan Lucas 983 -1098
9. Steve Torrence 972 -1109
10. David Grubnic 955 -1126

Summary: Only Class In The 2010 Countdown That Was Most Unaffected By The Countdown

Funny Car Countdown Results:

1. John Force 2621
2. Matt Hagan 2579 -42
3. Ashley Force Hood 2449 -172
4. Jack Beckman 2439 -182
5. Bob Tasca III 2395 -226
6. Del Worsham 2307 -314
7. Ron Capps 2284 -337
8. Robert Hight 2277 -344
9. Tony Pedregon 2251 -370
10. Tim Wilkerson 2242 -379
11. Cruz Pedregon 1103 -1518

Funny Car Regular Points:

1. John Force 1700
2. Matt Hagan 1579 -141
3. Jack Beckman 1496 -204
4. Robert Hight 1368 -332
5. Bob Tasca III 1348 -352
6. Ashley Force Hood 1336 -364
7. Ron Capps 1246 -454
8. Tim Wilkerson 1206 -494
9. Del Worsham 1196 -504
10. Cruz Pedregon 1103 -597
12. Tony Pedregon 1008 -692

Best Result: Tony Pedregon Finishes In The Top 10

Worst Result: Cruz Pedregon Is Denied A Top 10 Finish

Overall Summary: Outside Of The Different Championship Winners, The Class Stayed Almost The Same

2009:

Top-Fuel Countdown Results:

1. Tony Schumacher 2571
2. Larry Dixon 2569 -2
3. Antron Brown 2522 -49
4. Cory McClenathan 2490 -81
5. Brandon Bernstein 2438 -133

Top-Fuel Regular Points:

1. Antron Brown 1473
2. Larry Dixon 1343 -139
3. Tony Schumacher 1311 -145
4. Brandon Bernstein 1105 -186
5. Cory McClenathan 1094 -375

6. Spencer Massey 2437 -134
7. Morgan Lucas 2353 -218
8. Doug Kalitta 2325 -246
9. Shawn Langdon 2299 -272
10. Clay Millican 2093 -478

6. Spencer Massey 1051 -403
7. Morgan Lucas 1035 -444
8. Shawn Langdon 984 -513
9. Doug Kalitta 798 -533
10. Clay Millican 713 -594

Best Result: Tony Schumacher Wins 6th Consecutive Championship And 7th Overall, Whit Bazemore Finishes In The Top 10 In His Only Season In TF

Worst Result: Antron Brown Loses Championship By 49 Points When He Would Of Won It By 139, David Grubnic Is Denied A Top 10 Finish

Summary: Countdown Helped Add To History Helping Tony Win His 4th In A Row And 5th Overall

Funny Car Countdown Results:

1. Robert Hight 2547
2. Ashley Force Hood 2481 -66
3. Ron Capps 2433 -114
4. Tim Wilkerson 2430 -117
5. Jack Beckman 2406 -141
6. Tony Pedregon 2403 -144
7. Del Worsham 2352 -195
8. Bob Tasca III 2326 -221
9. John Force 2268 -279
10. Mike Neff 2235 -312

Funny Car Regular Points:

1. Tony Pedregon 1644
2. Ashley Force Hood 1632 -12
3. Ron Capps 1622 -22
4. Tim Wilkerson 1396 -248
5. Robert Hight 1379 -265
6. Jack Beckman 1373 -271
7. Bob Tasca III 1320 -324
8. Del Worsham 1292 -352
9. John Force 1281 -363
10. Mike Neff 1262 -382

Best Result: Robert Hight Wins The Championship, Makes Up For Losing In 2007 On Regular Points

Worst Result: Tony Pedregon Loses What Would Have Been 3rd Championship By 144 Points When He Would Of Won It By 12, Makes Up For Winning The 2007 Countdown On Luck

Overall Summary: Outside Of The Different Championship Winners, The Class Stayed Almost The Same, The Result Justifies The 2009 And 2007 Championship Winner And Runner Up

2008:

Top-Fuel Countdown Results:

1. Tony Schumacher 2743
2. Larry Dixon 2445 -298
3. Cory McClenathan 2406 -337
4. Hillary Will 2405 -338
5. Antron Brown 2390 -353
6. Rod Fuller 2368 -375
7. Brandon Bernstein 2327 -416
8. Doug Herbert 2307 -436
9. Doug Kalitta 2209 -534
10. David Grubnic 2194 -549
11. J.R. Todd 983 -1760

Top-Fuel Regular Points:

1. Tony Schumacher 2417
2. Larry Dixon 1535 -882
3. Antron Brown 1527 -890
4. Cory McClenathan 1462 -955
5. Rod Fuller 1384 -1033
6. Hillary Will 1358 -1059
7. Brandon Bernstein 1336 -1081
8. Doug Herbert 1203 -1214
9. Doug Kalitta 1043 -1374
10. J.R. Todd 983 -1434
11. David Grubnic 982 -1435

Best Result: Tony Schumacher Wins 5th Consecutive Championship And 6th Overall, David Grubnic Finishes In The Top Ten

Worst Result: J.R. Todd Is Denied A Top 10 Finish

Summary: Tony Schumacher Won 15 Races, He Was Not Going To Be Stopped Under Any Points System. What's Most Impressive? His 882 Point Lead Under Regular Points Would Have Been The Biggest Lead In NHRA History, There Was Only A 326 Point Difference

Between His Ending Countdown Points Lead And Regular Points Lead; The Team Owned Top-Fuel.

Funny Car Countdown Results:

1. Cruz Pedregon 2581
2. Tim Wilkerson 2468 -113
3. Jack Beckman 2457 -124
4. Robert Hight 2442 -139
5. Tony Pedregon 2440 -141
6. Ashley Force Hood 2385 -196

7. John Force 2303 -278
8. Ron Capps 2302 -279
9. Mike Neff 2284 -297
10. Gary Densham 2217 -364

Funny Car Regular Points:

1. Tim Wilkerson 1639
2. Cruz Pedregon 1556 -83
3. Robert Hight 1506 -133
4. Tony Pedregon 1504 -135
5. Jack Beckman 1365 -274
6. Ashley Force Hood 1310 -329
7. John Force 1184 -315
8. Ron Capps 1184 -315
9. Mike Neff 1155 -484
10. Gary Densham 1122 -517

Best Result: Cruz Pedregon Wins His 2nd Championship

Worst Result: Tim Wilkerson Loses Championship By 113 Points When He Would Of Won It By 83

Overall Summary: Outside Of The Different Championship Winners, The Class Stayed Almost The Same

2007:

Top-Fuel Countdown Results:

1. Tony Schumacher 3186
2. Rod Fuller 3167 -19
3. Brandon Bernstein 3149 -37
4. Larry Dixon 3135 -51
5. Bob Vandergriff Jr. 2358 -828
6. Doug Herbert 2292 -894

Top-Fuel Regular Points:

1. Rod Fuller 1617
2. Larry Dixon 1478 -139
3. Tony Schumacher 1472 -145
4. Brandon Bernstein 1431 -186
5. J.R. Todd 1242 -375
6. Bob Vandergriff Jr. 1214 -403

7. J.R. Todd 2273 -913
8. Whit Bazemore 2182 -1004
9. Melanie Troxel 1173 -2013
10. Doug Kalitta 1045 -2141
11. David Grubnic 1023 -2163

7. Melanie Troxel 1173 -444
8. Doug Kalitta 1104 -513
9. Doug Herbert 1084 -533
10. David Grubnic 1023 -594
11. Whit Bazemore 989 -628

Best Result: Tony Schumacher Wins 4th Consecutive Championship And 5th Overall, Whit Bazemore Finishes In The Top 10 In His Only Season In TF

Worst Result: Rod Fuller Loses Championship By 19 Points When He Would Of Won It By 139, David Grubnic Is Denied A Top 10 Finish

Summary: Countdown Helped Add To History Helping Tony Schumacher Win His 4th Consecutive And 5th Overall And Hurt Dave Grubnic

Funny Car Countdown Results:

1. Tony Pedregon 3178
2. Robert Hight 3159 -19
3. Gary Scelzi 3092 -86
4. Ron Capps 3067 -111
5. Jack Beckman 2358 -820
6. Mike Ashley 2337 -841
7. John Force 2191 -987
8. Jim Head 2163 -1015
9. Del Worsham 1050 -2128
10. Ashley Force Hood 960 -2141

Funny Car Regular Points:

1. Robert Hight 1408
2. Ron Capps 1394 -14
3. Tony Pedregon 1373 -35
4. Gary Scelzi 1230 -178
5. Jack Beckman 1219 -189
6. Mike Ashley 1201 -207
7. John Force 1093 -315
8. Del Worsham 1050 -358
9. Jim Head 996 -412
10. Ashley Force Hood 960 -448

Best Result: Tony Pedregon Wins His 2nd Championship

Worst Result: Robert Hight Loses Championship By 19 Points When He Would Of Won It By 14

Overall Summary: Different Championship Winners, The Class Stayed Almost The Same

2006:

Top-Fuel Points:

1. Tony Schumacher 1681
2. Doug Kalitta 1667 -14
3. Brandon Bernstein 1565 -116
4. Melanie Troxel 1471 -210
5. Rod Fuller 1384 -297
6. David Grubnic 1285 -396
7. Larry Dixon 1151 -530
8. J.R. Todd 1105 -576
9. Cory McClenathan 1036 -645
10. Hillary Will 1035 -646

Funny Car Points:

1. John Force 1636
2. Robert Hight 1524 -112
3. Ron Capps 1503 -133
4. Eric Medlen 1407 -229
5. Tony Pedregon 1370 -266
6. Tommy Johnson Jr. 1322 -314
7. Gary Scelzi 1204 -432
8. Phil Burkart 1034 -602
9. Whit Bazemore 956 -680
10. Cruz Pedregon 956 -680

2005:

Top-Fuel Points:

1. Tony Schumacher 1981
2. Larry Dixon 1566 -415
3. Doug Kalitta 1538 -443
4. David Grubnic 1407 -574
5. Morgan Lucas 1357 -624
6. Doug Herbert 1353 -628
7. Brandon Bernstein 1344 -637
8. Scott Kalitta 1142 -839
9. Cory McClenathan 1096 -885
10. Rod Fuller 801 -1180

Funny Car Points:

1. Gary Scelzi 1516
2. Ron Capps 1508 -8
3. John Force 1484 -32
4. Eric Medlen 1411 -105
5. Robert Hight 1379 -137
6. Tommy Johnson Jr. 1294 -222
7. Tony Pedregon 1239 -277
8. Del Worsham 1208 -308
9. Whit Bazemore 1192 -324
10. Cruz Pedregon 1074 -442

2004:

Top-Fuel Points:

1. Tony Schumacher 1994
2. Doug Kalitta 1668 -326
3. Brandon Bernstein 1531 -463
4. Scott Kalitta 1440 -554
5. David Grubnic 1368 -626
6. Larry Dixon 1242 -752
7. Cory McClenathan 1152 -842
8. Doug Herbert 1098 -896
9. Rhonda Hartman-Smith 840 -1154
10. Scott Weis 803 -1191

Funny Car Points:

1. John Force 1883
2. Del Worsham 1586 -297
3. Gary Scelzi 1565 -318
4. Gary Densham 1405 -478
5. Eric Medlen 1375 -508
6. Whit Bazemore 1338 -545
7. Tim Wilkerson 1218 -665
8. Tony Pedregon 1192 -691
9. Cruz Pedregon 1188 -695
10. Phil Burkart 1159 -724

2003:

Top-Fuel Points:

1. Larry Dixon 1994
2. Doug Kalitta 1664 -330
3. Tony Schumacher 1523 -471
4. Darrell Russell 1301 -693
5. Cory McClenathan 1150 -844
6. Kenny Bernstein 1111 -883
7. David Baca 1041 -953
8. John Smith 938 -1056
9. Doug Herbert 912 -1082
10. Rhonda Hartman-Smith 870 -1124

Funny Car Points:

1. Tony Pedregon 1768
2. Whit Bazemore 1628 -140
3. John Force 1504 -264
4. Del Worsham 1387 -381
5. Gary Densham 1343 -425
6. Gary Scelzi 1159 -609
7. Tim Wilkerson 1117 -651
8. Ron Capps 1105 -663
9. Tommy Johnson Jr. 1051 -717
10. Dean Skuza 1039 -729

2002:

Top-Fuel Points:

1. Larry Dixon 1951

Funny Car Points:

1. John Force 1776

2. Kenny Bernstein 1758 -193
3. Tony Schumacher 1428 -523
4. Doug Kalitta 1425 -526
Cory McClenathan 1425 -526
6. Darrell Russell 1343 -608
7. Doug Herbert 1333 -618
8. Andrew Cowin 1132 -819
9. Rhonda Hartman-Smith 997 -954
10. John Smith 846 -1105

2. Tony Pedregon 1698 -78
3. Del Worsham 1439 -337
4. Gary Densham 1412 -364
5. Whit Bazemore 1208 -568
6. Ron Capps 1148 -628
7. Tommy Johnson Jr. 1128 -648
8. Scotty Cannon 1121 -655
9. Dean Skuza 1001 -775
10. Johnny Gray 941 -835

2001:

Top-Fuel Points: Funny Car Points:

1. Kenny Bernstein 2102
2. Larry Dixon 2007 -95
3. Doug Kalitta 1598 -504
4. Mike Dunn 1594 -508
5. Gary Scelzi 1581 -521
6. Darrell Russell 1505 -597
7. Doug Herbert 1206 -896
8. Tony Schumacher 1153 -949
9. David Grubnic 843 -1259
10. Rhonda Hartman-Smith 822 -1280

1. John Force 2000
2. Whit Bazemore 1748 -252
3. Del Worsham 1490 -510
4. Ron Capps 1451 -549
5. Tony Pedregon 1406 -594
6. Bruce Sarver 1283 -717
7. Frank Pedregon 1149 -851
8. Gary Densham 1147 -853
9. Dean Skuza 1128 -872
10. Tommy Johnson Jr. 1127 -873

2000:

Top-Fuel Points:

1. Gary Scelzi 1890
2. Tony Schumacher 1624 -266
3. Larry Dixon 1603 -287
4. Joe Amato 1422 -468
5. Doug Kalitta 1413 -477

Funny Car Points:

1. John Force 1992
2. Ron Capps 1551 -441
3. Jerry Toliver 1513 -479
4. Tony Pedregon 1444 -548
5. Jim Epler 1242 -750

6. Kenny Bernstein 1275 -615
7. Cory McClenathan 1249 -641
8. Bob Vandergriff Jr. 1001 -889
9. Doug Herbert 963 -927
10. David Grubnic 861 -1029

6. Scotty Cannon 1114 -878
7. Whit Bazemore 1088 -904
8. Del Worsham 1056 -936
9. Bruce Sarver 1035 -957
10. Dean Skuza 995 -997

1999:

Top-Fuel Points:

1. Tony Schumacher 1488
2. Gary Scelzi 1380 -108
3. Joe Amato 1345 -143
4. Mike Dunn 1326 -162
5. Doug Kalitta 1307 -181
6. Kenny Bernstein 1260 -228
7. Doug Herbert 1259 -229
8. Larry Dixon 1210 -278
9. Cory McClenathan 1149 -339
10. Bob Vandergriff Jr. 1131 -357

Funny Car Points:

1. John Force 2071
2. Tony Pedregon 1604 -467
3. Whit Bazemore 1413 -658
4. Frank Pedregon 1028 -1043
5. Dean Skuza 997 -1074
6. Jim Epler 960 -1111
7. Del Worsham 928 -1143
8. Jerry Toliver 923 -1148
9. Ron Capps 891 -1180
10. Tommy Johnson Jr. 881 -1190

1998:

Top-Fuel Points:

1. Gary Scelzi 1781
2. Cory McClenathan 1640 -141
3. Joe Amato 1522 -259
4. Kenny Bernstein 1385 -396
5. Mike Dunn 1344 -437
6. Doug Kalitta 1098 -683
7. Larry Dixon 1093 -688
8. Jim Head 1083 -698

Funny Car Points:

1. John Force 1663
2. Ron Capps 1528 -135
3. Cruz Pedregon 1445 -218
4. Chuck Etchells 1430 -233
5. Whit Bazemore 1281 -382
6. Tony Pedregon 1256 -407
7. Tim Wilkerson 1143 -520
8. Dean Skuza 1117 -546

9. Bob Vandergriff Jr. 993 -778
10. Bruce Sarver 957 -824

9. Al Hofmann 1044 -619
10. Del Worsham 905 -758

1997:

Top-Fuel Points:

1. Gary Scelzi 1837
2. Cory McClenathan 1660 -177
3. Joe Amato 1597 -240
4. Scott Kalitta 1301 -536
5. Kenny Bernstein 1279 -558
6. Bob Vandergriff Jr. 1083 -754
7. Larry Dixon 1071 -766
8. Mike Dunn 1044 -793
9. Jim Head 955 -882
10. Shelly Anderson 889 -948

Funny Car Points:

1. John Force 1865
2. Tony Pedregon 1411 -454
3. Whit Bazemore 1405 -460
4. Chuck Etchells 1298 -567
5. Ron Capps 1174 -691
6. Randy Anderson 1167 -698
7. Cruz Pedregon 1166 -699
8. Dean Skuza 1083 -782
9. Kenji Okazaki 959 -906
10. Gary Densham 924 -941

CREW CHIEFS WHO HAVE TUNED IN BOTH NITRO CLASSES:

INTERVIEW WITH TODD OKUHARA:

Todd Okuhara began his tuning career as an assistant crew chief working under great minds like Roland Leong and Ed McCulloch. He began his career as a crew chief in 2006 and he collected a win with driver Whit Bazemore. In 2007, he was Jack Beckman's crew chief and Gary Scelzi's toward the last half of the season and he tuned both cars to top 5 finishes, even getting Gary Scelzi into the countdown just missing a championship win. After a tough 2008, he switched to Top-Fuel in 2009 working with Phil Shuler and together they have become one of the toughest crew chief duos by 2012; winning won 11 times and challenging for every championship down to the wire. 2012 they find themselves in prime position for the championship, already having won 3 times; a championship is not far behind for Todd Okuhara.

PK: What does it take to be a successful crew chief in this class?

TO: You have to have the resources to obviously do what you wanna do and people, I think that's the biggest thing, the people. The crew and how well they prepare the car, not just at the race track, but more importantly between races. The better your team is, you have more time to tune the car than to troubleshoot; that's the most important part.

PK: Do you race the track or the opponent?

TO: I would say 95% of the time it would be the race track, but there's times where you're a little behind and your opponent has a little advantage you have to chase a little bit. Most of the time I just try to race the race track.

PK: How hard is it to run a 3.728? I was a witness to that pass and you could just tell it was a pass unlike all the others.

TO: You probably get those conditions 2 or 3 times a year and throughout the year I think about what I will do, what I will try, and if you're in the position to do it. We were qualified real good before that run, so we went ahead and did thing we never done before and it worked. It's something that you work on a lot, but don't get a chance to do it a lot.

PK: Can you take me through what you do as a crew chief prior to a run?

TO: There's weather conditions, track conditions, that you look at hours before a run and you kinda have to guessitmate what the conditions are gonna be like during the run and hopefully you have the setup for that. Most of the changes we make is probably 10-15 minutes before the run.

PK: Your dragster leaves aggressively, wheels up and is always exciting to watch. Does it affect the chassis at all?

TO: There's always gonna be the fatigue fact in the chassis of our runs the more fatigued it gets, but these cars are built for that type of trauma I guess you can say. We have confidence in 200 runs a year that from the first run to the 200th run that it will be fairly close to being the same.

PK: Over the course of a weekend the goal is to make 8 passes down the strip. Outside of explosions and any major after run engine damage, what is the maximum expectancy of the parts you have to replace due to wear and what and when do you replace?

TO: Every part has specific number of runs that we put on it and no two parts are really the same. If we get 10-12 runs on a crankshaft that would be good, 6 runs on tires that would be good, we restriped the blower every 4 runs. It just depends on the part and everything has a run timeline.

PK: With the 3 Dragster's that make up DSR's Top-Fuel operation, what is the deal with the tune. Do you all write you own or does the team have a baseline that each crew chief adjusts how they see fit?

TO: Basically all ours cars have the same parts, but every car has a different personality. How the driver drives, does his burnout and stuff, and we have to take the into consideration; just do what basically our car tells us it wants. Bottom line we have to make these cars perform and Don's (Schumacher) not gonna want to hear about why it just worked for their car and only their car went down the track, we have to do what the car tells us to.

PK: What is the cost of 1 pass?

TO: I say it's close to 15,000 dollars a pass.

PK: The price to race in the sport's top class keeps rising and has almost kept the independent team out of racing completely. What do you see for the reason the costs have skyrocketed and what would you do to put a cap on or decrease the costs making it friendlier to small budget teams?

TO: I think if you tried to restrict these cars or put a cap on these cars, I actually think it would be more expensive. We put a specific number of runs on everything and if we ever had a cap, a budget on it where we had to get 2 more runs out of a crankshaft or tires, I think that it might save you a couple races here and a couple races there, but one big malfunction of parts would cost you more than that. I think first to run at the level that we wanna run, doing it the way we run is probably the most cost effective.

PK: I have to say that I do admire how you race heads up all the time against your teammates with no funny business. Is there ever any influence on how you tune based on how your car is running?

TO: For me, yeah. When there's 2 DSR cars running and I know 1 car is gonna go past that round, I think yeah, you tend to be a little more aggressive with it because you still wanna beat your teammate, but you don't feel so bad losing to them.

PK: Your talent puts you in a very elite class with only a handful of tuners who have been capable of running successful championship contending programs in Top-Fuel and Funny Car. Your career best in Funny Car for a quarter mile is 4.662/333.66, also the last quarter mile National E.T. and Speed Record, finishing 2nd in the points. In Top-Fuel, your best is a 3.728/332.18, the speed is a National Record, and a 2nd place finish. What class do you personally feel you understand and/or enjoy more?

TO: I like both classes, I tune the Dragster and I still have a hand in some of the Funny Car stuff out there. I like both, but there's been some rule changes in Funny Car since I moved and I guess I'd be way more comfortable tuning the Dragster because I am doing that right now.

PK: Will you ever transition back to Funny Car and how much of a learning curve is it for you when you decide to switch classes?

TO: I hope I don't have to switch, I'm happy where I'm at. The Top-Fuel car every race you learn something new, it's comfortable because you learn one thing and okay what's the next.

PK: How different is the frame of mind for a crew chief when you have a slow start that turns into almost overnight success in comparison to when you have a hard charging season from start to finish and what type of season do you find more welcoming to your habits?

TO: If you're in the countdown you get to race the last 6 races, typically with the weather that time of year you go out there and you run your car hard. It's pretty exciting then to go to races and have it be so hot you smoke the tires. I always told the guys we wanna be competitive during the year, try things, and hopefully by the time the countdown comes around we can just race for it.

PK: Do you feel that the sport is on a good path for the future ahead?

TO: If you look at the racing yes. There's a lot of good quality cars out there, in my opinion it's looking good right now.

PK: What are your feelings on the sport's decision to move to 1000 feet?

TO: Fully support it. We've done a lot of research on it, how much safer it is, the cars shutting off at 1000 feet and what the speeds are at 1320 verses racing to 1320 and having to shut off after that. The most shutdown area, the more time for the driver to get the car under control and that's a big plus.

PK: If the sport was to return to 1320 feet, what steps would you take in slowing these cars down to make sure that a quarter mile return was a safe return?

TO: I would think that going back to quarter mile from what we've seen is a mistake, it's more dangerous with the shutdown and everything that we have. I don't even think about stuff that would take us back to 1320, I think it's safer now, I fully support that and I think that's where we need to keep it.

PK: The move to 1000 feet turned back the clock on the incremental performance in Top-Fuel for a short time, but the E.T. record in 1000 feet is the quickest a dragster has been to 1000 feet in the history of the sport. Your tuned your driver, Spencer Massey to a 3.728 and could add up to being the first ever 4.3 second run. Saying that we will eventually hit 3.6 and 335 MPH in 1000 feet, is there any need for the NHRA to be concerned?

TO: I think when you talk about speeds anyone is gonna be concerned about it. For our job we're supposed to think about how to make the cars run quicker, faster, better, will it ever get to that? I don't know, but we went 3.72 and we already think we can go quicker yet. I'm sure the NHRA will be concerned about the speeds.

PK: The move to 1000 feet gave the sport an extra 320 foot window to slow down. If we stay the course with 1000 feet could the time ever come where the increase in performance for these cars ends up that they can begin to greatly diminish the extra 320 feet, thus drivers facing the same possibility of danger that they faced when it was 1320 feet?

TO: I guess it's always possible, I think that the changes they made with the shutoff devices are huge. In 1000 feet you're about high 200 at the 1320, where in 1320 feet I've seen drivers shut their motors off at 1600 feet. I think it's safe for a while right now.

PK: Have you had any aspirations to drive?

TO: Not a fuel car no. I see the concepts put together, I don't wanna drive it.

PK: Do you have any aspirations to be a crew chief, or own a team in another class?

TO: Hopefully I never have to be.

PK: What programs do you run in-house?

TO: I pretty much do all the blower dyno for all the teams here and that probably keeps you the busiest in the shop when I'm not tuning the race car.

PK: What is your favorite race track?

TO: I think Vegas is probably my favorite. Just being from Hawaii that's the race where I can see a lot of my friends and family.

PK: What is your favorite track in each nitro class?

TO: The Same, Vegas.

PK: What win and single run mean more to you than all the others?

TO: I don't really have one. I just go out there and try and do more.

COUNTDOWN ATTITUDES: FEELINGS FROM THE MOST POSITIVELY AND NEGATIVELY AFFECTED DRIVERS ABOUT THE COUNTDOWN:

INTERVIEW WITH ANTRON BROWN:

Antron Brown burst on to the scene in 1998 and by 2012 is one of the most popular drivers in the NHRA; certainly doesn't hurt that "Big Daddy" Don Garlits is one of his fans. He spent the first 10 seasons of his career proving how good a Pro Stock Motorcycle rider he was by collecting 16 Wins, 2 U.S. National victories and 2 championship runner up finishes. In 2008, he moved to Top-Fuel Dragster, a move that hardly any former Pro Stock Motorcycle riders have ever made, and he drove like he's been in the class for years. Currently into his fourth season, he has won 16 times in the class, won the U.S. Nationals, has been a consistent championship contender, and he has left first almost 70% of the time in the class, cutting lights in the .040-.070; you can't get much better than that. As long as Antron Brown continues to drive/ride well, anything, he's proven to be a quick adapting racer who digs down deep to try and beat anyone and everyone; something he has done a lot, so a championship will soon be his.

PK: In 2009 you were 49 points out of the top spot and finished 3rd. Under the old points system, you would of won the championship by 139 points. What are your overall feelings on the countdown and is it a good system for the NHRA?

AB: I think the countdown is good for our fans, but it takes away from the marathon that we need to have a hard earned championship. It is just brings in a different strategy.

PK: I am not a fan of good teams being told the best they can finish is 11th. Since, the NHRA resets the points at the start of the countdown to make the points race tighter, I feel that the NHRA should qualify everyone for the countdown who has run every countdown qualifying race. It would eliminate anyone getting locked out of a top ten and a top ten finish can still be a goal for everyone. Would you modify the system for teams that peak at the wrong time and get locked out of the all-important top ten when they may perform better than a locked in top ten finisher?

AB: I would take only 8 to the countdown and would only let the count down racers race each other for a true playoff feel to develop a champion. Or just race the old traditional way.

PK: What does it take to be a successful driver in this class?

AB: Team player, determination, integrity, willingness to keep learning.

PK: What is your favorite race track?

AB: I like all the race tracks on the tour. It is nice to go to all of them. It is a good challenge.

PK: You are one of the best in the class for having a really great light at any time. How do you stay so focused and what do you attribute to being the most important factor?

AB: I just feed off my team. I work and train hard to stay at a high level to be able to bring the same game at each race.

PK: Do you have any aspirations to drive in another class, or be a crew chief, or a team owner in any class, or even return to Pro Stock Motorcycle?

AB: I would be love to be a part owner or owner of a team one day when I retire from driving. That would be a huge deal for me to accomplish that. I would love to race Funny Car one day also. I love where I'm at right now.

PK: What is your private ride and does your career as a driver/rider influence any of your daily driving habits?

AB: I drive a Toyota Sequoia SUV. I love it. I just cruise around town with the sunroof open and enjoy the view. Racing every weekend makes you enjoy driving slow to see what is happening around you.

PK: What Top Fuel and Pro Stock Motorcycle win, and single run mean more to you than all the others?

AB: The Top fuel run that sticks out is racing Del Worsham at US Nationals in 2011 in the finals and beating him by a nose and bringing that race win home! Pro stock bike the win that sticks out is 2001 when we doubled up and won the All-Star race and Indy in the same weekend!

PK: Do you find yourself in awe that in such a short time, you've won 16 races in Top-Fuel equaling your record in Pro Stock Motorcycle?

AB: Yes I do. I'm so blessed to be a part of such a great team that is why we have had so much success in a short time. True Team Work!!

PK: What are your feelings on the sport's decision to move to 1000 feet?

AB: It is not a decision that I liked, but it was the right decision for the safety of our sport. The speeds we run now, a lot of tracks shut down areas are not long enough so the extra 320 feet of stopping room really helps. The racing has gotten a lot closer and better for the fans.

PK: How would you feel about any of your kids having aspirations to race?

AB: I would be happy and scared at the same time, but will support them in whatever they wanted to do. That is what I really think is important for them to have is a support system to encourage them.

INTERVIEW WITH TONY SCHUMACHER:

Tony Schumacher's career has been so dominating that when you think of Top-Fuel Dragster you think immediately of Tony Schumacher, just like when you think of Funny Car, you think of John Force. A 7-Time Champion, 67 National Event Wins, 8 U.S. National Wins, and over 600 round wins, he has already had a career that is not complete, possibly over complete, but numbers don't mean as much to him as his pure passion to drive. He has accomplished many impressive things such as a 76 round win season and a 15 national event win season which he fittingly one the Driver of The Year Award for, but two things on his resume may never be forgotten in the sports history. "The Run" is where he set the National E.T. Record running a 4.428 in the final run of the season to win the championship, and winning the title from being 336 points back earlier in the season; two feats that this sport and its fans may never see again. Tony Schumacher will forever be a feared racer for as long as he races.

PK: What does it take to be a successful driver in this class?

TS: Nine amazing people, we call 'em A + guys. When people ask me I say, "I idiot proofed my racecar." The fact is I wouldn't wanna drive my car with my high school buddies working on it, that's what I'm saying. When it comes down to absolutely having to win at a certain given time, I want those nine guys; that's how you win races you surround yourself with people that get it. Nobody shows up for a paycheck, they show up because an A + is absolutely mandatory.

PK: Can you take me through what you do on a run from the burnout to the completion?

TS: We start the car, crew chief will get everything set that he wants to set, make sure the cylinders are all working everything where we wants it, then he'll give me the to go sign. I'll roll through, lock the clutch, and I'll give it gas. Now the fuel has a throttle stop, so it won't allow me to open it all the way, whatever they predetermine.

Lift off that, put the clutch in, and get on the breaks softly to keep the fuel from flowing out the front; overflow. Put it in reverse, let it settle down, and back it up real smooth not riding the clutch, so you don't get anything to hot.

Back up, they'll stop me, I'll put it back in forward and I wait. I'm probably a foot back from the pre-stage beam and they set everything up and make sure everything's where they want it. When I pre-stage, they step away, I pull the fuel pump on, step on the clutch and stage. At that point the light comes on, I open the throttle and I get the car where it wants to be; it's not always in the middle of the racetrack. I put the car where it has to be on the racetrack and keep it in the groove and pull the parachutes.

PK: What is your favorite race track?

TS: Man that is a really tough question. I won Indy a lot of times, so I enjoy going there, but I really like going to Denver and Sonoma. A couple of beautiful places, the mountains are bitchin'. Englishtown is the biggest east coast race, but I like fishin' so I end up going the other way.

PK: You are one of the best in the class for having a really great light at any time. How do you stay so focused and what do you attribute to being the most important factor?

TS: I attribute having great other teammates. If you look at my history we won a lot of championships with .060 and .090 lights, we didn't have to have .030's and .040's now. You gotta understand that when my car's a tenth faster than everybody, I only need a .090 light, but as the cars are getting more uniform, we all have to step it up. Why are my lights good? Cause I read the rulebook and those guys are fast, it makes me go fast.

PK: Do you have any aspirations to drive in another class, or be a crew chief, or a team owner in any class?

TS: No. I like to go for a Funny Car ride, but I enjoy the kings of the sport; Top Fuel.

PK: What is your private ride and does your career as a driver/rider influence any of your daily driving habits?

I have an (Ford) F-250 diesel. I've seen more people get hurt in cars than other people, I drive very slow. I got a beautiful family; we wear our seat belts and follow the rules of the road. I get to go fast out here, going 56 mph not's gonna impress me; going the speed limits fine.

PK: What are your overall feelings on the countdown and is it a good system for the NHRA?

TS: I understand why they did it, there was a time where me and John Force ran away with a lot of championships; we'd lock it up by the time we get to Reading, people didn't need to watch the last four to five races. However, the year they went to it we rocked the NHRA before that by having to comeback by a 336 point deficit and winning by setting the world record on the last run of the year. It's absolute staggering irony that after the most intense year ever that they switch to the countdown the following year and then we had to do the same thing next year winning the last run of the year because of the countdown.

PK: Did "The Run" influence any of your feelings as a driver as far as feeling pressure. "Either I run my fastest pass right now, or I smoke the tires and lose the championship."

TS: I'll tell the whole world a secret, none of us dream of winning by three car lengths, no baseball player dreams of winning by 40 points and no football player hopes for a blowout game; we all have the same American dream. It's absolutely mandatory that we perform a miracle, that's why it's great and we do it. That was a gift when we had "The Run", the world record, and we had to win, it the kinda stuff we dream of. Most guys choke on it, but nobody had to tell me to try harder and I didn't have to tell them to try harder. That was a blessed moment in the history of the sport in my life and i'm telling my grandkids what I did, and what that team pulled off, at that given moment stemmed from 10 years of getting to that moment and being so good that on that moment you were good enough to pull it off; that's what makes it great.

PK: I think it should have been the top moment of the 60 moments last year. I mean how many times can that happen?

TS: That was a media deal and for all the fans and with all the guys and (Don) Garlits, I'm just happy to be in the same sentence as them. It didn't win us a car or a prize, and to be in the top five like that was great; that was a great moment in racing.

PK: What are your feelings on the countdown as far as drivers that are locked out of the top ten and perform better than a locked in top ten car?

TS: Bad timing. I'll give you a great example of that, I should have won 10 races since last year; except the other guy went faster on that particular run. If it wasn't that way I would of beat 'em; there's alotta if's out there. I can't tell you how many times I get beat by the quickest run of the weekend and the guy can't do it again, but he did it that time and that's the same thing. This is the thing with, you go up, you win, win, win, and right now we're not winning, we're leading, but we're not winning and if you can't hold your team together and sometimes you gotta get through those rough moments.

A lot of times you'll see a good team fire people when there not running good, and then they turn it around and run really good again. If they led earlier, maybe they would have been in the top ten. It's hard to say, it's in their shoes and that's the reason for their decisions.

PK: Going into 2009 your team was unfairly considered a huge underdog. How much pressure did that put on you as a driver and a team?

TS: I loved it! If you want to see this driver make mistakes take the pressure away. I'll make 'em, we all do, I just don't like to make them when it's absolutely mandatory when we need to win and that's what we proven we're good at. I like to be known as that driver where if you have the highest pressure situation, pick me to put in that car. People don't assume I'm gonna make a mistake and it's good to do that and that doesn't come from me, it comes from when I sit there and look at those nine guys, there so good at what they do that I don't wanna be the guy that didn't get it done.

PK: What are your feelings on the sport's decision to move to 1000 feet?

TS: You know, that's a really tough question, I grew up on quarter mile; we all did. I also grew up on watching (Scott) Kalitta race and when he got hurt, killed, there was a period of eight to 10 years when we got in a car they were scary; that's intense. There still scary, we're still going fast, but there was a time where I pretty much thought, "We're gonna crash," that ain't good for anybody. If you look at the last '60s early '70's Formula 1, guys were getting killed constantly, cars were going faster than the safety had kept up with. At some point we had to make the change, I am of fan of racing to 1,000 feet because there's still drag racing and if we stayed quarter mile the insurance would of pulled the plug on drag racing; so we benefit from it in the long run.

PK: What championship, win, and single run mean more to you than all the others?

"The Run" is the greatest run in the sport, but winning (the championship) in '09, beating my old guys by two points that was pretty good because the team that we were told you could not beat, and we beat 'em. There's a lot of good moments, beating them in Houston the first time we met up beating them on a holeshot getting it done. For me it's sucking it up and rising to the occasion in that given moment.

PK: You share something in common with yourself. You originally broke the 330 mph barrier running 330.23 in the quarter mile at Phoenix in '99. You ran the same exact number to break the barrier in 1000 feet earlier this year at Concord. Is there any difference in the way that it feels setting the barrier between and extra 320 feet and a minus 320 feet?

TS: You are hauling ass to get there 320 feet earlier. 291 to halftrack I think that's wicked fast. I like to drive with the front wheels in the air, I like when it's scary, Morgan's (Lucas) getting used to it. He's my competitor, but it's fun to talk to him cause he's got a bad ass car right now.

PK: Can you say the same for a 4.42 vs. a 3.75?

TS: The difference is when the 4.42 came up you can't see the scoreboard where when you're on a 3.75 you can see the scoreboard as you go by. The 4.42 I wouldn't of moved my eyes cause I had to set a world record. After watching Beckman set a world record (4.66 FC) right in front of me and get beat on a holeshot, that would have been the worst way to go, to go out there and set the world record and lose on a holeshot, lose the championship, and you could of pulled a hat trick off; there was a lot of stuff going through my mind. Take away the world record and just look at the 4.420 and the 3.75, the 4.42 I'd be expected to crash every time; it's just the way it was and everybody felt that way, it wasn't just me.

PK: Have you accepted, I believe that your still equal, that you one day may have more # 1 qualifiers than you do wins, at 67?

TS: Yeah.

PK: Either way you're a win waiting to happen and your teammates seems to give you the best competition, especially Antron.

TS: Yeah, he's my worst adversary, but we taught him how to do it. It's not like they developed their own tune up, when they all moved over here they, you know. The most difficult thing for me is that we spend years developing stuff and whoever my dad brings out as a new team, gets it and it's really, it's a tough thing to swallow.

INTERVIEW WITH JACK BECKMAN:

Jack Beckman has made a name for himself as a very, very tough competitor. A former instructor at Frank Hawley's Drag Racing school, he has helped over 7,000 students find their way onto the track. He is a cancer survivor and looks like he's lately been living his life to the fullest. A former Super Comp National and Divisional Champion, he is licensed in 12 classes, and drives one of the most feared Funny Cars in the class. One of the meanest racers on the track and one of the nicest off, it's easy to see why Jack Beckman is drives the popular cars with swarms of fans that follow.

PK: The Countdown hasn't really affected you much and I like the Countdown more when it hasn't affected anybody. What are your overall feelings on the countdown and is it a good system for the NHRA?

JB: The countdown is an alogus (Latin; does not mathematically compute) to a yellow flag in NASCAR racing, it bunches everybody up and they stay in the same order. I agree with you, if they stay close to the finish and if it didn't cost somebody with a big lead the race; then it had a good value. I think to truly understand where we're at in this sport you have to look at it from many different angles, the car owners, the drivers, the fans, and the organizations. We gotta face, it's a new generation of fans. Their attention spans are way shorter than it was forty years ago, more channels on television, the internet, and NHRA recognized that they had to do something even if it was an artificial they had to something to keep people's interest to the final race of the year.

Just the fact that we have a countdown that can be called playoffs, kinda makes the last six races slightly more exciting because even though the round points are the same, they are worth more during those last six races. I'm old school, I think if somebody wins the first 15 races they should be able to go to the Bahamas and show up at Pomona and get their trophy, but I completely understand why we gotta keep the fans interested until the final day of the season.

PK: I am not a fan of good teams being told the best they can finish is 11th. Since, the NHRA resets the points at the start of the countdown to make the points race tighter, I feel that the NHRA should qualify everyone for the countdown who has run every countdown qualifying race. It would eliminate anyone getting locked out of a top ten and a top ten finish can still be a goal for everyone. Would you modify the system for teams that peak at the wrong time and get locked out of the all-important top ten when they may perform better than a locked in top ten

JB: What they (the NHRA) did was put a glass ceiling under 10th place and it's a ceiling for 11th on down, the best 11th can finish is 11th; take Johnny Gray last year. (who finished 7th under a no countdown points system) NHRA's defense to this was that post Indy no driver had ever come out of the top ten and won the championship, and my observation is that sometimes a top ten finish opens the door for sponsorship next season. What I think would be a better idea is cut everybody's points in half after Indy, if someone's got a 10 round lead it shouldn't go to 1 and a half rounds; they still carry a 5 round lead. If you got lead going into Indy, you deserve to keep a lead going out of Indy and that person in 11th, 12th, and 13th still have a viable chance at racing for a top ten spot. With your (PK) system, the problem mandating that they gotta attend every race is what if you have a Jim Head or Gary Densham if they don't have the backing to go to 16 races; maybe they ran really well at 10 of them and are in 12th place.

They may wanna attend the last 6 if he could still salvage a top ten finish, but if it was mandated that he had to attend the first 16; they might only go to 2 of the last 6. I think you do something to tighten up the points, but don't cap it where only a certain number of teams are eligible for the championship.

PK: What does it take to be a successful driver in this class?

JB: A mediocre driver could win in a great car, but a great driver can't win in a mediocre car unless you get incredibly lucky four times in a row on race day and that almost never ever happens. First off it takes a great car, I can't even start the thing without four guys there and you're depending on nine other people. I think to be an effective driver, maybe this is a slightly different approach maybe an enormous ego drives someone be hungry and passionate, but my personal opinion is that you better check your ego and recognize that you're doing it as 10 people as not one person. Being a driver's the best on the planet, you get almost all the credit when you seldom deserve it and almost none of the blame when you often deserve it; it's a good gig. I always look at my job in a Nitro Funny Car as very, very different than my job was in my Super Comp Dragster.

My job is not to mess up what the crew did to the car, if I do my best their number comes up on the scoreboard; anything outside than I make it look worse than the car that they gave me. Check your ego, try to stay as calm as possible, and I love the way (Tony) Schumacher puts it, "Be a machine in that racecar."

PK: Can you take me through what you do on a run from the burnout to the completion?

JB: It would be a little snug to be honest with you, oh you mean metaphorically, ok. It takes 2 minutes and 15 seconds, but to describe would take 4 and a half minutes. When I'm in the car strapped in at the water box, body up, before their gonna start the car I make sure I am in forward gear, the mag switches are off, I make sure my arm restraints to the point I can reach everything, get to the harness releases and the parachutes, and then I push the clutch in and hold the break. They windmill the motor to clean it out, they'll nod at me when it's time to start, I turn the mags on, they spin it over, it fires up, I pull the fuel pumps full volume; I told you this was gonna take 4 minutes. I make sure I'm on the break and on the clutch, when they drop the body and motion, break off, I control the speed with the clutch and I roll up and aim for the crew chief.

When he tells me to nail it I crack the throttle, it's got a stop on it so it's only gonna open to a 23 drill bit, not very much and I'm always looking right out in front of me at the track and trying to keep that thing pointed straight on the burnout. We're not always gonna backup in our burnout marks, we're not always gonna do a burnout in the center of the lane, so your job is to try to make the burnout marks go straight down track and at some tracks that's very difficult; the car wants to washout. Lift, clutch in, break on, stop, break off, reverse, backup follow the guy backing me up to get in my tracks, stop, pull forward, stop, body up, they trim the fuel pumps, do all the shit they need to do, body down. Roll up to the crew chief which gets me six inches from the pre-stage beam and stop, and at that point I start trying to get into focus mode. Deep breath let it out, when he motions me forward its visor down and I try to control my breathing from that point on.

Roll up slowly as soon as I light the pre-stage expect in the final at Topeka. Clutch in, break on, wait for the other car, when I'm ready to go in, I'll go fuel pump on, clutch out then I lock my eyes down on that top amber bulb; you can see the stage come on out of your peripheral I inch in and when it comes on stop. I like to think that I'm in sniper mode, I'm locked on something and I'm not moving; your calm, but you're focused. When that light comes on boom, go, and I find my spot out on the racetrack and from that point your reacting to what the car does. You gotta keep it in the groove; you gotta do your best to keep it in the groove and there's several different mindsets you take up there.

If the forecast is for good weather and it's the first two qualifying runs and it does something stupid, you shut off. If you think you're gonna get one run, you better get it to the finish line. If it's race day, you get it to the finish line. Then there's that mindset that we don't beat up any equipment and then there's that mindset that we own this stuff and we need to get this to the finish line to either get in the show or get the win light.

PK: What is your favorite race track?

JB: Anyone where I can get four win lights on Sunday. I love Pomona because as a kid I went to the races there, as an instructor at Frank Hawley's I stood up there and flipped the switch 23,000 times. I love Vegas because as a Sportsman that's the track that runs National Events that I ran the most at. Bristol's bitchin' cause you cannot beat that echo, Denver's amazing because it's carved into the side of a mountain, Chicago's a great facility, Sonoma the road course, there all pretty cool for different reasons. E-Town's a legend that's what I love here and I said it in the press release, "if you are a Funny Car driver, when your done driving and you got your resume complete, it's gotta have an E-Town Funny Car win."

This event now gets convoluted, the Summer Nationals are now in Topeka, but in 1970 the schedule went from four events to seven events and this race was your Summer Nationals. Before '71 this was the place where guys making a living match racing and pushing fiberglass all across the county, this was one of the main stays.

PK: Do you have any aspirations to go back to Top-Fuel or tune?

JB: Yes, yeah, one day I would love to get back in a dragster. I love to have to opportunity to drive a car that could win a national event and maybe say that you were one of the people that were able to win in both categories, and I always been a Top-Fuel guy. Since I was seven years old they were the kings of the sport, the first time I saw them push start at Orange County in 1973; instantly hooked. I always thought the Funny Cars were bitchin' from an entirely different stand point; they put on the show, but the Top-Fuel Dragsters were the shit back then. When I was given the opportunity to drive a Funny Car I took it because there were no other driving opportunities and I'm so glad I did and I wouldn't wanna switch now because I think the Funny Cars are so challenging, but one day I would love to get back in a Top-Fuel car.

PK: Do you wanna tune?

JB: I'm not that smart and I mean that sincerely; it's a different kind of intelligence. Rahn Tobler, because I asked a lot of questions about tune up stuff, and he looks at me and goes, "Hey, my last driver ended up taking the crew chief job is that what you wanna do?" and I said, "Trust me, I couldn't start the damn thing by myself if I was crew chief." I like to understand how things work because I'm mechanical, but the crew chiefs think in an entirely different dimension.

PK: What did you do before this?

JB: Four years in the Air Force then I was an elevator guy for 11 years, and then I taught at the drag race school.

PK: What is your private ride and does your career as a driver influence any of your daily driving habits?

JB: A '96 Nissan pickup with 251,000 miles on it and the only influence it might have is it's downright ready for a parachute cause it doesn't wanna stop and then a 2001 PT Cruiser with 140,000 and it wouldn't do 150 mph if you dropped it out of an airplane. I'm gonna have to say no, they don't influence how I drive. I still got my '68 El Camino that runs 12.50's, 10.15/134 on nitro, and I still got my Super Comp car; the one I won the championship with in 2003.

PK: What win, and single run mean more to you than all the others?

JB: That's so difficult to say because there's some wins when you look back there tough to remember, but there's so many that mean so much for different reasons. This last win in Topeka means a lot because with all the crew changes and things that happened, I thought it might take us a year to get back to the winner's circle. When you're wondering if it's gonna happen again sometimes you don't know that your last win was your last win. Look at Tony Schumacher, they haven't done a thing wrong they just keep getting beat in final rounds, you just never know. My first win in a Nitro car was unbelievable, but my first win ever at the '98 Winternationals in Super Comp in a borrowed car, that's awesome.

My 15 national event wins, I have to say that probably five mean a tremendous amount for different reasons.

PK: Were you a fan with the move to 1000 feet?

JB: Because I'm a purest when I first read it on the internet I was so upset for a half hour, then I started thinking about NHRA took such a risk we are defined as the quarter mile people and they took us away from that. I think it was maybe one of the more brilliant moves that they have made because there's two goofy things about it which makes me believe that one day we probably do need to go back to quarter mile. One is we have two different finish lines now, and the other is you can't compare numbers with quarter mile numbers, but if we ever go back to quarter mile their going to reduce the power so much that you also won't be able too. The awkward thing is just having two different finish lines, but it fixed two things immediately, it cut the speeds down on the cars, and gave us more shutdown area every race track. I have to say if I was in their circumstances, I'm not sure I would have been smart enough to make that call.

PK: Do you think that there is any concern that the NHRA was trying to back them down when they were at 337 in the quarter, now there at 332 at 1000?

JB: Keep in mind, apples to apples, at the same speed at 1000 foot that you were running in a quarter mile, if a driver lifts when they were gonna lift at 1000 foot and get the chutes out, you're doing 270 mph and decelerating at the quarter mile. That is an enormous difference than doing 337 and accelerating.

PK: Could there ever be a point where the increase in performance for these cars ends up that they can begin to greatly diminish the extra 320 feet?

JB: Absolutely. Plus, remember that the cars are an extra 170 pounds heavier now than they were seven years ago; absolutely. You got tons more, literally, kinetic energy going there, so yea we're gonna reach another point in our sport where something needs to be done. The question then becomes do we slow down and stay at 1000 foot, or do we really slow them down and go back to the quarter mile.

PK: We can't go eighth mile?

JB: You know what? Never say never because you'd see 3.3 second times outta Funny Car, 3.0 outta Top Fuel; it'll still be unbelievably exciting. I think if at that point I rather them slow us way down and back to a quarter mile. If they go back to a quarter mile a good speed out of a dragster would be a 305, 298 out of a Funny Car. People say that sucks, they didn't think that sucked back in 1992. I mean this sincerely I am still a huge fan of the sport, I can't fucking believe they give me a paycheck to drive a Nitro Funny Car; I don't think it jaded me or changed me. I still recognize that this is the most bitchin' thing going, if it ends tomorrow I'll be on the other side of the ropes, but I love the sport.

You get some people that get that fire suit on and start thinking their shit doesn't stick, and eventually you don't have this job anymore. It's a great sport and the drivers need to keep in mind what keeps our sport, well obviously the cars are amazing, what makes our sport unique is that the fans can get close to us. Don't get the stick up your ass and get this force field around you and I always tell people any driver that ever bitches at how many people are outside the ropes, shouldn't have anybody outside the ropes. It's as big a part of your job as driving the car.

PK: I know it was a whole rocky situation between all the changes between your team and the NAPA team, is everything smooth now?

JB: Sunday evening, we went up in Tobler's crew chief lounge and we all had a shot and we all celebrated; that should tell you how it went. Nobody likes to lose, but half Capps' crew guys were my crew guys, everybody came over and said we were happy for you. Clearly they didn't wanna lose, it costs them money to lose, but they were happy for us. Everybody's still pretty tight, you wanna win; but burnout to turnout you don't have a friend on this planet. Before and after you wanna be able to respect them and this is a huge part of our lives.

INTERVIEW WITH RON CAPPS:

Ron Capps started driving a Funny Car in 1997 and has become one of the most consistent national event and championship contender since. He has always been one of the best on reaction time and driving as he has won 34 times in 73 final rounds and won over 440 elimination rounds. He's a fan favorite and shows unbreakable dedication on the track and his reward for that will be tying Don Garlits National Event win record of 35. Ron has proving that he can successfully drive a Top-Fuel Dragster, Funny Car, NASCAR, and a dirt track car, so he's a threat in basically anything he drivers. He's finished 2nd in the championship three times even missing the top spot by just 8 points, but I personally feel time is running out in the era that leaves him without a championship as this may be the year that he finally holds that enormous trophy and gets the championship monkey off his back for good.

PK: What are your overall feelings on the countdown and is it a good system for the NHRA?

RC: Yeah, it is. I wasn't so sure the first year, in '07 and I was leading the regular points going into it, then we saw the lead disappear and never saw it again. To be honest with you it's done its job, when I first came into to Funny Car John Force was clinching titles by Dallas and back then there probably three, four or five races after Dallas before Pomona. He was clinching so early in the season people got bored, so this mixes it up. I been on both ends of it, I been leading going in and I been terrible, barely in the countdown and I had a chance. You love it when the countdown comes around becomes it almost evens everything out, I like it.

PK: I am not a fan of good teams being told the best they can finish is 11th. Since, the NHRA resets the points at the start of the countdown to make the points race tighter, I feel that the NHRA should qualify everyone for the countdown who has run every countdown qualifying race. It would eliminate anyone getting locked out of a top ten and a top ten finish can still be a goal for everyone. Would you modify the system for teams that peak at the wrong time and get locked out of the all-important top ten when they may perform better than a locked in top ten finisher?

RC: My teammate Johnny Gray is a great example of that last year how he could of won the championship had he been in it. Robert Hight, the year that he barely got in, perhaps maybe he shouldn't of been in and won the championship. It's tough, but you gotta race by what rules you have. The countdown's created this whole playoff atmosphere, I don't mind it.

PK: What does it take to be a successful driver in this class?

RC: Consistency, alertness, I think mainly you gotta be able to be able to hear the car and feel what the cars doing. People think to be a successful drive you just stand on the gas and hang on to a bar when in actuality it's the driver that catches them when they do something wrong. Catch it when it breaks track and you peddle it, know when something's not right and shut it off and keep it from blowing up and causing more work for the guys. I think all those make you a successful driver.

PK: What is your favorite race track?

RC: My favorite race track is probably Sonoma. I grew up there in central California, I lived in the area for a while, that atmosphere and the people up there remind me when I used to go to Fremont Dragway when I was a kid with my mom and dad. I won there three of four times, for me it's a great race track for me to go back to.

PK: You are one of the best in the class for having a really great light at any time. How do you stay so focused and what do you attribute to being the most important factor?

RC: I don't think people understand that the car has a lot to do with it and how the crew chief has the clutch set up and that depends on how the car reacts. Again it goes back to being consistent and how you roll in and stage the car. We're talking inches when you roll it into stage after you light the pre-stage bulb, so it's very crucial that you try and do the same thing every time. The really good drivers I look at are the ones that don't roll in deep to make their numbers look better and those I respect more when I race cause I know when they have a good light, and I look, I even look at 60 foot times to see how much a driver rolled it in.

Those are the guys I really get up to race cause I know it's sorta like a poker game up there in Top-Fuel and Funny Car. Who's gonna roll in deep, if the guys gonna roll in deep on 'ya and it looks like a holeshot when it's really not a holeshot.

PK: Out of all the stats I did on your career you averaged around a 60 percent (Left First) your entire career and that's pretty good.

RC: Early in my career I put the top light out on drivers I thought I could mess up mentally and it worked a lot of times, but really as you grow older and wiser you learn that you just try and do the same thing every time.

PK: Do you have any aspirations to return to Top-Fuel, crew chief, or own?

RC: Yeah, I think one day, right now I'm stuck on trying to win a championship in a Funny Car. I had offers to go back and drive one the last few years, but I don't want to until I win a championship; but I love to go back and do what Del did. (return to Top-Fuel and win the championship)

PK: Your part of an elite club, you're not the only guy to drive in both classes, but you are one of the few that have won in both.

RC: Yeah, what's cool is a few years ago I got to drive Tony's (Schumacher) car on test day and it was right after he set the speed record in the quarter mile. We stuck around and Tony had to go somewhere for the Army and we were testing and at the time Alan Johnson asked me to drive Tony's car right after it set the speed record and in Topeka it went something like 337 and it was just amazing to jump in a Top-Fuel car after being in a Funny Car for so long.

PK: Are they easier to drive?

RC: Well I wouldn't say easier, well, physically yeah because you don't move the wheel as much. You gotta be very precise with your movements.

PK: What is your private ride and does your career as a driver influence any of your daily driving habits?

RC: I have a Cadillac CTS-V, the first year, 2004 they came out with it.

PK: What win, and single run mean more to you than all the others?

RC: As far as a win the first time I doubled up for Don Prudhomme, me and Larry won the Winternationals in '98. That was probably the biggest win, my family were there, Snake has never doubled up.

PK: Are you a fan of 1000 foot?

RC: I am now because we can't lengthen some of these tracks, but if we were gonna go back and I had a choice, and you gotta remember I'm not a crew chief, but I think you gotta make it something that's easy to police and that's the hardest part. I drive the Nostalgia Funny Cars a lot and those go faster and faster, but I have to say limiting the fuel. They got one pump on 'em, 21 gallon maximum I think it is and those cars run 5.75, 5.80's the good ones and they seem to be kind stuck there. I would have to say keeping the fuel limited to one pump and maybe having those pumps checked periodically would probably be the best thing.

PK: How much is a run?

RC: I hear its $8 to $10,000 per run, that's what I heard; I don't know how accurate that is.

PK: Can you provide an example of what a driver and a crew chief would roughly make in a season?

RC: It's a good question as of late. When I was at Don Prudhomme's driving the Copenhagen and Skoal cars I was making between $250 and $400,000, and that was back '99, 2000. You gotta remember at the time there was not a whole lot of paid drivers out here because a lot of drivers owned their own cars, there's more now. At the time there was Larry Dixon, myself, I think Gary Scelzi, not to many guys were around. I always had big sponsors and I do a lot of stuff away from the track and that's where you earn your money more than anywhere else. Crew Chiefs are probably between $250 and $400,000 now, some are more.

INTERVIEW WITH JOHNNY GRAY:

Johnny Gray has proved that he can be successful in many different classes, Top Alcohol Dragster, Top Alcohol Funny Car, Comp Eliminator, Pro Stock and Funny Car. Currently in his second year since his return to Funny Car, he came back to drive for Don Schumacher, and it has really accelerated his Funny Car career. He just missed the countdown last season, but unofficially could have finished well into the top ten. This year he is well on target for making the countdown and contending for the championship with a team that's very capable of winning it. At 59, Johnny Gray is showing no signs of slowing down and will only continue making competitors nervous.

PK: Last season you finished 11th in the points and had an amazing countdown, earning more points than anyone. If you qualified in last place for the countdown you could of finished 2nd. Under the old points system you would have finished in 7th place last year. What are your overall feelings on the countdown and is it a good system for the NHRA?

JG: I don't particularly like the countdown, because I was in the position where it hurt me real bad last year. We struggled a little bit getting the season going, and did not make the top ten, but at the end of last year I had one of the fastest cars out here; it was all for naught. Basically all we did was aggravate people that were in the countdown.

PK: I am not a fan of good teams being told the best they can finish is 11th. Since, the NHRA resets the points at the start of the countdown to make the points race tighter, I feel that the NHRA should qualify everyone for the countdown who has run every countdown qualifying race. It would eliminate anyone getting locked out of a top ten and a top ten finish can still be a goal for everyone. Would you modify the system for teams that peak at the wrong time and get locked out of the all-important top ten when they may perform better than a locked in top ten finisher?

JG: There could be several ways to go about changing it, but we start the season, we know what the rules are, so you abide by 'em and you run that way. Do I particularly like the countdown? No, if you're gonna do anything reset the points let the top 16 in the countdown, reset the points and see where everybody ends up and give them 20 points or 10 points for the position they were in and just reset everything.

PK: In 2000, you tuned yourself, you tuned your own Funny Car and you did fairly well with it. Have you ever gone back to tuning?

JG: No, I have made suggestions. My crew chief and I, Rob Wendland, use to run against each other all the time in alcohol and I always tuned all my own alcohol cars. We raced each other in Dragster and Funny Car when I ran alcohol and he tuned other people. My alcohol cars were pretty competitive.

PK: Will you ever return to Pro Stock?

JG: I'm 59 years old, and if there's one thing I learned never say never.

PK: What are you in charge with on your son's team?

JG: I own the engine shop, I own the team, and I have some input in what we do with the engines.

PK: What else do you run in-house?

JG: We do everything in-house. The only thing we do not do in-house is build the chassis. We design, cut our own heads, intake, everything.

PK: Do you have any aspirations to drive in another class you haven't yet?

JG: Not really. I'm not gonna say that the day won't come where I might play with a Pro Mod car a little bit. I'm not a Dragster guy; I really care nothing about Dragsters. I ran a Dragster in '93 for just a little just cause I wanted to be the first gasoline powered dragster to run 200 mph and it was just a project, then I sold that. I went to Alcohol Dragster cause Mike Spitzer who builds those cars wanted me to run one and I tried it a year and it ran real well; it was a very competitive car. I think we ended up 5th or 6th in the points, but it was a very competitive car there just not fun to drive and after a few discussions my wife let me go to Alcohol Funny Car and I loved it.

I actually got in a lot of trouble in Denver, Colorado because Jay Payne who's a really good friend of mine and he was busting my chops for quitting the Dragsters when he was the Dragster champ and getting into Funny Cars. I made the comment to him that I really rather get the tow truck and pull me around the pits in the Funny Car than go make a run in my Dragster. Now Jay drives Pro Mods, and Funny Cars, I always told him if you ever go make a run in a Funny Car you put the Dragster out there and let weeds grow up in it. I asked him where his Dragster was he said, "In the backyards, weeds were growing up in it." Some people like the Funny Car, some people don't. I feel real comfortable when they lower the body and I'm in my own little world in there.

PK: Have you ever found yourself in the habit of trying to shift the Nitro Funny Car in a run like you had to in Alcohol Funny Car?

JG: No, you're just hanging on. I'm not gonna say there real hard to drive; a Funny Car is relatively easy to drive if it's on a really good pass. When it's not right, then it's really hard to drive. If it leaves the line real good, gets up on the tire, makes a real nice clean run, they are relatively easy. When they start moving around they get hard to drive.

PK: What win means the most to you?

JG: Probably my Brainerd win in the Fuel Funny Car. This is my second stint back in a Funny Car, maybe even my third; Don brought me out to drive the Wonder Wagon. At my age you don't get to win a whole lot anymore, and you know your time is short in these things so to go win Brainerd in a Fuel Funny Car was a big win.

INTERVIEW WITH TONY PEDREGON:

Tony Pedregon got hired to drive a second car for John Force in 1996 and has cemented his name in the class ever since. He is 2nd on the all-time Funny Car win list with 43, but that is not what drives him to be successful. He has pure passion for the sport and having a successful program no matter the capability. In 2004, he stated his own team after winning a championship the year before, and by 2012 he has managed to win another championship, 16 wins, and improved his overall record to over 500 round wins and almost a 70% left first reaction time average. He has always been an expert at marketing agreements and keeping himself in the Funny Car as 2012 is a year that looks like he can finally return to championship contending, race winning status.

PK: In 2007 you won the championship in the countdown when under a regular points system you actually finished 35 points out and in 3rd. In 2009 you would of won the championship by 12 points under regular points when in the countdown you finished 144 points out and in 6th. There's no denying that you are a 2-Time champion under any system. What are your overall feelings on the countdown and is it a good system for the NHRA?

TP: I think so, it could work either way and in the end I think the purpose of the countdown is to generate excitement. I'm a sports fanatic; I follow football and basketball, so we got a regular season and a playoff. I'm good with that, the pros and the cons of it.

PK: I am not a fan of good teams being told the best they can finish is 11th. Since, the NHRA resets the points at the start of the countdown to make the points race tighter, I feel that the NHRA should qualify everyone for the countdown who has run every countdown qualifying race. It would eliminate anyone getting locked out of a top ten and a top ten finish can still be a goal for everyone. Would you modify the system for teams that peak at the wrong time and get locked out of the all-important top ten when they may perform better than a locked in top ten finisher?

TP: I think they should have a wildcard or two, maybe having some other race within a race to get the last two spots. I don't think it should be a popularity contest like they have that (Traxxas) shootout with the final spot, it doesn't make sense, but we're glad to have Traxxas that's bringing that show back. I think instead of 12 cars you got a lot of good quality cars, so why wouldn't you have a consolation and bring a few other cars in. I think they should and there still at a disadvantage, they got a lot more catching up to do, but I think with the corporate involvement that you have at this level you should allow some other teams to make it in.

PK: What does it take to be a successful driver in this class?

TP: You gotta be dedicated, you gotta have more mental toughness, maybe physical attributes. What we do is a short amount of time, we don't go around on a track, we mentally have to be right at the fraction of a second when we leave the starting line; in the short amount of time you gotta pay attention to those things.

PK: What is your favorite race track?

TP: I like Vegas, I'm always gonna be partial because I was able to nail down my championship there, my first one and I made a pretty good move in '07 when we were able to win that 2nd championship. I love Sonoma, I like racing up there, I probably like the area more than anything. I say Vegas still, number one.

PK: You are one of the best in the class for having a really great light at any time averaging almost 70% (Left First) your entire career. How do you stay so focused and what do you attribute to being the most important factor?

TP: Fear of losing. I conditioned myself at a very young age and I don't like losing and whatever I can control I try and be good at. I live this stuff and I don't know if you're physically fit it's gonna make it any better, but I try to stay healthy. I think this is a mental game and I think you gotta be sharp. I take that approach, I don't like losing.

PK: Do you have any aspirations to go back to Top-Fuel?

TP: No, at this point I love watching them, but I see how those chassis flex, I want no part of them if I have my way. I like Funny Cars, I like the way they look, I like there wheelbase, there hard to drive, there not very pleasant to drive sometimes, I like that challenge.

PK: What about being a crew chief?

TP: I enjoy getting involved with the car to some degree; I think I'm stronger in some areas than other areas, not just in the seat, but as a team owner. I think that presents some challenges. It's hard to say, it's not outta the question, but I hope I can stay a team owner even when I'm not driving anymore.

PK: What is your private ride and does your career as a driver/rider influence any of your daily driving habits?

TP: No, thank goodness it doesn't. It's a Toyota Sequoia actually and I'm very family oriented, I got kids, so it's practical. I got a hot rod that I've been working on for six years and I hope I finish it this summer, but that's my toy, it's got an LS7 (motor) and it's 540 horsepower. Maybe when I finish it the people that I know that wanna hear that cool answer I'll give them that one, but for now it's the family car.

PK: What championship, win, and single run mean more to you than all the others?

TP: It was probably the final in Vegas of '07 because all the other cars that were close in the countdown right behind me got beat in the first round. I kept telling myself I could go into this last race one, one and a half, two rounds ahead and by the time I got to the final, at that point I realized, not technically, but I could wound these guys here if I just win this one round. That final round, I think I raced Ashley (Force), it was a big one.

PK: Do you race the track or the opponent?

TP: Both. I factor in both for anybody that says track, mistake, for anybody that says opponent, mistake.

PK: Over the course of a weekend the goal is to make 8 passes down the strip. Outside of explosions and any major after run engine damage, what is the maximum expectancy of the parts you have to replace due to wear and what and when do you replace?

TP: Too often! They need to do something so we put less stress on the parts and we don't go broke. Billet block, billet cranks, they have a very short lifespan. The rods, the pistons, some of the parts after we get x amount of runs, whether we want to or not we still have to take them out of service.

PK: What is the cost of one pass and what parts are needed?

TP: $7500 to $10,000. It's an expensive sport.

PK: The price to race in the sport's top class keeps rising and has almost kept the independent team out of racing completely. What do you see for the reason the costs have skyrocketed and what would you do to put a cap on or decrease the costs making it friendlier to small budget teams?

TP: You gotta somehow contain the amount of power these cars make, whether you do it with fuel, blower overdrive, or compression. There's a lot of ways that make sense to do it, but nobody's really motivated to do that for some strange reason.

PK: Do you feel that the sport is on a good path for the future ahead?

TP: I'm a perfectionist and my reply is gonna be that there's always room for improvement. Is it going where it needs to be? Well, as long as there's growth, growth is good, but I think it could be better.

PK: What are your feelings on the sport's decision to move to 1000 feet?

TP: Until there (NHRA) willing to do something to slow the cars down it seems to make sense. In terms of the marketability of the sport, I think there's a way to maintain this level of safety and race some races in a quarter mile. Not here, (Englishtown) but there's some places where we could go the quarter mile in. Some of the other teams will tell you that the cars are gonna blow, no, these cars blow up at 700 feet if you run it wrong. I'm a quarter mile guy where we can race a quarter mile, I gotta walk into the boardroom and I gotta sell a program and hey, it's tough to sell a quarter mile let alone a thousand feet.

PK: What does it take to be a successful team owner in this class?

TP: You gotta be pretty well rounded. You gotta be educated, you gotta understand business, you have to understand racing; not both, but you have to combine the two. You have to be real creative and work like heck to stay here.

PK: You always have done a great job at finding sponsors and keeping yourself out here.

TP: I gotten real creative and it's frustrating sometimes because I know there are so many different areas where I would like to be a little bit stronger, but I hustle. I been able to manage and maintain being here, but it could always be better.

PK: Can you provide an example of the financials and the amount of parts that are needed to compete at top level for a season?

TP: It's well in the millions and I think that's a moving target. You could make it work with a couple million, some guys make it work with a lot less, but in the end to compete with a team like Force and a team like Schumacher I wouldn't say you need as much, but it wouldn't hurt to get close. I think in the end a guy like me and a guy like Cruz could do more with a little bit less, could we do more with a lot less? We've done it, but it's hard to do it consistently.

PK: Are you at the ability where you can operate as an effective two car team?

TP: Yeah, I mean it's getting better, we're not we're we'd like to be, but we plan on getting there. We're at the midway point of the pre countdown and we need to get it together.

PK: But you are exactly where you need to be for the countdown as you seem to be getting better every weekend and can peak at the right moment.

TP: Yeah. We need to make it, we need to continue it, we need to make it stick tomorrow.

PK: Can you provide an example of what a driver and a crew chief would roughly make in a season?

TP: I would say that depends on the season. A lot of it is based on a bonus, the car performs better, they get more. Some of them could make a couple hundred thousand, some of them could make even more than that if they have a great season. I'm not saying it's what I pay these guys cause I just don't have that type of program anymore.

PK: Do you kids have any aspirations to drive?

TP: If they do I'm gonna talk them out of it. I'm gonna put a doctor's outfit on 'em.

1320 VS. 1000 FEET: A FULL DEBATE:

INTERVIEW WITH DON GARLITS:

Don Garlits is a name that you can mention to any drag racing fan and images of innovation, wins, championships, success and respect comes to mind. He was voted # 1 drag racer of all-time by the NHRA in 2001, he's won a total of 17 championships and 144 events when you look at his entire career over many sanctioning bodies. In the NHRA alone he has a resume that most drivers would be envious of as he's won 3 championships and 35 events, including 8 U.S. National Wins. Don was also the first drag racer to earn national records as the first to 170, 180, 200, 240, 250, 260, and 270 miles per hour in the quarter mile as well as being the first to break the 200 MPH barrier in the 1/8 mile. Don started his career in 1950 and once he won his first race in 1955, he made it very difficult for anyone to beat him.

After winning 17 championships, 144 events, and many match races, he hung up his helmet in 1987 to only pick it up 14 years later in the pursuit of accomplishing two things that would make his resume perfectly complete. He wanted to run a four second pass and record a 300 MPH run and at the U.S Nationals in 2001 his already well rounded resume was made compete. With the help of Gary Clapshaw loaning his equipment and his crew chief Lonnie Strode, he ran a 4.720 at 303.37 MPH. In 2002 he would again return, this time with his own equipment after an upgrade to his decade old trademarked mono-wing Swamp Rat XXXII to meet current safety specs in order to run 3 events. Don would go on to record two more 4 second passes and 1 more 300 MPH run with a 4.881, and a 4.763 with a major improvement in speed running 318.54 MPH in the Richard Hogan tuned machine.

In 2003, He worked with chassis builder Murf McKinney and designed Swamp Rat XXXIV, which was also a mono-wing. He would go on to record ten more 4 second runs (4.737, 4,776, 4.778, 4.761, 4.788, 4.790, 4.805, 4.809,4.80 4.943) and 6 more 300 MPH runs, 306.85, 307.44, 310.77, 310.91, 319.98 and a huge 323.04; again with Hogan tuning. In his brief return he did not just run a four second pass at over 300 MPH, he ended up running 13 four second passes with 8 of them being over 300 MPH, and I have a feeling that it makes Don even more proud to know that he has runs under 4 seconds and over 300 MPH in the quarter mile with his own equipment. Since his retirement he has inducted continued to induct member in to the drag racing hall of fame that he created in 1991 and has 233 members.

62 years after first stepping into a race car, he still is actively involved in the sport and makes an attempt to win 1 more event in stock every now and then. He is a founding father in preserving the history of drag racing with his museum in Ocala, FL since 1976. His innovations in safety for a driver, being the first to endorse a fire suit, to his technological innovations to the dragsters have made the sport safer for the racers. Drag racing may never have another drag racer that was not only so dominant on the track, but has given himself, his ideas, and his innovations unselfishly for the improvement of the sport. It's easy to see why drag racers and fans alike are left in awe when they thing about how truly impressive Don Garlits really is.

PK: After the infamous transmission explosion on the starting line in 1970 with Swamp Rat XIII, you helped implement the revolutionary change where the engine would remain behind the driver in a Top-Fuel Dragster. Although you were not the first to develop a rear engine dragster, you were the first to campaign one successfully on the track. How long was the entire process from the development to the success that was found with tweaks to the suspension? In the early stages, was there ever a point where you thought that having success with a rear engine dragster was more of a dream than a reality?

DG: The process took over 3 months and in fact I had given up, built Swamp Rat XXV, the best Slingshot we ever built, which hangs in the Showroom of Summit Racing in Georgia. My wife caught me in the process and demanded I get back on the rear engine project. Two days later we stumbled on the problem, the steering was too fast and the rest is history. The fact of the matter is; I had a very nice rear engine gas car in 1957 that didn't handle and my buddies, back then, round track racers advised me to speed up the steering which I did and my Brother was almost killed. We scrapped the project!

PK: Of all your innovations, what do you feel is your greatest?

DG: The rear engine project was my most important as to safety, but the Drag Racing Museum is more important as to saving the history of the sport.

PK: Which Swamp Rat is your favorite?

DG: Swamp Rat I is my favorite, it made me famous and I raced the car for over seven years, then in 1979 restored the "Old Girl" and took it to the US Nationals, drove it down the strip at over 165 MPH, which started the whole nostalgia thing!

PK: What are your overall feelings on the countdown and is it a good system for the NHRA?

DG: I liked the original way the points were complied, I don't care if a team wins early, too damn bad, if you are a winner, you are a winner!

PK: What does it take to be a successful Top-Fuel crew chief?

DG: A successful crew chief today needs to be able to translate the downloaded information to the tuning of the racecar. During my championship years in '85 and '86, I built the car from scratch, built the engines, tuned the car and drove it, that is not possible today and that is why there are only a few teams competing. The "money" guys made it better! What a joke! I knew the limitations of my car and engine and I didn't exceed those limitations! Translate that to; "Very little oil on the Dragstrip"! Oh, I forgot to mention, we didn't have diapers to hold back small amounts of oil! Any oil at all went right on the strip! Today almost all engines put down some oil, but the diapers catch all but the catastrophe explosions!

PK: Can you provide an example of what type budget you were working with or the budget that was necessary for a championship caliber team in such as yours in the '85 and '86 seasons and

DG: Budget in 1985 and 86 was a little over 900K per year, up from the 150K to 200K the years before.

PK: The price to race in the sport's top class keeps rising and has almost kept the independent team out of racing completely. What do you see for the reason the costs have skyrocketed and what would you do to put a cap on or decrease the costs making it friendlier to small budget teams?

DG: No one will like this! No oil ever on the drag strip, plus remove the "diapers" so we really know when the engine has expired. Much smaller wings and tires, a break rule so if one car oils the strip, the other car is not beat. All rules off the engine such as cubic inches, etc. NHRA owns and controls the fuel pumps and they are reduced in size dramatically. Smaller blowers at reduced overdrive ratios. I could go on, but you see the drift.

PK: Do you race the track or the opponent?

DG: I raced the opponent, but never tried to overpower the track or overstress the engine, beat lots of faster cars this way; many went up in smoke against me!

PK: Of all the runs you made down the quarter mile, what was the most memorable?

DG: The 303 MPH run in Gary Clapshaw's T/F Car at Indy in 2001 was definitely the most memorable!

PK: You have 144 event wins and won 17 championships; is there a single win and championship that stands out above the rest?

DG: The win at Ontario in 1975 that clinched the 1975 NHRA Winston World Championship and the 250 MPH run at this event. The record stood for 7 years! Most important, the entire NHRA

Crew was against me and for Beck, there is no way I should have won. Today the NHRA has done a complete 180 and I love the entire crew from President Tom Compton to the little guys that help you park your rig!

PK: What is your favorite race track?

DG: Indy, won 8 times there and should have won 10 times!

PK: Will there ever be one last attempt in a dragster?

DG: I will never drive another Top-Fuel Dragster.

PK: What are your feelings on the sport's decision to move to 1000 feet?

DG: I was for the 1000 foot move after Kalitta's accident, as NHRA was going to slow the cars down. Because of the powerful, rich Top-Fuel Teams they have not been able to do this and return to quarter mile racing. The fans hate 1000 foot racing and the stands show this, but NHRA is between a rock and a hard spot, they don't want to hurt anybody, but the teams control the technology! I could fix the problem, but all my racing friends would hate me and at the same time my fans in the stands would love me! It is a very tough situation.

PK: Would you make any improvements to today's dragster?

DG: I would make improvements to Top-Fuel. I would mandate an enclosed cockpit such as the one Schumacher is trying to run and the one I did run in 1986. Then I would encourage the teams to run the mono-wing configuration, as it helps the cars go straight during clutch lock-up. I would also make the Top-Fuel cars run much smaller fuel pumps to help with parts attrition.

PK: The move to 1000 feet turned back the clock on the incremental performance in Top-Fuel for a short time, but the E.T. record in 1000 feet is the quickest a dragster has been to 1000 feet in the history of the sport. Spencer Massey ran a 3.728 and could add up to being the first ever 4.3 second run. Saying that we will eventually hit 3.6 and 335 MPH in 1000 feet, is there any need for the NHRA to be concerned?

DG: Of course there is need for NHRA to be concerned, I have made this statement several times; there is no place in side by side auto racing for 8000 horsepower engines. What we need is; one event each year at a really long track like Gainesville, no timers in the center of the track, one car at a time, quarter mile racing, all gloves are off, no rules except for safety and let's see just how fast and quick we can go! You are ordered to leave the track after the first oil-down. Run as hard as you can with any parts available, but don't blow up! No spectators past the halfway mark. No points, no money, just trophies and the record certificate. This would be kind of like Bonneville.

PK: The move to 1000 feet gave the sport an extra 320 foot window to slow down. If we stay the course with 1000 feet could the time ever come where the increase in performance for these cars ends up that they can begin to greatly diminish the extra 320 feet, thus drivers facing the same possibility of danger that they faced when it was 1320 feet?

DG: If some restrictions are not implemented very soon, we will have to go to 1/8th mile racing and then watch the paying fans disappear!

PK: Your mono-wing design has always been a topic of debate for you and the NHRA. I personally feel it looks better, but I also remember that you state it is stronger and safer that the current trend of wings. Why is there such resistance against it when we are dealing with a class where wing failures have killed racers and even had racers leave the class because of the fear of a wing failure and being a victim of 7000-12000 pounds of downforce that has no support?

DG: The mono-wing came at a very bad time; NHRA was trying to slow the cars top end speed down. My mono-wing car gained 65 MPH during the last half of the run at Gainesville in 2003 during the 323.04 run. This was a full 3 MPH more than any other car at that time. NHRA could see the handwriting on the wall, this new design was going to increase the top speed of the fuel dragsters and this was the opposite of the NHRA desired safety goals.

PK: If the sport was to return to 1320 feet, what steps would you take in slowing these cars down to make sure that a quarter mile return was a safe return?

DG: The Top-Fuel cars would have the following rules changed to allow them to return to quarter mile racing;
1. Any oil down, anytime, disqualifies the run, time trial or elimination, the same as the rear tires crossing the barrier lines.
2. Much smaller fuel pumps, probably around 50 to 60 gallons per minute
3. A smaller, single element wing, at least 24" lower and moved forward about 12 inches
4. Return to a smaller blower, perhaps a 12-71 or even a 10-71 with blower speed restrictions
5. Smaller Goodyear tires, the tires are just too good!
6. NHRA needs to put the break rule into effect, if the winning car cannot return, the loser is reinstated
7. 20 to 30 minutes between rounds
8. In Eliminations, the engine you start with is the engine you finish with, no engine changes!
9. Teams; no team can have two cars in the same class as it leads to hanky-panky. A team could field a car in every NHRA class if they wanted to, but not two or more cars in the same class.
10. From this point forward, any time a car exceeded 300 MPH in the quarter mile, the fuel pumps or the blowers, for the entire fuel class would be reduced in size. I might even go so far as to take complete control of the fuel pumps by NHRA owning them and giving them out at the race and collecting them back up at the end. We would need a fuel

pump factory trailer on site to handle the pumps and do the flow work on site.

PK: Do you feel that the sport is on a good path for the future ahead?

DG: If something similar to what I recommend is not done soon, we will not have fuel racing very long as the big tracks will not be able to afford it any longer. My rules will increase the fields and make the racing much less expensive. I think this covers everything, but I don't envy Tom Compton, or NHRA and the job they are confronted with to try and save the sport.

PK: What are your private rides?

DG: My personal rides, first is the 1940 Ford 4 door sedan, black with a Hemi Desoto for power, all "Old School", no AC, Auto Trany or PS, just the way they were back in the day! Then of course for comfort and long trips, my 2011 Dodge Charger "Mopar" with all the bells and whistles, black and Hemi power, of course!

WHAT DOES IT TAKES BE A SUCCESSFUL DRIVER?

INTERVIEW WITH LARRY DIXON:

When Don Prudhomme retired from driving in 1994, he personally picked Larry Dixon to fill his shoes; Larry did that and much, much more. After 16 years of driving for Snake racing and later Alan Johnson Racing, he won 3 championships, and won 62 races in 108 final rounds, 2nd best for wins and finals in Top-Fuel. He's also done things that some drivers have never done such as win 637 elimination rounds out of 914, 66.9%, win the U.S. Nationals 4 times, qualify for 377 races with an average qualified spot of 4.56, finish in the top 5 12 times, and something no one can touch; being the first to break the 4.4 barrier with a 4.486 in 1999. 2012 finds him outside the driver's seat, but with a resume as impressive as his; it should not take long to find a sponsor. Once he's back driving he can contend for a championship, his 18th consecutive top ten finish, and continue to prove why he is one of the best drivers in the classes history.

PK: What are your overall feelings on the countdown and is it a good system for the NHRA?

LD: Yes. I think the NHRA has done a great job to get people to talk about points in the middle of the season. At the top where they might be losing ground on 2nd, and around the 10th spot fighting to get in. That wouldn't have taken place in the past. Having won a championship in both formats I can say they were both equally rewarding.

PK: I am not a fan of good teams being told the best they can finish is 11th. Since, the NHRA resets the points at the start of the countdown to make the points race tighter, I feel that the NHRA should qualify everyone for the countdown who has run every countdown qualifying race. It would eliminate anyone getting locked out of a top ten and a top ten finish can still be a goal for everyone. Would you modify the system for teams that peak at the wrong time and get locked out of the all-important top ten when they may perform better than a locked in top ten finisher?

LD: No. The points position you find yourself in is a report card on how your season is going. If you're up, you have good marks, down, not so much. My feeling is, this isn't 5 year olds playing soccer. Everyone doesn't deserve a trophy. If you're not in the top 10, you shouldn't get a prize.

PK: What does it take to be a successful driver in this class?

LD: Effort. I believe to be successful driving is no different than excelling at other sports or businesses. Whatever effort you feel necessary to be better than your opponent.

PK: Can you take me through what you do on a run from the burnout to the completion?

LD: Everything you do in the car needs to be repetitive. The burnout, the speed backing up, staging, even the time your foot is off the clutch, etc. That creates consistency. The team needs to have everything the same so as when a crew chief makes a change, he can see it. The driver is another piece of the puzzle to help make that happen

PK: What is your favorite race track?

LD: Indy, Pomona, Gainesville. Having to pick one over another would be like trying to pick your favorite kid. I can't do that.

PK: You are one of the best in the class for having a really great light at any time. How do you stay so focused and what do you attribute to being the most important factor?

LD: Fear of failure. Not wanting to let my team down.

PK: Do you have any aspirations to drive in another class, or be a crew chief, or a team owner in any class?

LD: Although I love all the classes, I'm a nitro guy, that's where I was born and raised, I don't see me changing now. I have a lot of respect for the job that the top tuners do on the tour and I don't put myself anywhere near that level, but I enjoy listening to the thought process. As far as ownership goes, I'll let you know how that goes real soon…and it might not be only in the nitro classes.

PK: What is your private ride and does your career as a driver/rider influence any of your daily driving habits?

LD: I must get it out of my system on weekends. I drive a Chevy Silverado pickup truck and I just cruise around in it. Definitely enough for me on the streets.

PK: What championship, win, and single run mean more to you than all the others?

LD: The next one. Not my line, but Tom Brady's. It fits perfectly with where my head is always at, the next one.

PK: Do you feel that the sport is on a good path for the future ahead?

LD: Yes. I think our sport of NHRA Drag Racing is coming out of this economic downturn faster than the other motorsports as our numbers to go racing weren't as wildly inflated as some of the others. NHRA Drag Racing has great value and I believe companies do and will recognize that moving forward.

PK: What are your feelings on the sport's decision to move to 1000 feet?

LD: I was for it at the time because that was the easiest fix for the moment until the proper modifications were made to the cars and the facilities.

PK: If the sport was to return to 1320 feet, what steps would you take in slowing these cars down to make sure that a quarter mile return was a safe return?

LD: It looks like the restrictor plate has shown some promise, so I would say in that area. Get rid of the pressure/air in the motor and you cannot burn the same amount of fuel. The cars that are running fast in the nitro classes are spending a lot of time and money right now in that area. If the nitro classes were limited to say an 8:71 supercharger, they probably wouldn't go as fast.

PK: The move to 1000 feet turned back the clock on the incremental performance in Top-Fuel for a short time, but the E.T. record in 1000 feet is the quickest a dragster has been to 1000 feet in the history of the sport. Spencer Massey ran a 3.728 and could add up to being the first ever 4.3 second run. Saying that we will eventually hit 3.6 and 335 MPH in 1000 feet, is there any need for the NHRA to be concerned?

LD: The NHRA ALWAYS needs to be concerned. That is their responsibility to keep the team/us in check. We need that. Crew chiefs will always push the envelope, that's their jobs and responsibility.

PK: The move to 1000 feet gave the sport an extra 320 foot window to slow down. If we stay the course with 1000 feet could the time ever come where the increase in performance for these cars ends up that they can begin to greatly diminish the extra 320 feet, thus drivers facing the same possibility of danger that they faced when it was 1320 feet?

LD: I would imagine that's a possibility. That's why we need the NHRA to keep the teams and our sport in check.

PK: Once and for all, can you set the record straight on all the rumors that you were fired from AJR?

LD: What can be said was said in the release AJR sent out last December. They have 2 great drivers they picked to drive their cars and I wish them the best. Del landed on his feet with the Kalitta/Patron team and it's on me to find a new home for 2013.

PK: Do any of your kids have any NHRA aspirations?

LD: My kids love the sport as I did growing up. If one or all wanted to go NHRA Drag Racing, I couldn't be prouder.

PK: What was it like running the sports first 4.4 back in 1999?

LD: That was a barrier that my crew chief at the time, Dale Armstrong wanted. I was extremely proud that I was part of it.

INTERVIEW WITH SPENCER MASSEY:

Spencer Massey started his career driving in a championship contending Top Alcohol Dragster in 2006 and moved up to Top-Fuel by 2008; he won the 2008 IHRA Top-Fuel championship. He was hired by Don Prudhomme to drive his Top-Fuel Dragster in 2009, Don's final year of owning a team in the NHRA, and he represented Don well by winning 2 races and finishing in 6th place. He was then hired to drive for Don Schumacher in 2011 and last year he narrowly missed winning the championship, walking away with 4 wins and 45 elimination round wins; they are running even stronger in 2012. You may want to say he is so dominating because he has been blessed with great crew chiefs and Dragsters, but I kid you not, he exceeds in his job of just cutting okay lights; he almost embarrasses his opponents by being one of the best, if not the best as he bleeds pure passion for being the best he could be always.

PK: What are your overall feelings on the countdown and is it a good system for the NHRA?

SM: I actually love the countdown; it makes it to where you have to work hard to get to the top ten in the middle of the season, or any part of the season. Once you're in the countdown everybody pretty much gets re-zeroed up to certain points for whatever position you're in, but it makes it that much more of a dogfight towards the end. An old system, meaning that the driver could of walked away with it where we start the countdown, Indy or the next race after Indy, to where the championship could have been already locked up and made it a not interesting final few races; so I love the countdown.

PK: I am not a fan of good teams being told the best they can finish is 11th. Since, the NHRA resets the points at the start of the countdown to make the points race tighter, I feel that the NHRA should qualify everyone for the countdown who has run every countdown qualifying race. It would eliminate anyone getting locked out of a top ten and a top ten finish can still be a goal for everyone. Would you modify the system for teams that peak at the wrong time and get locked out of the all-important top ten when they may perform better than a locked in top ten finisher?

SM: I would change it, I like what we got going on. Obviously there's times where teams are getting backed into the corner and that times happening like right now in our 2012 season. You look at the alBalooshi car where the Al-Anabi guys, there in a position where they need to step up. You look at some of our (DSR) cars, there are a lot of good cars out there that are on the bump right now and it's getting to the point where they have to step their game up and make it into the countdown. Once they get into the countdown then it happens all over again because there's ten of us that are pretty much equaled out and we can all win that championship. That's what makes it so exciting, I wouldn't change it for anything.

PK: What does it take to be a successful driver in this class?

SM: It takes dedication, devotion to your racecar, to the crew guys, to being focused, to just knowing what to do; knowing your job, knowing your game. When you get up there, you know you have to be the best or very best, of the very best because right now this is what it is. Knowing exactly what your job is to do, who your racing, the situations on the track, cutting a great reaction time and keeping it in the groove and then, hopefully, celebrating at the end; at the finish line.

PK: Can you take me through what you do on a run from the burnout to the completion?

SM: To start out Todd (Okuhara, Crew Chief) tells me to go out there, do my burnout, have fun and do my thing and I say, "Alright man, let's do it" and we fire the car up. I set the fuel pressure to a certain pressure during the burnout, Todd will tell me to pull forward and I watch Phil Shuler's (Crew Chief) motions as he's pulling me through the water box and he tells me to stab the gas. I'll do the burnout generally till I pass the Christmas tree, the 60 foot marker, I'll shut it off, roll over to Scotty Okuhara, he'll look over the motor, look at the dash, we'll start backing up. He'll put me in my tire tracks as I'm backing up, he'll tell me to stop and then he'll pull me up to the beams. He'll walk back and as him and Todd look over the motor, set the fuel, set the idle, I'm sitting there positioning myself getting focused, getting ready.

Staring at that tree, looking at the groove, getting ready for my job at hand, which is about to be driving an 8,000 horsepower Top-Fuel Dragster. As soon as Todd tells me to go in, I'll flip my visor down and slowly let the clutch out until I start rolling forward to pre-stage the beam on, and I'll pre stage; I'll stop. Wait on the other competitor or if he's already there, (staged) I'll stop, take my foot off the clutch and slowly start inchin it in until I turn on the stage bulb. Whenever I stage I'll take all my focus from the staging beams to the amber beams and watch 'em for any sign of flicker, and as soon as they flicker, as fast, as hard, as quick as I possibly can on the gas, off the break to the steering wheel. Manhandle the 8,000 horsepower machine all the way to the finish line, get to the finish line, hit the parachute button or reach up and hit the levers, whichever ones easier done, and get off the throttle, get on the break as fast as I can.

As soon as the parachutes hit at the car starts to settle down I'll reach over, shut the fuel off, let the motor go ahead and die, make the turnoff, jump out, and if the win lights on hopefully we're celebrating in the final round. Here comes my guys, either going to service the car or celebrate in the winner's circle.

PK: What is your favorite race track?

SM: My favorite racetrack would definitely have to be my home track at The Texas Motorplex. (Dallas) It was my very first time I ever saw a nitro car run, or smell the nitro or anything back in 1986 when it was first opened. It was my first time to win a race in the

Junior Dragster's was at that track, my hometown track; I gotta love it.

PK: You have only been completed two full seasons in Top-Fuel and for those entire seasons you left first 89%, and 84% of the time. Over your career it's very fair to say you react first about 85% of the time. You are the best in the class for having a really great light at any time, even when the tune is not enough; you still deliver with holeshot wins even in the final. How do you stay so focused and what do you attribute to being the most important factor?

SM: I say being a good factor is starting in the Junior Drag Racing categories. Going from that to bracket racing, Super Comp cars, or Doorslammers, knowing the tree, just knowing the staging procedure from burnout to the time you're gonna leave. No matter what kind of car you're driving, from Super Stock, Junior Dragster, Super Comp, to Top-Fuel Dragster's, it's the same job you do no matter what. The more consistent you are the most consistent the Crew Chiefs can be, which make for a better race car and I feel like it all comes from just bracket racing. The more you see that tree, the more you're comfortable with it, the better you're gonna be because it's gonna be more natural and more automatic.

PK: Do you have any aspirations to drive in another class, or be a crew chief, or a team owner in any class?

SM: I always wanted to drive Top-Fuel Dragster's because they been the kings of the sport since, well forever. All my heroes I ever looked at, that's what they drove. The fastest and quickest cars in NHRA Drag Racing is Top-Fuel and that's what I always wanted to drive. Don't get me wrong, I'll drive anything with four wheels on it and you never know. My goal would obviously be 20, 30, 40 years down the road or 5 years down the road would be to own my own Top-Fuel team, to drive my own Top-Fuel car, to even drive the rig or motorhome from race to race and yes, I would love to tune it.

I even try to help out on Top-Alcohol Dragster teams now and tune the Top-Alcohol Dragster that I used to drive. I would love to get in there and help Phil Shuler and Todd Okuhara out and tune our car, but they already have a handle on it so maybe one day I could be a part of it and get my hands dirty with em.

PK: What is your private ride and does your career as a driver/rider influence any of your daily driving habits?

SM: My daily driver is a 2009 Chevrolet pickup; it's a crew cab, four door. I have it actually lowered from stock 3 inches in the front and 5 inches in the back with some "22's on it, it looks awesome. My favorite color is black, I don't know why, I guess I worn black my entire life, so I have it blacked out and it just looks clean. I put it in my stacker trailer that I pull behind my motorhome and it's a 2009 45 foot Sport Coach Legend and it's a very nice motorhome. I drive it to every race, basically live outta the thing going from race to race, so it's my daily driver I drive it more than I drive my pickup truck.

Influence from Drag Racing to street? I drive probably maximum 60 MPH from racetrack to racetrack, because I get to go 330 MPH on the racetrack. It's where I get to slow down from race to race where I get to go 330 at the racetrack.

PK: What win and single run mean more to you than all the others?

SM: That one's kinda a tough one, there's a lot of great runs, a lot of great races that stick out. Obviously my very first win in Top-Fuel was amazing with Don Prudhomme winning in Joliet. (Chicago) A huge race last year was Reading against Del Worsham, we took him out in the final round where he actually ran the record setting run back then at a 3.73 and we won on a holeshot, and as a driver winning on a holeshot; that's as good at it gets.

PK: How does it feel to drive such an aggressive Dragster, especially recently when you ran a 3.728 and earlier in the year when you ran 332.18 mph?

SM: Driving a car like that, that performs like it does that just puts a lot more confidence in myself as a driver, for the crew, for the Crew Chiefs, and just to know exactly what we have to do out there, that's just to go down the racetrack. Whenever we have to step up and run numbers, we can and Todd Okuhara, Phil have proven to myself and to everybody out there in Drag Racing and to Don (Schumacher) that they know how to get a racecar down the track. Not only can they get it down a hot racetrack, they can get it down a cool racetrack and what do ya know; it's the quickest and fastest car in the NHRA right now. It just helps me as a driver to be that much more focused and to stay on my toes and do my job right, cause those guys are doing their job right every time.

PK: What are your feelings on the sport's decision to move to 1000 feet?

SM: I like 1000 foot, I drove in IHRA in 2008 when we were still quarter mile and drove in NHRA in 2008 as well for one race when we were at 1000 foot, so I actually been back and forth between thousand foot and quarter mile in the same season; I like it. It's a tighter format because it makes reaction times become a bigger situation or that much bigger of a deal, the Crew Chiefs have to focus because right now we're running so close and it's kinda because the 1000 foot era. Beforehand the extra 300 feet would allow something to smoke the tires, engine to expire, it helped out on a lot of parts failures, it helped out on tire failures. In turn, I think it helped a lot from saving cars from going down the road and well, not crashing, not having anything bad go on with them, so I feel like it's safer, I feel like it makes it for better racing; I love it, I'm ready to go 1000 foot right now.

INTERVIEW WITH CLAY MILLICAN:

Clay Millican has had a career in the IHRA that could make anyone speechless; 6 consecutive championships and 51 wins. On the NHRA side of things his record unfortunately has yet to really be made, but time is running out when it comes to the sport thinking it can keep him winless of a national event. 2012 finds him driving the best and most consistently quick NHRA Top-Fuel Dragster he has ever driven. With almost a career left first average of 75%, he often leaves on his opponents and is more often outrunning them. One of the nicest Top-Fuel racers you will ever meet, you should meet him at your next NHRA event, it may even be the place he finally holds an NHRA trophy.

PK: What are your overall feelings on the countdown and is it a good system for the NHRA?

CM: I think it is a good system. It makes it exciting for the fans. Who's going to get in, who's not? Who is going to get it all together at the end of the season and be the champ?

PK: What does it take to be a successful driver in this class?

CM: Understanding the situation you are in each run and doing what needs to be done accordingly.

PK: What is your favorite race track?

CM: This one is easy Rockingham.

PK: You are one of the best in the class for having a really great light at any time leaving almost 75% of the time on your opponents. How do you stay so focused and what do you attribute to being the most important factor?

CM: I think too much emphasis is put on reaction time by the media. So much of the actual number you see has to do with how the driver stages the car. Also car set up has a huge amount to do with what the reaction time number is. For me it is all about being consistent. The things I do to be consistent that is just something I study I a lot.

PK: What is your biggest NHRA and IHRA moment?

CM: IHRA: Beating Shirley for our first win. Getting my head shaved on the starting line at Martin Michigan after beating Big Daddy's all time when record. Win number 50 at Rockingham knowing that would be my last full season in the IHRA. All six of our Championships are all very special. NHRA: making it to three straight finals.

PK: Do you have any aspirations to drive in another class, or be a crew chief, or a team owner in any class?

CM: My aspirations are simple. I want to continue making a living in the sport I love, so I guess my answer is by any means necessary. I love this sport!

PK: What is your private ride and does your career as a driver/rider influence any of your daily driving habits?

CM: I am just a simple country boy I do not have any fancy rides at all. I drive a 2008 Dodge dually. When you drive as fast as I do for a living driving fast on the public roads just isn't that fun. I just don't really drive fast and I am always wearing my seat belt.

PK: Over the course of a weekend the goal is to make 8 passes down the strip. Outside of explosions and any major after run engine damage, what is the maximum expectancy of the parts you have to replace due to wear and what and when do you replace?

CM: I am just going to list out what our standard replacement schedule is.
- Crankshafts: 6 to 8 runs. Cost: $3900
- Connecting Rods: 10-12 runs cost. Cost: $160 each
- Pistons: 6 to10 runs. Cost: $65 each
- Head Gaskets: 1-3 runs. Cost: $160 pair
- Rod and Main Bearings: 1 run Cost: $400
- Oil: 1 run: 8 gallons. Cost: $160
- Spark Plugs: 1 run: 16 Cost: $80
- Plug Wires\ Caps: Replaced after each event: Cost per run: $43.75
- Clutch Disc: 5 per run: used 1 run: Cost: $160 each
- Clutch Floaters: 4 per run: used 1 run: Cost $50 each
- Fuel: 20 gallons per run: Cost $25 per gallon
- Ring and Pinion Gear: used 20-30 runs: Cost $3000
- Rear Tires: 4-6 runs: Cost: $1100 set

The real cost starts to come from salaries, travel, shop equipment, rent, etc. etc.

If you average out the cost of each run over a season it will be about $15k per pass down the track.

PK: The price to race in the sport's top class keeps rising and has almost kept the independent team out of racing completely. What do you see for the reason the costs have skyrocketed and what would you do to put a cap on or decrease the costs making it friendlier to small budget teams?

CM: The reason cost continue to climb is simple, these cars continue to go faster and faster. There is no real simple way to make the cost go down. For every rule that is changed we as racers look for other areas to make up for what we lost. Nitro racing is as close and competitive as it ever has been. Nitro racing now looks like Pro Stock, almost every lap is side by side, close and competitive.

PK: What are your feelings on the sport's decision to move to 1000 feet?

CM: I do not think the NHRA had any choice. A lot of tracks we race on were built for cars going 200 mph not 330 mph. It was becoming more difficult to stop at some of those older tracks.

PK: If the sport was to return to 1320 feet, what steps would you take in slowing these cars down to make sure that a quarter mile return was a safe return?

CM: I do not think we will return to 1/4 mile racing. I do not know of an economical way to slow these cars down. The fans will expect to see 330 mph 1/2 mile runs. The cars are over 320 now in the 1000'. As I said earlier rules to slow the cars down make the cost go up.

PK: Can you provide an example of the financials and the amount of parts that are needed to compete at top level for a season?

CM: An easy way to think of the budget need for a single car team is $125k per race. So let's do the math:
23 races x $125 = $2.875 MILLION
- 2 chassis complete
- 12 complete short blocks
- 16 sets of cylinder heads complete
- 2 complete rear ends
- 2 sets of wings, front and rear
- $175K in clutch disc and floaters
- 23 crankshafts
- 6 super chargers
- 4 Injectors

- 6 sets of rear wheels 3 sets of fronts
- $40k in tires
- $30k in RacePak computer equipment
- 4 sets of MSD Mags
- 200-300 Pistons
- 150-250 Connecting Rods
- 175 sets of Rod and Main Bearings
- 1 complete race rig but you really need 2. It is basically impossible to haul all you need in one rig without being overweight.
- At least 6 people who eat sleep and breathe nothing but your race car.

This is a very incomplete list it is literally just a start of what you need to go NHRA Top Fuel Racing. Bring your BIG Checkbook.

PK: Can you provide an example of what a driver would roughly make in a season?

CM: I would say that is all over the board. Some drivers actually pay the team owners to be the driver. Some drivers bring sponsorship with them so they can drive. There are a few paid drivers out there and their salary would be based on experience and how well they work with the teams sponsors. So I guess my answer is there is no real standard going rate.

I can tell you this most crew chiefs will make more than their driver does. NHRA is not NASCAR where the roundy round guys make millions. Your average Top Fuel guy is making a living.

PK: How did you get to drive a Top-Fuel Dragster?

CM: My whole life story in one sentence. I convinced Peter Lehman he needs to become a Top Fuel Team owner and let me drive.

PK: I know your son, Dalton, is a championship winner with ATV's and Motocross. What sanctioning body does he race for and does he have any NHRA asirations?

CM: My son Dalton won the 450A National Championship in the AMA ATV National Motocross Series in 2011. Dalton loves what he is doing but wants to move into a Top Fuel Car if and when our team could ever add a second car.

INTERVIEW WITH WHIT BAZEMORE:

Whit Bazemore; love him or hate him, the controversial drive spoke passionate truth and behind the wheel you could not find a better driver. In Funny Car he was always a contender for any round and event win, winning 20 races and 289 round wins out of 486; a nice 59.7%. After 14 top ten finishes, he switched to Top-Fuel with good results winning 17 rounds, and going to 1 Final, and finishing in the top ten; his 15th overall and 14th consecutive. Whit has stayed active in the sport as he recently completed a stint as a pit reporter and a weekly radio reporter on the NHRA. He still has many fans that would love to see him race again, something he has never ruled out.

PK: In 2007 you finished eighth in the points in the countdown. Under the old points system you would have actually finished 11th, only because you did not run the last 2 events. What are your overall feelings on the countdown and is it a good system for the NHRA?

WB: Overall, I feel the countdown has livened up the show a little bit, which is a good thing. But it doesn't necessarily reward the best team over the entire season, which is what a championship truly is, so I disagree with it. It would have been nice to have had it a few times earlier in my career though!

PK: I am not a fan of good teams being told the best they can finish is 11th. Since, the NHRA resets the points at the start of the countdown to make the points race tighter, I feel that the NHRA should qualify everyone for the countdown who has run every countdown qualifying race. It would eliminate anyone getting locked out of a top ten and a top ten finish can still be a goal for everyone. Would you modify the system for teams that peak at the wrong time and get locked out of the all-important top ten when they may perform better than a locked in top ten finisher?

WB: I would do away with the countdown completely and liven up the show in different ways. And, yes, I do think the show needs some help!

PK: What does it take to be a successful driver in Top-Fuel and Funny Car?

WB: These days, really only money and the ability to not lose concentration at critical moments, which is not all that hard.

PK: What was your favorite class?

WB: Funny Car.

PK: How big of a learning curve was it as a driver when you made the switch?

WB: The racing in Top-Fuel was great and very challenging as the level of competition was very high, but actually driving the car was easy. I found it boring compared to the Funny Car. It took two runs in testing to learn not to over steer it, which is the biggest difference between the two.

PK: What is your favorite race track?

WB: Favorite track would have to Denver and Bristol. My favorite race would be Indy.

PK: You are one of the best for having a really great light at any time. How do you stay so focused and what do you attribute to being the most important factor?

WB: The biggest thing is being motivated to win at all costs and to hate losing.

PK: Do you have any aspirations to return, or be a crew chief, or a team owner in any class?

WB: I would want to return as a driver for a top funded team that wants to win at all costs. But I don't foresee that happening, as even the top teams are budget crunched and take on pay or sponsored drivers, which is totally understandable.

PK: In what class would you return in?

WB: Funny Car or Top-Fuel.

PK: What is your private ride and does your career as a driver influence any of your daily driving habits?

WB: I drive slowly these days. I have an Audi wagon and a Honda van. The family thing, you know. My business has a big 15 passenger Ford van. I'm really into vans these days!

PK: What win and single run mean more to you than all the others?

WB: 2001, Indy when one side of the wing came off at night. We set both ends of the National record when it would have been easy to just crash the thing. Winning Indy twice was huge for me and are my best memories of racing.

PK: The price to race in the sport's top class keeps rising and has almost kept the independent team out of racing completely. What do you see for the reason the costs have skyrocketed and what would you do to put a cap on or decrease the costs making it friendlier to small budget teams?

WB: The answer is not to necessarily make it easier for small teams to compete, but to raise the total value of the sport, so that more companies want to participate by backing drivers and/or teams. The sport has not grown in years. In '97, we won $75k at Indy, which was not bad. I think it still pays about the same 15 years later! The sport has to give everyone value, from the teams to the sponsoring companies.

If it costs $3mil to run a competitive car, but the ROI (return on investment) for a sponsor is only $2mil, then there is a problem. It is one reason team owners would rather have a guy who might get beat on holeshots 5 or 6 times a year, but who they do not have to pay, than someone who is better, but will not race for free. And right now, the value of the sport is not where it should be. It is why Amato, Bernstein, Prudhomme, etc., are not fielding teams. If they could field a team, and make a good profit, do you think they would still be racing? My bet is yes.

PK: Do you feel that the sport is on a good path for the future ahead?

WB: No. Like I said, there needs to be growth, and it is pretty stale at the moment.

PK: What are your feelings on the sport's decision to move to 1000 feet?

WB: Personally, I do not like it.

PK: If the sport was to return to 1320 feet, what steps would you take in slowing these cars down to make sure that a quarter mile return was a safe return?

WB: One, it will never happen, but the sport would be way better off with less HP, less downforce and a longer track. If you could smoke the tires, like in the old days, and get the car to recover and still win, then there would still be a place in the sport for drivers who have that ability. Not everyone does; in fact, I would say that today, very few of them do. It would put the driver into the equation more than they are now, it would be better all the way around. When I raced I was dead set against slowing the cars down, but now I see the situation differently.

PK: The move to 1000 feet turned back the clock on the incremental performance in Top-Fuel for a short time, but the E.T. record in 1000 feet is the quickest a dragster has been to 1000 feet in the history of the sport. Spencer Massey ran a 3.728 and could add up to being the first ever 4.3 second run. Saying that we will eventually hit 3.6 and 335 MPH in 1000 feet, is there any need for the NHRA to be concerned?

WB: The nature of the sport is that the cars will always go quicker and faster, unless new rules are implemented to keep that from happening. So if they are concerned, all they need to do is slow them down. But, performance has not increased all that much over the past ten or eleven years. We ran a FC sub 4 second 1,000 foot time way back in 2001! So, you could say the cars have not progressed much at all in that time.

PK: The move to 1000 feet gave the sport an extra 320 foot window to slow down. If we stay the course with 1000 feet could the time ever come where the increase in performance for these cars ends up that they can begin to greatly diminish the extra 320 feet, thus drivers facing the same possibility of danger that they faced when it was 1320 feet?

WB: Look, racing is always going to be dangerous. People race and get killed. It will never be 100% safe, and it is frustrating when a car goes off the end of the track at high speed and then the track and the NHRA get sued. Regarding E-town, if a car has carbon brakes and is not on fire, then the driver must be good enough to get it stopped without the parachutes. If not, is it the tracks fault? I don't think so.

Now, not all tracks are as safe as they can be. Poles, scoreboards, etc. are still an issue at some places. Those concerns should be dealt with by the professional drivers, as they are the ones with the most to lose.

PK: Can you provide an example of what a driver would roughly make in a season?

WB: I can only tell you what I made, which I think was decent by drag racing standards. But compared to other forms of racing, it is way behind. This is because of lots of reasons, not least of which is that a good driver must be judged by more than reaction time. But these days, that is about all there is!

PK: What have you been doing since stepping away from driving?

WB: I recently started a high end cycling tour business, so I have been doing a lot of work related to that, including racing my bike.

WHAT DOES IT TAKES BE A SUCCESSFUL CREW CHIEF?

INTERVIEW WITH VIRGIL HARTMAN:

Virgil Hartman is best known for tuning his daughter, Rhonda Hartman-Smith, to 4 consecutive top ten finishes in the NHRA, 5 top ten's in the IHRA, including 3 top five's and 3 wins in 7 finals with a Dragster he built. He also tuned and built the Funny Car that his son, Richard, started his career in to 1 final; Rhonda also drove a Funny Car he built and tuned and she had a successful season in the California Independent Funny Car Association. He also tuned Rhonda's husband, John Smith, to 2 top ten finishes and 1 final in the NHRA, as well as 2 finals in the IHRA; but there are some unknowns about how hands on he really is. All of the clutches, cannons, fuel systems, and their management systems he also constructs them all, as well as having his innovations bought by companies, used by companies and many championship winning Pro Stock and Pro Stock Motorcycle Teams. Recently, you can find him working at his shop producing parts for companies and you can find his son as a current Top-Fuel crew chief that even won the 2007 IHRA Top-Fuel Championship.

PK: What are your overall feelings on the countdown and is it a good system for the NHRA?

VH: I like it as there is now excitement and drama in the last 6 races of the year

PK: I am not a fan of good teams being told the best they can finish is 11th. Since, the NHRA resets the points at the start of the countdown to make the points race tighter, I feel that the NHRA should qualify everyone for the countdown who has run every countdown qualifying race. It would eliminate anyone getting locked out of a top ten and a top ten finish can still be a goal for everyone. Would you modify the system for teams that peak at the wrong time and get locked out of the all-important top ten when they may perform better than a locked in top ten finisher?

VH: I like the system as it is. It allows the top ten teams to go for wins and/or test for the following year without fear of losing their top 10 status. It also adds drama to the final couple of events prior to the countdown.

PK: What does it take to be a successful crew chief in this class?

VH: Besides being a problem solver you must be an above average people motivator.

PK: You are responsible for the first husband daughter team to race against each other and finish in the top ten twice in the NHRA. Was it a challenge tuning both teams?

VH: Tuning the two cars was not hard; working with added people was a challenge.

PK: Do you race the track or the opponent?

VH: The track, but you are always aware of who you are running and their tendencies. If they have a weakness you want to be prepared to use it to your advantage at the most opportune time.

PK: Can you take me through what you do as a crew chief prior to a run?

VH: You lay out a battle plan according to the available equipment, its condition and the people available for an event. Once you have this plan, you set the car up for the first run according to the track location, prep and weather to give you the best opportunity to make a quick pass. After the pass you gather information, define problems and make adjustments accordingly within the parameters of you overall plan.

PK: Throughout my research, I been getting numbers as low as $8,000 and as high as $15,000. What is the cost of 1 pass and why such a variance?

VH: A slippery slope here. You must add all of your costs per year and divide the total by the number of runs. Some teams don't count all appropriate costs, others add outside expenses to the costs. Less runs may give a higher cost per run but a lower overall cost for the year. I am an owner/crew chief and my cost per run will be lower than with a hired crew chief because I pay the bills and a lot of my decisions factor in the costs.

PK: The price to race in the sport's top class keeps rising and has almost kept the independent team out of racing completely. What do you see for the reason the costs have skyrocketed and what would you do to put a cap on or decrease the costs making it friendlier to small budget teams?

VH: Most racers in their desire to win will spend whatever it takes to accomplish winning. Their creation of more systems and equipment and the need for more crew persons to maintain that equipment creates the extra costs. To cut the costs you just need to make the cars simpler, and that will also reduce the performance; but who has the fortitude to make such a decision. Tom Compton was brought in to save the NHRA from the very bad financial shape it was in, and he did save the organization; but he does not have the knowledge, or anyone around him to stand up to the larger teams to simplify the cars. Everyone there is afraid they will lose what little they have if they make any moves to improve the situation.

PK: How different is the frame of mind for a crew chief when you have a slow start that turns into almost overnight success in comparison to when you have a hard charging season from start to finish and what type of season do you find more welcoming to your habits?

VH: Drag racing is an "in the moment" sport, and if you have done it for any length of time at any level, you understand that there are times when everything you do leads to success and other times no matter what you do success eludes you. You must understand that you are doing something you relish and just enjoy every moment.

PK: Do you feel that the sport is on a good path for the future ahead?

VH: No, not in the professional ranks. I see a lot of family participation at the local tracks with the junior dragsters and lower bracket classes, but not many that are willing to dedicate their life to becoming a pro.

PK: What are your feelings on the sport's decision to move to 1000 feet?

VH: I like it and wish it had come years sooner.

PK: If the sport was to return to 1320 feet, what steps would you take in slowing these cars down to make sure that a quarter mile return was a safe return?

VH: I hope it never does, but the performance levels need to be lowered in all classes.

PK: The move to 1000 feet turned back the clock on the incremental performance in Top-Fuel for a short time, but the E.T. record in 1000 feet is the quickest a dragster has been to 1000 feet in the history of the sport. Spencer Massey ran a 3.728 and could add up to being the first ever 4.3 second run. Saying that we will eventually hit 3.6 and 335 MPH in 1000 feet, is there any need for the NHRA to be concerned?

VH: NHRA is concerned, but the racers are several steps ahead of them on all fronts.

PK: The move to 1000 feet gave the sport an extra 320 foot window to slow down. If we stay the course with 1000 feet could the time ever come where the increase in performance for these cars ends up that they can begin to greatly diminish the extra 320 feet, thus drivers facing the same possibility of danger that they faced when it was 1320 feet?

VH: I believe the speeds the cars are going are too fast for any confined track area, no matter what the distance. You will see 300 mph in the 1/8th mile in the near future. Too much acceleration and speed and it needs to be stopped.

PK: Have you had any aspirations to drive?

VH: I drove all my cars when I started drag racing on the street and track. As the rules required more safety gear, especially driver's suits, I became more disenchanted with driving. I have driven up to TAD and TAFCs, but it is just another job to be done on a racing team. I enjoy building and developing things more than racing on the track today, and for about 15 years now.

PK: Do you have any aspirations to be a crew chief, or own a team in another class?

VH: I dabbled in all my extracurricular activities until I had the misfortune of seeing my oldest son electrocuted at an industrial site in front of me in 1993. During the funeral process I decided that if I wanted to do anything in life from then on I would do it immediately, no putting anything off that I really want to do. I have satisfied my desires in drag racing and at present have no desires to race.

PK: What programs do you run in-house?

VH: I own two junior dragster teams.

PK: What is your favorite race track?

VH: The one that I am at, whenever or where ever.

PK: What are your private rides?

VH: My wife drives a 2012 Chrysler 300 and a 1956 Chevy 210 sedan. I have a 2000 Chevy pickup, 1939 Chevy 2 door sedan, 1932 Ford hi boy roadster, 1966 Mustang coupe, 1988 Chevy 1500 bagged, shaved, show truck, building a 1937 Ford coupe and 1965 C10 pick up. And for my spare time I ride a Honda VTX1300C, wave runners and a 24' pontoon boat.

PK: What does it take to be a successful team owner in this class?

VH: Dedication and putting the race team as your #1 priority. When nothing else matters, you will be successful, just like any business or job.

PK: Can you provide an example of the financials and the amount of parts that are needed to compete at top level for a season?

VH: These are basic numbers for a full time NHRA team to run once the initial investment of car, transporter and support equipment is bought:
- $900,000: Survival to get to all the events, make the qualifying runs, only win a round or two all year.

- $1.4 million: Same as above, but better performance and win about 10 rounds.
- $2 million: Mid pack performance and win about 15 rounds, a couple semi-finals.
- $3 million: A few top 5 qualifiers, consistent 1st round winner, many semi-finals, maybe a couple finals.
- $5 million: A contender

As your budget expands, the sources of income also expand along with the expenses. Money comes from sponsorships, souvenir sales, hospitality, personal appearances, and product endorsements.

PK: Can you provide an example of what a driver and a crew chief would roughly make in a season?

VH: Some drivers pay up to $1.5 million to drive, some get paid, usually by the sponsor directly. Crew chiefs get anywhere from $2,000 for a weekend to $300,000 a year. A couple have been paid $750,000 for the year.

PK: How is Rhonda and when can we see her driving again?

VH: Rhonda is doing great enjoying her kids and family life. She gets offers, but the situation has to fit to allow her to be involved with her kids.

PK: Do you currently work for any teams or do you assist Richard at all with his team?

VH: Richard and I talk about his car/team at times, but that is his deal and he has always wanted to do things on his own, and I am in agreement on that. We do at times team up together on outside ventures, some racing and more on the business side. I do telephone consultations with about 15 teams at many different levels of the sport. I seldom go to the track anymore because I have an addiction to the sport and will jump right back in with both feet at a moment's notice. I crew chiefed a TF team at a national event last year along with the Bullet Bod NFC at a few races, but that is about all.

I have teams that park their rigs at my facilities all the time and I see many of my racing friends throughout the year at many functions away from the tracks.

INTERVIEW WITH TODD SMITH:

Todd Smith has made quite a name for himself as a crew chief throughout his career and stays relevant for jobs for one reason; he knows how to run you a competitive team. He not only knows how to run a successful program, he can do it if his employer runs a Top-Fuel Dragster or a Funny Car. Since 2000, he has played a huge hand in helping to keep teams contending for race wins, and not only for a top ten points finish, but for a top five points finish as we seen with teams such as Darrell Gwynn Racing and Kenny Bernstein Racing. 2012 he was given an opportunity that I would think honored him and scared that crap out of him; fill the shoes of Rahn Tobler and tune Jack Beckman to championship contending performances. It only took his 5 races to win and the Funny Car is more than just competitive, it's a championship contender; like most of Dragsters or Funny Cars that Todd Smith has tuned.

PK: What does it take to be a successful crew chief in this class?

TS: Good mechanical abilities, knowledge and understanding of all aspects of your car and how they relate to each other, attention to detail, lots of experience, good at math, common sense, and the one I like the most, the ability to make crucial decisions, on short notice, under extreme pressure and look for successful results.

PK: Do you race the track or the opponent?

TS: I do both. I look at what the track condition will allow us to run, then I look at how the other guys are running and I come up with a number and go with it. We got a target number we'll just shoot for it.

PK: You certainly have proven you can make Jack Beckman a championship and race win contender in such a short time. Was it at all intimidating when Don Schumacher gave you the offer the fill Rahn's void?

TS: Uh no, not intimidating, felt fortune for the opportunity.

PK: Can you take me through what you do as a crew chief prior to a run?

TS: I have a checklist of all the parts of the car that require tuning adjustments, I monitor weather and track conditions, and then continually build scenarios in my mind while adhering to my checklist. I communicate these final changes to my assistant and he in turn relays those to the crew. We watch the other cars in the session and decide on any last minute changes.

PK: Over the course of a weekend the goal is to make 8 passes down the strip. Outside of explosions and any major after run engine damage, what is the maximum expectancy of the parts you have to replace due to wear and what and when do you replace?

TS: We have stuff we call consumables that you're gonna change either every run or every 4-6 runs depending on what it is. After the run these are all the things that come out of the car and go back in:
- Blower belt—one run
- Blower wear strips—2-4 runs
- Head gaskets—2-3 runs
- Pistons—2-3 runs
- Piston Rings—1 run
- Connecting rod—4-8 runs
- Connecting rod bearing—1 run
- Cylinder sleeves—2-4 runs
- Engine main bearings—1 run
- Crank shaft—6-10 runs
- Cylinder head service every run
- Intake valves—8-12 runs
- Exhaust valves—6-10 runs
- Intake valve springs—6-10 runs
- Exhaust valve springs—6 – 10 runs
- Valve springs retainers—10-15 runs
- Spark plugs—1 run
- Engine oil change—every run
- Clutch discs—2 runs

- Clutch floater plates—1 run
- Clutch pressure plates—flywheel facings—10 runs
- Rear differential gears and bearings—3-50 runs
- Rear tires—1-6 runs
- Nitro—20 gallons per run w/warm-up

PK: What is the cost of 1 pass and what parts are needed?

TS: 8 to $12,000 a run and refer to the last question for detail.

PK: The price to race in the sport's top class keeps rising and has almost kept the independent team out of racing completely. What do you see for the reason the costs have skyrocketed and what would you do to put a cap on or decrease the costs making it friendlier to small budget teams?

TS: Raw materials for building parts and pieces have seen significant price increases in recent years along with time and effort to make all the parts. The overall cost of doing business has gone up in every aspect, stuff that we can't control like insurance, fuel cost, and travel expenses. I just think it's the evolution of our class, it's a competitive class, and it just continually evolves. Everything gets more intense and you work harder at it and it costs more money to do.

PK: I have to say that I do admire how you race heads up all the time against your teammates with no funny business. Is there ever any influence on how you tune based on how your car is running?

TS: Every piece of consideration is up especially when you're running one of your teammates, but ultimately I try and run as hard as the track will let me.

PK: Your talent puts you in a very elite class with only a handful of tuners who have been capable of running successful championship contending programs in Top-Fuel and Funny Car. Your career best in Funny Car is 4.065/318.62 in a 1000ft., and in Top-Fuel your best is a 4.463/332.10 mph in a quarter mile and a 3.784/321.27. What class do you personally feel you understand and/or enjoy more?

TS: As far as understanding I would have to say the Dragster simply from time and experience, but right now I'm enjoying the Funny Car more because of the challenges and a new situation. I first worked with Dragsters in 1987, but I really like the Funny Car right now. It's nice to mix it up and do something different, you still apply the same process to tuning and stuff, but the numbers are different and the application is all different; but fun.

PK: Will you ever transition back to Top-Fuel and how much of a learning curve is it for you when you decide to switch classes?

TS: You never know what to expect in this business, each opportunity provides a set of circumstances and challenges of their own. I try to look at those opportunities as a learning experience and an avenue for more knowledge. As far as a learning curve between the classes, it really takes a couple races to get acclimated. If someone offers you a job you just look at it, the nice thing is if you can do both then you can be selective.

PK: How different is the frame of mind for a crew chief when you have a slow start that turns into almost overnight success in comparison to when you have a hard charging season from start to finish and what type of season do you find more welcoming to your habits?

TS: Having a good season from start to finish builds confidence as you go, usually means your off season was really productive; I prefer that type of season. However, if your season starts off slow and you are not achieving results you hope for, it can start to bother you if you let it. The key for me is I just always try to stay focused, focused and dedicated, whatever problem you have your gonna work through it, but ultimately you can't ever give up.

PK: Do you feel that the sport is on a good path for the future ahead?

TS: I have my concerns. Generally I think, it's seems as though America's younger generation have become less interested in their cars. If we can spark and interest with cars, hot rodding, and ultimately drag racing, I think the sport will make it. I think it will continue to progress. My generation didn't have so many things to get distracted and interested in. Now it's like yea, cars are cool, but cell phones and computers and whatever else young people could get into.

PK: What are your feelings on the sport's decision to move to 1000 feet?

TS: I believe it was a good decision. We have outrun some of the facilities on our circuit and something needed to be done in regards to that, it was the best and most economical solution at the time.

PK: If the sport was to return to 1320 feet, what steps would you take in slowing these cars down to make sure that a quarter mile return was a safe return?

TS: It's such a tough question; the whole topic is so sensitive. It's difficult to find a way to figure it out that's gonna pass with everybody. No matter what we do, if we do something, because we're going too fast somebody, somewhere is not gonna be on the right end of the stick.

PK: The move to 1000 feet turned back the clock on the incremental performance in Top-Fuel for a short time, but the E.T. record in 1000 feet is the quickest a dragster has been to 1000 feet in the history of the sport. Spencer Massey ran a 3.728 and could add up to being the first ever 4.3 second run. Saying that we will eventually hit 3.6 and 335 MPH in 1000 feet, is there any need for the NHRA to be concerned?

TS: Absolutely, they should always be concerned about safety and addressing those concerns at all facilities. Safety stuff should always take precedence with them and it does.

PK: The move to 1000 feet gave the sport an extra 320 foot window to slow down. If we stay the course with 1000 feet could the time ever come where the increase in performance for these cars ends up that they can begin to greatly diminish the extra 320 feet, thus drivers facing the same possibility of danger that they faced when it was 1320 feet?

TS: Yes I believe it is possible, but not likely. I believe our classes have been safer than they ever been and if the time came that we ever got to switch back I think our safety would be better than it is now. It's always improving and getting better. Racing's dangerous, accidents are always gonna happen, but we try to minimize them and we try to do that; drag racing has always done that always trying to make thing better and safer. If we had to go back, or if we progress where the last 320 feet don't even matter anymore and we used up that buffer zone, I think some of the facilities are gonna have to improve and we're just gonna have to improve safety.

PK: Have you had any aspirations to drive?

TS: Yes, when I first got into the business I really wanted to drive. My father (2-Time Competition Eliminator Champion Craig Smith) was a good driver and I just wanted to follow in his footsteps. The right situation just never came along and at that time I became more interested in what made the fuel cars run. I'm not built as a driver, not exactly 150 pounds.

PK: What programs do you run in-house?

TS: None at this time. I would like to run in-house any area, there all interesting to me. All the crew chiefs here have some area that they oversee, I'm sure something at some point will come up for me or when they need another hand. I'm just waiting to do it, I'll go into any area, they all interest me.

PK: What is your favorite race track?

TS: Pomona. A lot of history there with my dad racing and when I first started tuning I was working for a guy on the west coast and we would always make the Pomona race. It was always a special race to me; my dad had won there years ago and I just kinda fell in love with the place. Now, I just like going there, luckily we go there twice a year.

PK: What is your favorite track in each nitro class?

TS: Pomona, both classes.

PK: What win and single run mean more to you than all the others?

TS: Atlanta 2004 Top-Fuel, it was with an independent team (Carrier Boyz and Cory McClenathan) and we won and that's always hard to do when your lower funded or no funded to win a race. That's the win that sticks out in my mind. The single run that means most to me is semifinals, 2009 Top-Fuel at the world finals. (There win over Larry Dixon gave Tony Schumacher the Championship)

PK: What are your private rides?

TS: 2011 Chevy Silverado pickup.

PK: You have worked as a Crew Chief and an Assistant Crew Chief in your career. What is the difference between the jobs of a Crew Chief and an Assistant Crew Chief?

TS: The crew chief thinks mostly about his car and tuning that car. He has to shoulder all the final decisions that pertain to his car and his operation. He talks directly with the assistant on all the projects to be completed. The assistant basically carries out all the duties of day to day operations with the crew as well of ordering a large majority of the parts needed. He also communicates with the crew chief about race car set up.

TS: Why can't an Assistant Crew Chief hold a formal Co-Crew Chief Title? (Some teams such as DSR, makes a clear distinction that most Assistant Crew Chief's, are never labeled a Co-Crew Chief)

TS: Some teams don't have co-crew chiefs; like here you're either an assistant or you're a crew chief. Like Antron's team are co-crew chiefs, and I don't know the answer to that, Don might. When you got a crew chief and then an assistant and a crew it's really easier because you can follow a chain of command; everything is delegated down. It's easier when things go wrong, there's only one person to blame. In some situations when two guys work together as co-crew chief's, they thinking process my accentuate each other; one guy might be aggressive, one might be conservative one might be conservative and they meet somewhere in the middle.

WHAT DOES IT TAKE TO BE A SUCCESSFUL TEAM OWNER:

INTERVIEW WITH STEVE TORRENCE:

Steve Torrence has been racing since the age of 15 and has been going faster ever since. He beat cancer and returned to the sport with the attitude of taking no prisoners; that is exactly what he did. In 2004, he won the Top Alcohol Dragster National and Division 4 Championship. He moved up to the sport's premier class in 2006, scoring a top ten finish 4 years later in 2010, but it wasn't until the following season things really started coming together. With the support of his family and their contracting business, he starting assembling his own team; buying all the right parts, pieces, and talent with the endeavor to make a championship run in 2012 and beyond. As of this writing, he has won 2 races and is usually 1 of the top 3 quickest at any time; a championship run is what he wanted and it's exactly what his hard work and dedication has given him.

PK: What are your overall feelings on the countdown and is it a good system for the NHRA?

ST: I have a couple different ways that I look at it.
1. You will never have the chance to see someone make the "comeback" charge like Schumacher did a few years back. And whoever is the most consistent in the last 6 races has the best shot at the championship.
2. It ensures that we won't have a "runaway" champion that is decided before the season is close to being over. And usually makes it to be decided at the final race.

PK: What does it take to be a successful driver in this class?

ST: Consistency is key. Do the same thing every lap in the car. Quick on the tree, straight in the groove and repeat; become a machine.

PK: What is your favorite race track?

ST: Vegas.

PK: You have been going fast since 15 years of age. How many different classes have you driven in?

ST: Super Comp, Super Gas, Top Dragster, Top Sportsman, Top Alcohol Dragster, and I licensed in a Top Alcohol Funny Car.

PK: You are one of the best in the class for having a really great light at any time. How do you stay so focused and what do you attribute to being the most important factor?

ST: Practice! Being comfortable in the car, seat time builds confidence. My drive to be the best.

PK: Do you have any aspirations to drive in another class, or be a crew chief, or a team owner in any class?

ST: Possibly in the future as a multi-car team owner.

PK: What is your private ride and does your career as a driver/rider influence any of your daily driving habits?

ST: Denali 2500 Duramax truck

PK: What win and single run mean more to you than all the others?

ST: Right now, our win in Atlanta, the first of my career and being that it came with my family owned team.

PK: What is the cost of 1 pass and what parts are needed?

ST: 150,000 per weekend or close to 19000 per pass

PK: The price to race in the sport's top class keeps rising and has almost kept the independent team out of racing completely. What do you see for the reason the costs have skyrocketed and what would you do to put a cap on or decrease the costs making it friendlier to small budget teams?

ST: Layout of the schedule, crisscrossing the country. It's like any other sport, there is always someone that is going to have an advantage whether is funding or knowledge or whatever it may be. That's just life.

PK: Do you feel that the sport is on a good path for the future ahead?

ST: Need to bring in a younger crowd and reach out to other venues to cross market the sport, it's becoming stagnate and it's not bringing in enough "new" fans to replenish itself.

PK: What are your feelings on the sport's decision to move to 1000 feet?

ST: I like it, it's safer.

PK: If the sport was to return to 1320 feet, what steps would you take in slowing these cars down to make sure that a quarter mile return was a safe return?

ST: It won't go back to that.

PK: What does it take to be a successful team owner in this class?

ST: The same as any other successful business surround yourself with the best people possible, let them do their jobs, and support them.

AN EASY AND FAIRLY ACCURATE WAY TO CONVERT A 1000FT. E.T. TO A 1320FT. E.T.:

Following the tragic death of accomplished Funny Car driver Scott Kalitta in June of 2008, within a month the NHRA made a change that got everyone's attention. The counted distance for elapsed time and speed was shortening for the first time in the sports history, from 1,320 feet (Quarter Mile) to 1,000 feet. Met with equal amounts of praise and criticism, no one can deny that it's not safer in some aspects, but the real question for another time is if the sport is better because of it. I believe the easiest fix is a simple mental technique for fans that are just not used to seeing a 1000ft. time instead of a quarter mile time; even though it has been a full 4 years later, even I find myself still wondering what they would of ran if it was at the old standards.

NOTE: This method is for entertainment, it can never be 100% due to, well everything that can go wrong during a run. It's hard to say if many or any of the 1000ft passes would even make it to 1320ft under power without a fireworks show put on by Mr. 500 CID. This is my best attempt at a guide for fans like myself who like to wonder, and would like a ballpark, fairly accurate number without thinking a 3.90 in 1000ft. was about a 4.80 in 1320ft. in Top-Fuel; it's not.

TF: Spencer Massey ran a 3.728 in 1000ft. and it's the current unbacked National E.T. record. I would say add 0.70 (7 tenths) on to every run and it will ROUGLY provide a fairly accurate ballpark e.t. within 3-5 hundreds. You want to be a little more accurate? Try 0.67 (6 tenths, 7 hundreds). Now the margin of ever could be within a hundredth. 3.728 becomes 4.398, Spencer's run may have been that. Could have been better, could have been worse than the 4.398, but now you have a great estimate.

Proof On Theory: Look back at 2006 and Tony Schumacher's "The Run" orchestrated by Alan Johnson. He ran 4.428 and the 1000ft. time was a 3.759. Now using the theory you'll get the fairly accurate ballpark e.t of 4.429. Lastly, always remember if you take a look at pre 1000ft. racing e.t.'s, the 1000ft. times fluctuate and can still provide the same 1320 e.t.; main point is this is not meant to ever be exact.

FC: Robert Hight ran a 3.955 in 1000ft. back when 1320ft. was still the norm; it was a 4.636, unbacked. I would say add 0.70 (7 tenths) on to every run and it will ROUGLY provide a fairly accurate ballpark e.t. within 3-5 hundreds. You want to be a little more accurate? Try 0.68 (6 tenths, 8 hundreds).

Proof On Theory: Funny Car is a unique situation since the all-time 1000ft. record is still the best ever even after the 1000ft. era began, so I am using that model as the ballpark. 0.68 still seems like a pretty safe ballpark equation.

INTERNET AND ENTERTAINMENT DRAG RACING FIX:

You're a drag racing fan. You check your T.V. listings, find out when it's on, tune in, and make your living room a temporary equivalent to a "Sounds of the NHRA" audio cd for the time of the show. What's to do during the week when you want a drag racing fix, but have no idea how to get it when normal television shows drag racing only once in a blue moon. I am here to help, fear no more, as if you can get to a computer, you will never be more than a few clicks away from being right back into the world of drag racing. Sorry, no nitro smell from the internet just yet.

INTERNET:

NHRA—www.nhra.com—If I am going to list anything at all, it may as well be the # 1 source. Here you can find just about anything. Photos, schedules, press releases, stories, points, and just about anything you can think of that you know the NHRA would be in charge of having the information about. You will find driver blogs, driver profiles, (not anywhere as in-depth as you will find in this book) and daily driver reports from the day of racing. (If your driver participates is a better question) Last but not least, you can find out where your local drag strip is and begin racing and making your own stats for your career.

Competition Plus—www.competitionplus.com—From personal experience it is the best drag racing reporting site on the net that caters to every series. NHRA, IHRA, ADRL, and many more, with great editorials, drag race reporting, and some extremely talented photographers that do such a great job taken pictures from the events, that it is almost as good as being there yourself. This site also runs an annual new car paint schemes gallery, always fun to see all the new looks of cars, as well as a rumors section where they have a very, very good record of what they publish as a rumoring, turning out to be the actual truth.

Draglist.com—www.draglist.com—A fantastic site mainly in my opinion if you want an excellent in-depth database of a driver's career best in E.T. or MPH. It is constantly up to date and stretches as far back to the mid 60's. Without that site, it would be almost impossible to find almost all of the information in its database and do a great job at keeping history alive. Series doesn't matter, if it can be drag raced you have a pretty good chance of finding what you are looking for.

NitroMater—www.nitromater.com—For $1.00 you get to join a site with as of this printing 6,770 members that share your addiction. If it happened in drag racing this is the site to be a part of where you can view and contribute to drag racing discussion. Results, rumors, discussion about a team's performance/action, ask a question, it's all there and more. Like all message boards it has its share of arguments here and there, but it seems to be the most friendliest to anyone looking for pure drag racing discussion.

Drag Race Central—Dragracecentral.com—An excellent place for drag racing results for any series, especially when the sanctioning bodies website is down or does not update quickly serves as a great backup. An added bonus to this site that you won't really find are in-depth session by session testing results and not just summaries by the day.

ESPN3—www.espn3.com—Watch the national event live from your computer or smartphone on your time. Even watch the sportsman classes, not just Top Alcohol Dragster and Funny Car, but Top Dragster, Super Stock, Stock, etc.; something ESPN/ESPN2 almost never covers.

You can also look for your favorite teams on Twitter.com and Facebook.com and follow your favorites a little bit closer from behind the scenes. Many are on there, just search.

ENTERTAINMENT:

How about Drag Racing video games? I got everything you need to know! Make your very own fantasy stats as a racer in one of the sports premier classes thanks to these games. Here is the ultimate guide to Drag Racing gaming that can easily be purchased on ebay. com or amazon.com:

NHRA Drag Racing 2/NHRA Drag Racing 2 Limited Edition/ NHRA Gold: Now three different names, it's all the same game; except for the fact that Gold offers a few more developer paint schemes to choose from. NHRA Gold is simply what they changed the name to when it was bundled with NHRA Main Event. The paint schemes, the driver's, and the crew chief's in the game for your opponents are representative of the 2000 NHRA season. Fun to play, you can tune yourself, you can even pick a crew chief in the game that has championship strength; one disadvantage may be that you cannot pick an NHRA crew chief and just one they made up for the game. I feel it is the best Drag Racing game ever released. PC only 2000 release and all versions are compatible with every version of Windows.

NHRA Pro Stock Cars And Trucks: This game was released as the title shown and came in the NHRA Main Event package. This game operates in the exact way NHRA Drag Racing 2 does and is the only game you will ever race a Pro-Stock Truck on. PC only 2001 release and does not work on Windows Vista/7 as the company did not make a patch to fix the game crashing after a run.

NHRA Top Fuel Thunder: This game is basically a very detailed update to NHRA Drag Racing 2. Great to play. PC only 2004 release and does not work on Windows Vista/7 as the company did not make a patch to fix the game crashing after a run.

NHRA Quarter Mile Showdown: Very detailed update to the Drag Racing games. Great to play. PC, Sony Playstation 2 titled "NHRA Championship Drag Racing", 2006 release and and all versions are compatible with every version of Windows, expect for a no audio bug on Vista/7.

NHRA Countdown To The Championship: The first ever game that features the countdown points format and one you can race Pro Stock Motorcycle. Very fun game to play. Sony Playstation 2/PSP Only 2007 Release.

NHRA Drag Racing: The original PC Drag Racing release. This game is very good. PC only 2000 release and all versions are compatible with every version of Windows.

IHRA has a release of PC and Playstation games, but the competition is more of a run any class against any class. You get to build the cars though.

There are many PC Drag Racing games on the market and have a few series releases. Here are a few I recommend:

Hot Rod, American Street Drag, Garage To Glory: A great series if you want to build your car, and bracket race it.

IHRA Sportsman Drag Racing: The best bracket racing game I ever played. Built it, tune it, dial it.

MOBILE GAMES: (CELL PHONES, TABLETS)

The Apple operating system (ios) is the clear bread winner when it comes to Drag Racing Games. The Android operating system only offers one game, but it is a clear winner. Here is a review of games worth considering:

ANDROID:

Drag Racing: Buy cars, customize, race them. You have to shift well too. It's easy to be the best game when you are the only game, but this game was made well and worth playing.

Jeg's Perfect Start: A great practice tree game.

APPLE:

Dragster Mayhem: It has come a long way in its development and is a very fun and addicting game to play. Many upgrades, many realistic paint schemes, just accept that when you run your best it's in the 3.50's, yet the competition is tough.

Dragster: Much like Dragster Mayhem, not nearly as detailed. Still very good.

Quarter Mile Challenge Drag Racing: A great bracket racing game for solo runs. Fun.

Nitro Nation Drag Racing: Seems to be the Apple edition of Android's Drag Racing.

CSR Racing: A very detailed bracket racing game. Upgrade cars, parts, good competition.

You can also find useful apps filled with NHRA information. Just search NHRA in your proper OS market.

ACKNOWLEDGEMENTS:

Thank you to the following people for making this book and its content a success:

Jon Asher, Leah Vaughn, Don Garlits, Ted Yerzyk, Don Schumacher, Joe Sherk, Alan Reinhardt, Bobby Bennett, David Parsons, Todd Okuhara, Todd Smith, Antron Brown, Tony Schumacher, Jack Beckman, Ron Capps, Johnny Gray, Tony Pedregon, Larry Dixon, Spencer, Massey, Clay Millican, Whit Bazemore, Virgil Hartman, Steve Torrence, and you, yes you the reader. If you would like to see an annual edition of this book, spread the word, create a buzz, and if the demand is there, we will see what happens.

Would you like to see your manuscript become a book?

If you are interested in becoming a PublishAmerica author, please submit your manuscript for possible publication to us at:

acquisitions@publishamerica.com

You may also mail in your manuscript to:

**PublishAmerica
PO Box 151
Frederick, MD 21705**

We also offer free graphics for Children's Picture Books!

www.publishamerica.com

CPSIA information can be obtained at www.ICGtesting.com
Printed in the USA
BVOW031344270613

324503BV00002B/243/P